The Kanji (sign) for "prisoner of war."

ONE
DAY
AT A
TIME

A British
Prisoner of War's
account of
1,300 days
in a Japanese
slave labour camp

To Jean.

With best wishes

Arthur T.

ARTHUR TITHERINGTON

Published in 1993
The S.P.A Ltd.
Units 7/10 Hanley Workshops,
Hanley Road, Hanley Swan,
Worcs.

in conjunction with Arthur Titherington

British Library Cataloguing in Publication Data

A catalogue record for this book is available
from the British Library

ISBN 1 85421 205 2

Designed and Produced by Images Design and Print Ltd
Printed & bound in Great Britain by Hartnolls Ltd, Bodmin, Cornwall.

Arthur Titherington, aged 20.
Photograph taken in Nee Soon, Singapore, in February 1942.

Delicate art, trees bent with grace, and women,
drawn with the fineness of Eastern lace,

Black haired children, reflecting parents' face
belong to the men of that yellow race.

But, no mercy, light or dreams for men enslaved
by their greed for power

Only cold years, pressing upon youth, crushing
suppliant folds.

The shadowed years, making long passages
of brief time.

Frail bodies, relentless birch, hunger and
pain from these yellow men,

Cry for Hiroshima, Nagasaki . . . and so will
I, but you that will remember . . .

Cry like I, for the yellow, white and brown
who lived because of those dying towns.

In time will we reject our own, forget their
plight, will they become old men's tales?

Yet, from them we became alive, survived,
but not to bury them in our mind.

Anon.
(Written by a sixteen year old in 1945)

To Iris

⊣ACKNOWLEDGEMENTS⊢

For their considerable help and support during the writing of the earlier versions of my book, I have to thank David Horne and David Sear, both of whom offered constructive criticism when needed.

My thanks also to Mrs Tokiko Iwamoto for helping correct my Japanese spelling and for the discussions we had on Japanese life, even if we did not always agree.

I must also thank Robert O'Neill for the foreword. His summation is an exact reflection of all I set out to achieve with my book.

My special thanks to Alison Brown for her sketches, done entirely from a verbal description.

CONTENTS

LIST OF ILLUSTRATIONS

FOREWORD

By Robert O Neill

Chichele Professor of the History of War
All Souls College, Oxford.

It does us all good to read a book of the quality of this one. Many accounts have been written of captivity in war, but this one ranks particularly high because it combines immediacy and reflection. Arthur Titherington has been able to retain enough detail through memory and surviving records to give a vivid account of the dreadful experiences which he and his comrades endured at the hands of their captors for over three and a half years. At the same time, we have the benefit of a work completed over forty years after the events it describes, by a perceptive man who gives his readers of the 1990s answers to questions such as:

"What do you feel about it now?"

And "How do you regard the Japanese now in the light of what they inflicted on you then?"

The book gives us insights into four realms of experience which, however much one hopes that they will never be inflicted on other human beings again, are bound to recur.

The first is defeat. Here we learn what it was like for a young soldier to be sent out by his government on a hopeless mission and then see his own army disintegrate and face the stresses of having to surrender.

The second is captivity under rigorous conditions. We are given brief, mercifully brief, glimpses of the consequences not only of deprival of freedom but also of the denial of basic essentials for healthy life. We learn particularly of the balance and interrelations between the mind and the body while suffering as a prisoner under harsh conditions.

The third is life under a brutal or inhumane regime. Of this Titherington shows us, in adequate but not overwhelming detail, just how abominably one set of men under pressure are capable of treating one another who are completely in their control, when there are no effective sanctions of impartially administered justice to curb the powerful and protect the weak.

11

The fourth is comradeship in adversity. The author, frankly and credibly, gives us a clear view of what concern for one's fellow sufferers can and cannot achieve, and indeed of the limits to that concern itself when life is close to extinction. The book offers examples of the finite extent of comradeship as well as of the extraordinary acts of support and compassion of which men under extreme pressure are capable of rendering their fellows.

This book has real value as history. It gives the reader deep insights into the experience of captivity in the Second World War. But more, it challenges the successor generation to wonder how they would have coped, and whether they can conduct the affairs of the world so that this kind of suffering is not inflicted on their own or on those of future generations. And it gives us a salutary reminder of the depth which those of us who have lived mainly in peace and freedom since 1945 owe to men like Arthur Titherington and his comrades for what they have revealed of the nature of authoritarian regimes through their suffering and later telling of the tale.

I commend this volume warmly to readers concerned with the future as well as the past.

Robert O'Neill
31 August 1992

◦⟊ PREFACE ⟊◦

Taipei, 1983

I lay in bed at 4 a.m., six floors up in the Hilton Hotel. Darkness and silence. Even the air conditioning was muted.

I had returned to Taiwan to visit the hell-camp of Kinkaseki, to retrace my steps as a prisoner of war under the Japanese in the years 1942 to 1945. For some time I had thought of going back to the place which had caused me recurring nightmares, a place which had helped to shape my life and personality. That experience had drawn me back, inexorably, to this one spot. There had been a compulsion about it which could not be ignored.

I was determined to come to grips with this episode in my life, an episode that had put me several times on the very brink of death. But of equal importance was the desire to understand, if at all possible, why those three and a half years had to happen.

In the years following my release I felt compelled to read every book I could obtain dealing with all aspects of the Japanese, their society before the war and the events and decisions that had brought them into conflict with the West. To understand the incomprehensible. To find out why the Japanese had acted as they did.

Nothing has been written about my own camp, the No. 1 Prisoner of War camp on Formosa. Material relating to it is very difficult to find. There is no reference, for instance, among the list of camps mentioned by Lord Russell of Liverpool in his book *The Knights of Bushido* though other camps on the island are included.

However, what was available I found. I scoured the archives of the Public Records Office in Kew and obtained details of the War Crimes Trials, and discovered what had happened to the people who had tormented us so painfully and indelibly.

In the end I just had to return to Formosa. There was nothing else for it but to re-create the physical presence of the place.

So here I was, having brought my wife, now asleep beside me, halfway round the world on what might be considered

13

an obsessive pilgrimage.

I was afraid of the place, that much was true. The fear was almost tangible, and, had it been possible, I would willingly have returned home at that moment, away from my place of fear.

The scene on the quayside at the harbour of Kiirun returned to me as I lay in the darkness. The difference was that now I was physically much closer to the nightmare than I had been for years. At 4 a.m. in the darkness of an over-quiet hotel room in Taipei in 1983 the events that had taken place over forty years ago came flooding back. It was as if, by its very proximity, the ghosts of Kinkaseki were more tangible and more frightening.

I switched on the bed-side light. With the anonymity of the hotel bedroom furnishings around me it was possible to imagine I was anywhere in the world. But cloistered though I was in the comfort of the room, away from the street scenes of the wooden shacks and houses, the pavement eating places and the beaten up cars which lay abandoned on the sides of the roads, my mind was far from being at rest and sleep would not come.

As I lay there a phrase continued to return to my mind: "Sleep that knits the ravelled sleeve of care." I thought about my years as a prisoner and how sleep had been the nearest thing to escape. Sleep was the opiate, a release from hunger, exhaustion and illness.

PART
ONE
Betrayal

CHAPTER ONE

I am not afraid of tomorrow, for I have seen yesterday,
and I love tomorrow.

William Allen White. 14 November 1942

"Come on Tithy, we're there." The voice of one of my companions brought me out of my reverie.

'There' was a seaport on the north-eastern tip of the island of Formosa. A new place, and a welcome relief from the malodorous hold of the Japanese troopship, the *England Maru*. A ship of dysentery and death, but 'home' for myself and a few hundred others for the past few weeks.

In the background the noise and incomprehensible screams of the guards on the quayside and their cries of "*Hayaku, hayaku!*", cries which, for me, conjured up visions of headless bodies lying in the road, bayoneted women and children, the face of a young nurse who had killed herself, knowing, as she had told me, from the days of the war in China, what her race was to expect from the victorious Japanese as they entered Singapore.

"*Hayaku, hayaku!*"

They bludgeoned us into line and began their obsessive counting. Five-hundred and twenty-three of us, thirty-four officers, four-hundred and eighty-nine other ranks. We were left standing there, the drizzling rain steadily making us wetter and colder. There was little we could do except concentrate on remaining upright, and to speculate on where we were going from here.

"*Hayaku, hayaku!*"

A cry intended to hurry us along: to hurry us to work, to hurry us back from work, and to hurry us whilst we were still at work. In many cases to hurry some into the next world.

It was not quite the curse it seemed to be, though the manner in which it was delivered made it sound so. It simply meant: "Hurry up!" Or, to use the guards' version of English. "Speedo, speedo!"

We were to hear both versions of this cry thousands of times.

We must have presented a most unprepossessing sight as we were paraded through the town, with the Japanese guards swaggering at our side as we were marched past the crowds of Formosans who, it has to be said, appeared to be rather more interested in staying dry as they scurried along the wet streets on their way to and from their homes and offices.

The end of our march brought us to a railway station where we were herded into dark carriages with the window blinds pulled down, no doubt to prevent us looking out rather than to stop others looking in. Each carriage was divided into compartments containing about fifty men. We were prevented from moving from our wooden benches by the guards patrolling the space between the seats.

It wasn't too long before the train stopped at the station of a small town, which I was to discover later was called Zeiho. Lined up on a small square outside the station we were once again subjected to the usual counting procedure and the guards' incessant shouting. Finally we set off along a narrow street leading out of the town. For a while we made reasonable progress, prompted all the time by the harassing guards. But soon the hard road surface gave way to a track where the physical effort needed to force ourselves on became too much for some of the sick men.

Before long the rough terrain began to take its toll. The side of the track became littered with abandoned kit, dumped in a desperate effort to keep up with the column. To be a tail-ender was to invite the unwelcome attention of the guards. Men now began to fall from exhaustion. The reply from the guards was to kick them and, when that failed, to jab at them with their bayonets until in desperation the men would haul themselves to their feet, in many cases only to fall again, whereupon the treatment would be repeated.

The journey took ages. The sick and the lame fell back and the rest of us made every effort to help by carrying whatever kit they had. In some cases making the supreme effort of carrying the men themselves.

As we progressed along the track we passed through a number of hamlets consisting of just a few wooden houses, which, in some cases, appeared to be no more than huts. Outside these buildings members of the local population stood, silent and impassive as we passed.

By late afternoon we reached a small village where we were directed off the road and into the playground of the local school. Once again we were pushed into some semblance of a parade and were required to stand facing a small platform erected at one end of the playground. We didn't need a great deal of imagination to know we were awaiting a big event.

Instructions were given that under no circumstances were we to lean against the wall surrounding the playground, nor were we to sit. The more unfortunate amongst us, men who were by now in a state of complete collapse, were being supported on either side by their friends. It had already become an unwritten law that any man who was able should provide assistance where it might be needed. It was also firmly underlined in my own mind that from now on we were all truly going to have to be our brothers' keepers.

During the time we stood waiting for whatever event was to be provided for us, the guards were having a field-day. Using their own special talents they would suddenly pounce on a weary and recalcitrant prisoner who was unable to remain in an upright position.

Suddenly a lone voice screamed out a command. It was taken up by all the guards. There was a great bowing in the direction of a new figure entering the playground, all eyes were upon him as he mounted the platform. For some time he just stood there, his head moving first to the left and then to the right, looking us over in a most imperious manner. The whole thing was obviously meant to impress, not just us, but also his own men. It was not dissimilar to a scene I remembered from my first few weeks in Catterick before the war, when the Commanding Officer had taken the parade, only in his case he was seated astride a horse.

When all the shouting and the posing was over the Japanese officer addressed us. To us it was quite unintelligible. The guttural tone and manner of delivery conveyed nothing. The performance, however, conveyed a great deal. It was very stagey and was again part of an act which was meant to impress. It certainly sounded threatening, and if that was what he intended, then he succeeded.

An interpretation, carried out by another Japanese standing by his side, didn't really help very much. His English was almost as incomprehensible as the Japanese. It was possible, however, to understand we were being regaled with a long list of ever-increasing Japanese victories from all the battle locations in the Pacific. We were also being promised that: "Bread and meat would be available very soon now, after we have taken Australia." This magnificent event "was to be announced any day now."

There were rules for our behaviour in the new camp, one of the most important of which appeared to be "from now on you will show proper respect for Nippon and the Nipponese." No longer was the word Jap or Japanese to be used – in their place the words Nippon and Nipponese.

19

Furthermore, anyone who laughed at these, or any other references to "the Great Nation of Nippon" would bring down "great punishment on himself."

The work in which we were to be engaged was also mentioned, though at the time it didn't mean a great deal to any of us. We were to "work diligently." If we worked diligently "everything would be alright," he said. In fact the word diligently was repeated quite a few times; it seemed to be one of his favourite expressions.

There was a great deal of propaganda about many other things during the peroration, but most of it went over my head. I was tired before he started, by the end I was almost falling over. Some men had in fact fallen in spite of the efforts of their friends. Throughout the speech even the silent but forceful demands of the guards had failed to get them to their feet.

Eventually the speeches finished. We had been addressed by our Camp Commander, Lieutenant Wakiyama, known to us from then on as The Bunsho.

From the school we were taken a few yards down the road to the camp area in the mountains of Formosa and miles from any place of note. I was now in, and became part of, Number One Camp, Kinkaseki. I did not now then that this was where I was to spend the next two and a half years.

Within the confines of the new camp there were more parades and more counting. Then, a few at a time, carrying whatever possessions we had, we were taken into a small room full of Japanese all pushing and shouting at the same time. My few belongings were snatched from my hands and spread on the floor where two or three guards pounced on them. Items were picked up and examined before being thrown to one side. I had nothing of any value so I was allowed to retrieve what there was before I was pushed out of the door to join the other prisoners who had already been processed .

With the search completed we were split into groups of about thirty and led off to a two-storey wooden building. A guard indicated that my own group should occupy a particular section of the floor to the right of the doorway. It was now the early hours of the morning. We were supplied with a blanket and a piece of bread, and then instructions were issued to mount a guard in each squad "to prevent stealing." Considering all the stealing had been done by the guards themselves during the kit search, the precaution seemed superfluous.

The deaths which could be attributed to the past thirty hours or so amounted to ten men. Ostensibly from diphtheria, encephalitis and dysentery.

20

They were: L/Cpl. J.Griffiths, Bdr. F. Mckew, Gnr. S. Wearing, Sigmn. J. Adamson, Sgt. J. Shaw, L/Bdr. G. Ellerby, Gnr.A, Gunn, L/Sgt. H. Gore, Gnr. H. Warnock, and Gnr. K. Brain.

The road to the camp at Kinkaseki.

CHAPTER TWO

The Japanese had a small part to play in my life as a child, though I knew very little about it at the time. I was born in 1921 in Darwen, Lancashire. Weaving and spinning were the main livelihood, from the days when the work was carried out in the homes of the workers to the introduction of the large mills and power looms. Unfortunately, in the depression of the late 1920s, Darwen, like similar towns in the north of England, was badly hit by unemployment and it was general knowledge that one of the reasons was the Japanese intrusion into the world's market for cotton products. I suppose the word used today would be dumping. They were flooding the markets with cheap items, to the point where very few countries exercising any reasonable standard of working conditions were unable to compete. Even the very looms which were no longer working were sold to the Japanese, ostensibly for scrap. This was my first, if somewhat tenuous, brush with the Japanese.

As a child in the 1930's I was obviously not too aware of the economic needs and developments of my town, except those which they tried to drum into me at school. What I saw with my own eyes was that my family, just like many others in Darwen, went through hard times in those dark years after the 1926 General Strike. My father, engaged in transporting the products of the mills, was, more often than not, out of work, whilst my mother, a weaver for many years, was also a victim of the closures. We lived in a typical mill-town terraced house at Redearth Mount – my parents, elder sister, younger brother and myself.

As a youngster, however, I had just about as much adventure as a boy could want. There were natural playgrounds in the public-owned areas of the moors just a short walk away from my home. The high sweep of the Pennines could be seen from anywhere in the town, 280 acres of unresricted moorland, with Darwen Tower, a notable Victorian landmark, on the high peak. It was a magical place for me. There were also two public parks, one of which, Boldventure, my maternal grandfather had played a big part in laying out and constructing. Slightly less restricting, but a little further away, was Sunnyhurst Wood, another public owned area which could have been created, though perhaps unknowingly, for young boys.

The local cinemas were the other escape from everyday life, and if we couldn't afford the entrance charge we could always pinch in, provided somebody opened the exit doors from inside. Occasionally I went to the market place on Sundays and took in the sights and sounds of the public meetings which were Darwen's version of Hyde Park Corner.

It was on the market where I heard the meetings regularly held by Sir Oswald Mosley and his Blackshirt followers, making their anti-government and pro-German speeches. I simply came there to enjoy, from a distance, the scuffles and fights which broke out because of a difference of opinion between the Blackshirts and their audience. However, none of these things made any noticeable impression on me other than to create a vague suggestion of events beyond the confines of my own town. There was little doubt that as I grew older I became aware of the poverty around me. I can't actually say it made me unhappy, but I was conscious of the difference between families, even the families with whom I shared playing friends.

A decision was made in 1936 to move to Birmingham. Dad had left Darwen a few weeks earlier and found work almost at once. He found a house and we joined him the day before Christmas. Once again it was a big adventure for me, though the start in the new home was not at all auspicious. We spent Christmas day eating our festive food by candle-light and seated on boxes. The furniture had failed to keep pace with us, and the electricity authority had failed to connect the power.

Work in Birmingham was easy to find. For a while I settled down as an apprentice toolmaker. But I was restless. I wanted to travel. I wanted adventure, something other than a dull routine of going to work each day.

Unknown to my parents I tried to join one of the services. I wasn't really fussy about which one, they all seemed to offer what I was looking for. However, the Royal Navy and the Royal Air Force recruiting offices soon kicked me out after discovering that I was under age. So, in early June 1939 I took the fateful decision to go into the city and try my luck with the Army. I had no idea what regiment or corps I wanted to join. My only positive idea was that I wanted to be a dispatch rider.

On the morning of 5 June 1939 I entered the recruiting offices where the only person present was the recruiting sergeant who greeted me with: "And what can I do for you, son?

"I want to join the army," I replied. "I want to be a dispatch rider."

By now the sergeant was on his feet. Dressed in a smart uniform, with shining buttons and a sash across his chest, he seemed to be a towering man. "Then you will be wanting to go into the Royal Corps of Signals," he stated helpfully.

I had to admit I had never heard of them, but if it was going to make me a dispatch rider, so be it. "Yes," was my reply, as though I had known it all along.

"How old are you, son?"

"Seventeen," I replied.

"And when were you born?"

"Tenth of December 1921."

Things were going well for me, I thought, though I had also got this far on previous visits to the Navy and Royal Air Force recruiting offices.

The sergeant eyed me. "I'm sorry, son, you're not old enough. Why don't you take a walk around the block and come back when you are five days older?."

I hesitated. "Go on, off you go," he said, "take a walk around the block."

I was quite despondent. Again I was out on the street, and the unfairness of it all almost made me give up. However, I stood and thought about what he had said. It was obvious the answer lay inside the office with the resplendent sergeant, so back I went.

As I entered he got to his feet and I fully expected a greeting which would indicate that he remembered me, but no, it was as though I had never been in the place before.

"And what can I do for you, son?"

"I want to join the army. Don't you remember, I came in a few minutes ago?"

"Oh, did you, and how old are you? What's the date of your birth?"

"The tenth of . . . "

As I began to tell him he interrupted me with, "Are you sure it wasn't the 5th of December?"

Always under the impression that in such situations one was expected to tell the truth I was slightly nonplussed. I realised of course that he was trying to be helpful and, from then on, for the Army's purposes, my birthday was to remain 5 December, five days short of my real date of birth. It was not the last time I was to lie about my age in order to find the adventure for which I was looking.

On my arrival home that evening I had to break the news to my

25

parents, and mother's reply was somewhat typical: "Just wait until your father gets home." When I did tell him his first question was to ask what regiment I had joined. Like me he had never heard of the Royal Signals, but, after making sure it was what I wanted, said that as I had made my bed I must lie on it. In retrospect I was convinced he agreed with my actions, but not necessarily the way in which it was done.

My attempt to find adventure was still not guaranteed. During the first few days in Catterick I had to convince the Medical Officer I had never suffered from rheumatic fever. He was quite certain I had, which was of course quite true. However, I knew, just as well as he did, that if it could be shown that I had, in fact, suffered from that particular illness, I would be out of the army in quick time. He finally promised me, after three or four examinations, if I would confirm what he believed to be true, that I had had rheumatic fever, he would do nothing to jeopardize my remaining in the service. He stuck to his word, though I was rather surprised he should go to so much trouble. My parents would have confirmed his findings.

I enjoyed my first few months of training. I don't know if it was in spite of, or because of, my drill sergeant, but it was a great experience. There were the usual problems for any new recruit. I came up against the thick and the stupid, both among the commissioned and the non-commissioned officers. I discovered very quickly that because a man had a rank higher than that of private it didn't necessarily qualify him when it came to dealing with people. Some, like Sergeant Catanio and R.S.M. Stickley, possessed the ability. Others like Lieutenant Gee and Sergeant Major "Whadify" – we called him Whadify because his war cry was always, "Whadify came on parade with a belt like that" – did not possess this essential quality.

In the course of the next few months various people attempted to persuade me to change my trade from that of a dispatch rider to wireless operator, but I held out and remained faithful to my original desire. I was to discover that being a free and independent spirit had its compensations, but it also had more than its fair share of risks, and even fear. But that was in the future. The months before the war were spent square-bashing in Catterick, and then later, charging around the valleys and hills of Yorkshire on a W.D. motor cycle. I was learning to walk and ride the army way.

I heard the broadcast by Neville Chamberlain on 3 September 1939 with slightly mixed feelings: "That a state of war now exists between this country and Germany." There was a tremendous feeling of excitement. I hadn't seriously thought of war, but wasn't this the very adventure for which I had been looking? I suppose I ought to have felt fear, but I didn't. That was to come much later.

During the weeks following the announcement of the war we were required to dig trenches and air raid shelters in various parts of the camp for use by the civilian population in the married quarters.

Reservists were being called up and overseas postings were announced, which were of very great interest to the people who were on them, but disappointing to people like me who were not.

I was attached to various regiments in the Catterick area, and posted to various Holding Battalions in other parts of the country. I got the impression I was going to spend the whole of the war going round in circles in the U.K. Whenever a list went up for overseas posting I went into the Orderly Room and tried to persuade somebody that I ought to be on one of them, but continued to meet with a singular lack of success. I was suffering from the same old problem: my youth. Only this time it wasn't just a matter of five days. I needed to be at least a year older.

Looking at my army paybook one day I realised how easy it would be to change the 1 of 1921 to a 0. A quick stroke of the pen and it was done. I was a year older. Now, I thought, they couldn't keep me out of the war.

Within a few days I was put on orders for a move to France. In a mood of exhilaration I went home on embarkation leave, proud to be getting into the war. Dad thought there was something odd since I had been on leave quite recently. When I explained the situation he suggested I keep the information to myself.

A few hours after returning to my unit I was sent for by the Commanding Officer. His first question was very reminiscent of the day I enlisted in Birmingham: "How old are you?"

I lied, "Coming up to nineteen, sir."

His smile told me all I needed to know. I had been caught out. He asked for my Paybook and I knew the game was up. "Well," he said, "your mother doesn't think you are as old as that." My mother had apparently written to the C.O., or telephoned him, to put him right about my age. Of course I was annoyed. There was a war on. Soldiers went to war, and it was all so unjust.

It may well be that my feelings during those days are now difficult to understand. Old style patriotism has been somewhat tempered by the facts and true nature of war. However, for me, brought up in an era of exciting magazines which told stories of heroism at the battle-front – feats of great derring-do – war still offered the great adventure. I continued to apply for every overseas posting. I knew that sooner or later my age would catch up with things. Sure enough, early in 1941, whilst I was stationed in Bottesdale, Suffolk, as a member of a Signals

Unit attached to the 15th Scottish, a section was formed of wireless operators, drivers and dispatch riders, and I was included. I had no idea where we were going.

In due course we were issued with tropical clothing, including a pith helmet and a large white kit-bag in place of the more usual black one. It was a fair indication we were going to a tropical climate. Our briefing on the move had demanded we were not to discuss with anyone that we were going abroad. However, it didn't take very long before the whole village knew all about our posting though perhaps not our final destination.

We left Redgrave Hall, our billet, and were paraded on the railway platform at Diss in Norfolk, complete with our pith helmet hanging from our shoulders.

Our initial destination was Gourock in Scotland where we boarded a troopship, *H.M.S. Cythia*. From Gourock our journey took us round the Cape and across the Indian Ocean, calling in at interesting places like Sierra Leone, Durban, Bombay and Ceylon, each place providing a new and interesting experience. The troops on board were from a mixture of the services, and at various points along the route men left the ship to go their separate ways. On reaching Durban we were transferred to a Dutch ship, *The Neuw Zeeland*.

It became obvious that our destination was the Far East, though exactly where, and for what reason, we still didn't know. It was only through a lecture from a Medical Officer, after we had left Durban, we were given some clue.

He spoke about the various perils awaiting us in the tropics, of the need to pay great attention to matters of hygiene. We were appraised of all the possible illnesses we would soon be up against, and how important such matters were.

He concluded by saying: "If a Japanese bullet doesn't get you, then one of the tropical diseases will." It provided us with food for thought since at that time the Japanese weren't even in the war.

We arrived in Singapore in August 1941. There was certainly no war, nor any sign of war. Food rationing, black-outs and other restrictions were non-existent, and people seemed to be carrying on with their normal lives. It was quite exciting, and more like a holiday.

CHAPTER THREE

*A man who experiences no genuine satisfaction in life does not
want peace, men court war to escape meaninglessness and
boredom, to be relieved of fear and frustration.*

———————————— Nels S.Ferre. ————————————

My stay in the city of Singapore lasted only a few hours, so that, after a
brief look round, I entrained for northern Malaya and my destination,
Sungei Patani.

Our quarters were long, single-storey, wooden huts, each raised a
foot or two off the ground providing a cooling air-space underneath.
There was a full length veranda along the front of each hut – our shady
sitting out area. The roof, in keeping with the local style, was of attap.

In general it was not bad accommodation, rather more pleasant in
fact than the description wooden hut implies. The camp was contained
within a rubber plantation composed of serried ranks of trees, with their
thick foliage cutting out much of the sunlight. It was said by some of the
old hands that if one lived in such places for too long one began to suffer
from a disease known as "rubberitis", a fictitious malady which sent
men mad.

Two disciplines, of which we were appraised within the first few
hours of being in camp, was that the mosquito nets over each man's bed
had to be in place, and well tucked in, by 4 p.m. each day, and that all
rubber trees were 'sacred'. Any damage would cause the tree to 'bleed"
and valuable latex would be lost. Disciplinary action would be taken
should either regulation be broken. In view of the war which was to
follow, it is interesting to note that the locals had freedom to move
around the plantation in order to tap the trees every day, consequently
there was nothing to prevent them seeing, and hearing, about troop
movements.

In the beginning it was difficult to accustom oneself to the humid
climate of Malaya and many of us suffered at times from prickly heat, a
severe itching of the skin. We looked forward to the late afternoon
when, with some regularity, there would be a heavy downpour of rain.
This was the signal for us to strip of our clothes and stand in the cooling

rain. Apart from being a refreshing shower, it also gave relief from the irritating rash. However, despite the tribulations of becoming acclimatized, I must say I took to the life very well.

In Sungei Patani we could get a change from camp life by visiting one of the local cinemas where, through the cacophony of noise, we would try to get the drift of a Chinese film. In the local eating places we could dine on the ubiquitous fare available to troops all over the world, chips with everything, even if at times the "everything" looked rather dubious, since one of the eating places was the local brothel. I was warned off the main item on the menu rather early after my arrival in Malaya. I had acknowledged our Medical Officer, who had his nose in a book at the time, upon seeing me he turned and thrust the book towards me.

"How would you like to put your old man in that?" he asked, pointing to an illustration of a woman's vagina in an advanced state of venereal disease.

There were the usual servants attached to the camp, mainly of Indian extraction, each working for a group of soldiers as char and dhobi wallahs. These men were the camp followers who made themselves responsible for providing cups of tea – especially first thing in the morning.

They also made themselves responsible for washing and taking care of our clothes. There were others, such as the barber, whose particular accomplishment was his ability to shave a sleeping soldier, with an open razor and an almost 100% guarantee of not wakening him – an unnerving experience if one should by any chance come awake, to see an open razor just a few inches from one's nose.

I was fast becoming a Colonial soldier. Life was very interesting and, at times, quite exciting. Yet there were times when it troubled me greatly to think of the folks at home, with all their trials and tribulations, the war on their doorstep and their homes being bombed. I could not help but think that I had been cheated and that, despite all my efforts to get into the war, here I was surrounded by peace and plenty.

Late in November 1941 there was talk about some of us going on leave to the island of Penang, not many miles away. The suggestion found a great deal of favour, especially as I was one of the first people nominated. Little did I realise that leave in Penang was about to be replaced by an infinitely more volatile experience.

The first landing of the Japanese on the mainland of Malaya took place a little after midnight on 7/8 December 1941 on the beaches of Kota Baru. Just after 4 a.m. on 8 December the Japanese air force bombed the city of Singapore. Like the raid on Pearl Harbour there was no warning, and no 'official state of war' existed between the British Empire and Japan.

So, a Colonial soldier looking for a war had found one in the most unexpected place.

CHAPTER FOUR

Order Of The Day. Issued 8 December 1941.

———— Air Chief Marshal R. Brooke Popham. ————

"Japan's action today gives the signal for the Empire's Naval, Army and Air Forces, and those of the Allies, to go into action with a common aim and common ideals.

"We are ready. We have had plenty of warning and our preparations are made and tested. We do not forget at this moment the years of patience and forbearance in which we have borne, with dignity and discipline, the petty insults and insolences inflicted on us by the Japanese in the Far East. We know that those things were only done because Japan thought she could take advantage of our supposed weakness. Now, when Japan herself has decided to put the matter to a sterner test, she will find out she has made a grievous mistake.

"We are confident, our defences are strong and our weapons efficient. Whatever our race, and whether we are now in our native land or have come thousands of miles, we have one aim and one only. It is to defend these shores, to destroy such of our enemies as may set foot on our soil, and then, finally, to cripple the power of the enemy to endanger our ideals, and our possessions and our peace.

"What of the enemy? We see before us a Japan drained for many years by the exhausting claims of her wanton onslaught on China. We see a Japan whose trade and industry have been so dislocated by these years of reckless adventure that, in a mood of desperation, her Government has flung her into war under the delusion that, by stabbing a friendly nation in the back, she can gain her end. Let her look at Italy and what has happened since that nation tried a similar base action.

"Let us all remember that we here in the Far East form part of the great campaign for the preservation in the world of truth and justice and freedom; confidence, resolution, enterprise and devotion to the cause must and will inspire everyone of us in the fighting services, while from the civilian population, Malay, Chinese, Indian or Burmese, we expect the patience, endurance and serenity which is the great virtue of the East and will go far to assist the fighting men to gain final and complete victory."

CHAPTER FIVE

*I have never seen a document that was more crowded with
infamous falsehoods and distortions – infamous falsehoods and
distortions on a scale so huge – that I never imagined until
this day that any Government on this planet was capable of
uttering them.*

——————————— Cordell Hull. Secretary of State. U.S.A.———————————

*(Comment on a note delivered by the Japanese Ambassador after
the surprise attack on Pearl Harbour.)*

Lack of preparation for the war in the Far East has been well
documented. So too has the perfidious way the Japanese attacked, not
only in Malaya but at Pearl Harbour also, and before that Manchuria
and the greater area of China. As a young man, however, with a young
man's priorities, none of Japan's shortcomings, or her qualities, were
known to me. My awareness was limited to the knowledge that when
Japan was mentioned it was the place from where most cheap toys and
similar goods came.

On the afternoon of 7 December 1942 I was detailed to report to
Colonel W.E.S. Napier, Commanding Officer of the 80th Anti Tank
Regiment, under instructions to act as his dispatch rider. The Colonel's
Staff car was driven by Bombardier George Grundy and I followed on
my motor cycle. Our destination was northern Malaya, close to Jitra and
the border with Thailand. Even at this stage I was quite unaware of the
seriousness of the situation.

I soon discovered Colonel Napier was a man of action, determined to
be completely involved in the war. It was also obvious that he was a
brave man, and at times may even have been considered as foolhardy.
Not a 'seeker of gongs' he was, however, determined to be in the thick of
things when the need arose. He had no doubts about his responsibilities
and on the days when I or my friend Jack Saxon, another dispatch rider,
were on duty with him, we also were supposed to be not too far from the
action.

A dispatch rider occupies a rather unique role in an embattled army.
Whereas the driver of a truck, for instance, is accompanied by at least

one other person and an infantry man usually has somebody with whom the situation can be discussed, the dispatch rider is working alone most of the time and has to make decisions without the help of consultation.

When dispatches had to be delivered, off I would go, alone. To make matters worse, most of the maps with which we were issued had great blank areas. A road on the map would come to a sudden halt and the single word 'uncharted' would be stamped there. Many were the times in these uncharted areas when it was difficult, if not impossible, to know which was the correct way. When operating in a battle zone under these conditions there was always the chance that I would end up in the wrong side of the line. Such happenings came about all too often, partly due to the deficiencies of the maps, but also due to the very difficult terrain. In the middle of the jungle, and in the large areas covered by the plantations, the front was never quite so clear as in places like Europe or the Western Desert for instance. Certainly it was nothing like my map-reading days in Catterick before the war, when I was charging round the quiet villages of Yorkshire with six figure map references. What was needed here was a good inner compass.

There were times when the Colonel preferred to leave his staff car, which was all too easily recognisable. He would then complete whatever journey we were making as a pillion passenger on the motor cycle. Most of the time he seemed to know where he wanted to go, though there were the occasional worrying moments when I felt that each turn of the wheels brought us nearer to Tokyo than to a gun emplacement.

Now and again I found myself being shot at by my own side. At first I put it down to some infantry man being a bit nervous since I would, at times, be coming from the 'wrong' direction. But it was not until I was stopped by an infantry Brigadier who advised me to change my headgear that I realised what was going on. Apparently his men had already shot at, if not actually killed, a dispatch rider who was wearing the army issue crash helmet. Japanese military helmets, which I had not yet seen, were in fact very similar in appearance to the helmet I had been wearing. My issue helmet was discarded from that moment on, and I was quick to warn my friends of the danger.

One of the early battles in Malaya which almost cost me my life was on 14/15 December, just north of the crossroads at Gurun. Only a few hours earlier I had found myself on the wrong side of the line during the big Japanese breakthrough at Alor Star. I got out of that one by the skin of my teeth, only to walk into an even worse situation. We had moved south to the crossroads at Gurun where we made use of the local police station to set up our wireless communications in one of the offices, and to take advantage of a lull in the fighting.

Late in the evening I was instructed to report to the Commander of 6th Brigade, Brigadier Lay, his headquarters being about a mile or so to the north of the crossroads. My brief was to act as communications liaison under his instructions. Brigade headquarters were housed in a *godown*, an atap-roofed bungalow, set back on the left of the main road. On reporting in I was I was told to make myself comfortable. That night I attempted to get some sleep on a bench on the south side on the veranda, but it turned out to be a bad choice because every time I turned over I finished up on the floor. Finally that was where I slept.

In the early hours of the morning I was brought wide awake by the sound of shouting, mixed with the even more ominous sound of battle. I rushed to the end of the veranda where there were a number of infantry. When I asked what was going on I was given the bad news that the Japanese had broken through and were heading in our direction.

It soon became obvious that Brigade Headquarters was going to be a very dangerous place to be, but I couldn't leave without first obtaining permission from the Brigadier, so off I went in search of him.

The first person I found who appeared to have any authority was the Adjutant. When I asked that I be allowed to return to my unit he suggested I should speak to the Brigadier himself. Just at that moment Brigadier Lay came from inside the building. He was fully dressed and around his shoulders he was wearing a multi-coloured shawl. He was carrying a large walking stick and I thought he looked quite a daunting figure. I approached, saluted, and made my request that I be permitted to report back to my unit. There was, of course, no reason why he should remember me or why I was there.

When I made my request he replied: "Oh, now the fun has started I suppose you want to go home, is that it?"

My reply was perhaps rather bold, but nonetheless true, "Yes sir."

Having finally established why I was there he asked about my unit and their location. When I told him he said, "Take me there." Down the road went the Brigadier and the Signalman.

In General A.E.Percival's account of the War in Malaya, published after the war, the battle of Gurun is documented. Of the events that took place at 6th Brigade H.Q. on that day the General says: "The Brigade Major, Staff Captain, Signalling Officer and many others were killed. Only the Brigadier and one or two men survived."

Major General S.Woodburn Kirby (*History of the Second World*

War – The War Against Japan) also writes about the battle that took place in and around Gurun: "Not only was Headquarters 2nd East Surrey overwhelmed, the Commanding Officer and five other officers being killed, but also 6th Brigade Headquarters, the whole of which was lost with the exception of Brigadier Lay who was absent from his headquarters at the time."

The last time I saw the Brigadier that day he was standing in the middle of the crossroads at Gurun, the shawl still around his shoulders, waving his stick in the air to emphasize the instructions he was issuing regarding the deployment of the troops.

The part I was to play in the next couple of hours was, if anything, even more hair-raising than my rude awakening that morning. It was about half an hour after I had returned from 6th Brigade that I was ordered to return back up the road down which I had brought the Brigadier as a pillion passenger. I was to inform any retreating troops to stay off the road and use the plantation on either side. The reason given was cause for some consternation: the Royal Artillery, who had a number of 25-pounder field guns at the crossroads, were going to fire, open sights, straight up the road in order to knock out any armoured cars or tanks or anything else that might be coming towards the crossroads.

It was still quite early into the war but already I was beginning to find out that it was a most frightening affair. Also that being a dispatch rider in war wasn't the romantic, devil-may-care, freelance way of life I had imagined a few months ago. But even now my education was far from complete.

Going back up the road towards Alor Star was the most frightening thing I had ever had to do, aware that the Japs had broken through and that they would be heading in my direction. The fact that only a short time ago I had been provided with the intelligence that they were now only a short distance away, coupled with the possibility of a 25-pounder shell coming from behind caused me to be very concerned about my future. As I drove north I could already hear, in my mind, the sound of the shells as they pierced the air. I drove as close as I could to the deep ditch at the side of the road and as I came across any troops I passed on the instructions. Finally, just before I reached the point where I knew the 6th Brigade building was located, I turned and headed back towards the crossroads. My 16H, 496cc Norton motor cycle had never moved quite as fast as it did on that return trip, knowing full well that I was now driving full tilt into that same 25-pounder shell that had, mentally, chased me up the road. I never did discover if the shells were ever fired or, for that matter, if they achieved the effect that was hoped for.

On my return to the police station my unit was preparing to move out. The Japanese were now close enough to be reaching the area with mortar fire. We were on the retreat once more.

CHAPTER SIX

A young Apollo, golden haired,
Stands dreaming on the verge of strife,
Magnificently unprepared
For the long littleness of life.

Francis Cornford. 1886-1960

After we had evacuated the police station I drove south to 15th Brigade Headquarters where I met other members of my unit and was able to obtain some food and, of even more importance, a breathing space from the problems that had beset me over the past twenty-four hours. We were eventually joined by our Signals Officer, Lieutenant J. B. McKnight, who, after a few preliminaries, suggested we might care to volunteer to go back with him to the crossroads at Gurun in the role of infantry. I can't remember the initial response of the other men, but I just stood and looked intently at my bootlaces. I felt I had had all the luck that was due to me for that day.

"Come on now," he said, "you won't get any medals standing about here!" There was a brief silence.

Then a voice from behind me said, "No, and we won't get fucking shot either."

With that McKnight left us. I supposed he had returned to the crossroads alone.

In the absence of any specific instructions we had to decide what we were going to do next. Fred Campion, a dispatch rider friend of mine, and I decided we would head south while at the same time we would to pick up any wounded men and ferry them, provided they could ride pillion, to a medical aid station.

I came across a Ghurka Warrant Officer who had been shot through the stomach but was quite prepared to come on the back of my motor cycle, though it must have been a most uncomfortable ride. After depositing him at an advanced dressing station I realised I was quite close to Sungei Patani, my original starting point at the start of the war only a mile or so away. When I had left there with Colonel Napier a few

41

days before it had been necessary to leave behind all my possessions – both personal and military. Now seemed to be an appropriate time to retrieve them. Since I had been wearing the same clothes for a week clean clothes were becoming a most pointed need, and in any case I also wanted the personal items I had left behind.

On entering the barrack room in which I had been billeted I was disappointed to find that my kit had been looted, what hadn't been taken was spread all over the floor. I retrieved a few photographs but there was little else left.

I now owned just the clothes I was wearing and I needed a shower and some clean clothes. In my search of the camp area I entered the building that had served as the officers mess. There, sitting at a table were two officers, one of whom was Lieutenant McKnight, the man who had wanted us to return to Gurun. Obviously, discretion was the better part of valour for him also, and he had obviously decided to come south.

The job of dispatch rider was known for attracting the odd types, particularly those of the lone wolf variety. It manifested itself even in the way we adapted our regulation uniforms. Having got rid of the regulation dispatch rider's helmet we needed to find some other head-wear; I chose an Australian bush hat.

At times I suppose Fred Campion was perhaps the most outlandish dresser of all: an outfit consisting of an Aussie hat, an American wild-west type of shirt, a pair of bell-bottomed naval trousers and a pair of brown shoes. The finishing touches supplied by a black patent-leather belt and holster he had acquired from a police station, into which he stuck his army issue Smith and Wesson 0.38 revolver. Finally the whole ensemble was finished off by a pair of leather gauntlets. On one accasion when he was acting as dispatch rider to Colonel Napier, the C.O., he was told at the end of the day that he could report back to his Commanding Officer.

"But, sir", said Fred, "you are my C.O."

Apparently the Colonel thought Fred was a member of the Australian forces.

The need to obtain clean clothing was always one of our problems. We just didn't have access to a regular Quartermaster's store and we were obliged to grab whatever we could. Sometimes it might be military clothing, but more often than not it was from one of the many civilian shops in one of the towns or villages we passed through as we moved around.

There were times when life had its lighter moments even with all the problems of a war. On New Year's Eve of 1941-42 we decided, come what may, we were going to have a party. Even though at the last moment I had to go on a delivery of dispatches to each of the Batteries and Rear H.Q. I was not deprived of my own celebration. At each of the Batteries, and at our wireless trucks, I was offered a celebratory drink. So much so that after one or two slight accidents, due to my misjudgement, I arrived at Rear Headquarters rather worse for wear. I delivered my dispatches and was promptly invited to have yet more drink with a few friends. The following morning I awoke in a truck parked in a plantation. I had passed out and had been put to bed out of harm's way.

Our continuing retreat was preceded by a civilian exodus and this provided some odd but very welcome benefits at times. On one such forage I picked up a brand new civilian motor cycle, but my joy was very short-lived since the Colonel requisitioned it. Moreover, he in turn lost it a few hours later during the battle at Slim River. Most officers tried to obtain civilian cars due to the fact they were much less noticeable than the very obvious staff cars.

With the retreat there were other benefits, such as empty food shops, or houses with cooking and sleeping facilities, even if it was for only one night. On one occasion I slept on a billiards table in the club house of a golf course in Malacca. Another time a few of us had the use of a large limousine which, according to the name under the steering wheel, was the property of a princess. In most cases, such as houses or cars, or anything else we might have the use of for a few days, we often destroyed or burned them before leaving, a sort of scorched earth policy. It was quite disturbing at times but preferable to leaving them for the Japanese.

In Serenda we were using a house and other buildings on a palm oil plantation for a few evenings. When we were due to leave Lieutenant McKnight was given the task of destroying the diesel-driven electricity generating plant. The job had to be done quickly because we had word that the Japs were in the vicinity. In order, therefore, to facilitate a quick get-away I was detailed to stand-by with my motor cycle. Between us we tried every way possible to knock out the generator. We pushed, pulled, and twisted everything we could find but it just kept chuntering on. Time was running out and we could hear the sounds of gunfire coming closer. McKnight then produced some explosives originally intended for blowing up the house, so I suggested we blow up the generator and set fire to the house. We started a fire in the house, laid the charges in the machine room of the generator and lit the fuses. Without waiting for the explosion we made off in a cloud of dust. I had no way of knowing if the operation was a success, though McKnight said it was, and I accepted it. At least I knew the house was burnt down.

Wars throw up all kinds of inhumanity, as I discovered when I entered Malacca one morning. I was in urgent need of petrol, a commodity we normally found wherever we could. The petrol pump I found was fitted with a fairly stout lock preventing me from serving myself. In the midst of my frustrations an Australian soldier came along and asked if he could help. When I explained he did just what I had been avoiding: pulled out a revolver and shot the lock off.

"No trouble, mate, always ready to help," he said.

I filled the tank of the bike and we talked for a few minutes, during which I happened to say I could use a cold drink.

"No trouble, mate," he said again. He seemed to know his way around Malacca, and in a few minutes we were in a small shop not very far away. He explained to the Indian behind the counter what he wanted. There was a bit of an argument but I got my drink and was eagerly disposing of it when the next thing I knew the Aussie had drawn his revolver and shot the man. Whether he was dead or not I had no idea, and I didn't stop to find out. I left in a hurry, rather confused and not a little upset.

One of the big problems in Malaya was that of Fifth Columnists. In many cases they were actually Japanese. Unfortunately, we were not sufficiently knowledgeable at the time to know the difference between them and the local Chinese. It was also true, however, that many Fifth Columnists were members of the local populace.

One insidious way of helping the enemy was, on the surface, a most innocuous everyday event. By custom the local people, after washing their clothes, spread them out in the sun to dry. When laid out in a clearing it could be placed so that it formed an arrow. The point of the arrow would indicate a military target for the Japanese pilots and could be seen from the air quite clearly. When they were caught they were normally handed over to a member of British Intelligence. Unfortunately such people were not always available, and consequently there were many summary executions. It may well have been that the Australian at the petrol pump had experienced treachery from the civilians before, or had grown tired of not knowing who his friends were and consequently treated them all as his enemy.

The battle of Muar River was probably as bad as any in the whole of the Malayan campaign. General Percival, in his Official Account of the war, described it as "the most sanguinary of all battles."

In his book *Singapore, The Japanese Version*, Colonel Masanobu Tsuji, Chief of Operations and Planning Staff, 25th Japanese Army, Malaya, described it as "a great success" and "a glorious exploit", which sums up their military activities. He writes, "Increasing the weight of attack from the front, the Kunishi Unit also attacked from the direction of the coast and again intercepted the enemies' lines of retreat at the Easterly bridge of Parit Sulong, finally cutting them off and annihilating about one Brigade." He makes no mention of what happened afterwards.

General Percival's account was: "Our little force held up a Division of the Japanese Imperial Guards, they were attacking with all the advantages of aerial support, for almost a week. They saved another of our major forces from encirclement and probably annihilation. Eventually, some 550 Australians and 400 Indian troops out of 4,000 men who comprised the Muar force succeeded in rejoining. The wounded who could not walk were of necessity left behind, and it stands to the eternal shame of the Japanese that they were subsequently, almost without exception, massacred in cold blood."

At the time of the battle I was billeted at Yong Peng, an area just south of Muar, and I had to enter the battle area with dispatches on two separate occasions. There was another occasion when I found myself on the wrong side of the river, but this was not too difficult to do because the whole of the battle area was confusing. I had dispatches to deliver but no one seemed to know just where I was supposed to go. The exact location of the Battery seemed to be in some doubt, and after receiving rather mixed instructions and advice I headed just north of Muar River, which involved crossing over to the other bank. The aerial activity around Muar was considerable and it was a safe bet the aeroplanes were Japanese. The activity on the ground was even more intense with vehicles everywhere. The rifle and mortar fire was the worst I had experienced so far.

It wasn't long before I was completely lost, quite unable to find any bridge that would take me to the so called safe side of the river. I had, in fact, actually crossed, and re-crossed, the river without being aware of it. During my attempts to orientate myself I met a young officer who explained where the main crossing was, telling me I had better hurry. Following his instructions I found the main bridge and with a lighter heart drove to an area which afforded a better degree of safety, eventually succeeding in finding the Battery for which I was looking not on the north, but on the south side of the river. It was not until then that I discovered I had made my exit from the north of the river with only a few minutes to spare before the bridge was blown by the Royal Engineers. I later discovered that the officer to whom I had spoken was a Royal Engineer, hence his advice to hurry.

When I revisited Malaya in 1983 I made a point of staying in the Government Rest House at Muar, quite close to the river. It was the

Chinese New Year and celebrations were going on all around, including firecrackers. I felt once more those same fears I had experienced in the past. Outside the Rest House the river continued to flow by, broad and very fast moving. It was as if it contained all the emotions of forty years ago. I could still hear the rifle and mortar fire and there I was, still trying to find my way across the river to safety. I turned away and walked round the Rest House and across the nearby golf course, in an effort to drive the disturbing thoughts from my mind.

During the course of the war in Malaya many stories circulated about the cruelties inflicted on captured and wounded men, and about prisoners being tied up with barbed wire and then bayoneted to death. I don't think that I really believed them at the time, but all the same, it did nothing for my peace of mind on some of the lonely rides. As a young soldier I knew what fear was, but as long as I was afraid and free I was able to retain my determination to get through to the next day. The war was now about six weeks old, I had been on the go constantly and I was worn out, as much by the mental strain as by the physical weariness. I often thought of the two weeks holiday on the beaches of Penang I had missed.

Our campaign had been a series of retreats, the hardest type of war to fight. Each time we thought we might be able to settle, or prepare for a push forward, word came that we were to move back once again. Time and again we were outflanked by the enemy. Such actions were very difficult to observe and there was so often no option but to retreat. I had been on the go almost night and day since the beginning of the war and in that time we had covered over 400 miles in very difficult conditions through jungle, mountains, mud flats and thick plantations. I had crossed swift flowing rivers, rice fields and thick, almost impenetrable elephant-grass lands. I had lived almost solely off the land and the shops in the urban areas of Malaya.

I had been befriended by many local people, though I regret to say this had seldom, if ever, included any of the European residents. It now seemed I was on the last lap, but before I crossed the Causeway on to the island of Singapore there was one little secret I enacted outside the town of Johore Baru near the 39th milestone. It is an area that is now very much developed, the bulldozers having moved in many years ago. During the retreat I had entered, and slept in, many deserted houses. I had also been in many deserted shops and in the process I had collected – I like to think they were 'liberated' – various items I thought might be of value, things like watches, rings, necklaces and other pieces that looked like gold or silver. I also had a superb ivory Mah Jong set. Of necessity they had to be small because I carried them in one of the panniers on my motor cycle. I don't know why I decided to bury the loot at that particular location. I may have just stopped there to have a smoke or a rest, but it seemed as good a place as any and easy to return to when the time came. I paced out the spot in true pirate fashion and wrapped my loot in an anti-gas wallet before burying it. That was the last I saw of it.

Crossing over onto the island there was less than three weeks to go to the end of the conflict. I was a little older, and considerably wiser, than the child who had sat in the canteen in Catterick on the day war was declared and thought the whole thing was a *Boy's Own* type of adventure. I think I grew into a man the first time I lay in a ditch in Northern Malaya and felt the whole of the Japanese army was making the war a personal matter between me and them.

The Signal Section had settled temporarily in a house in Nee Soon at the north end of the island. This was to be my last billet as part of the Section. But for now there was far less running about to do, so I was able to catch up on my eating and sleeping. Our greatest danger was from air raids. The skies were virtually open to the Japanese all day long, an almost every time we looked up it seemed there was a flight of twenty-seven planes, the usual formation of the enemy air force, plus shelling from the now all too close field guns. The usual shelter from air raids was in one of the deep monsoon drains and culverts on the side of the road. During one such raid I took cover in a deserted pineapple canning factory. The place was stacked from floor to ceiling with canned pineapple of every description, sliced, chunks, crushed and juiced. I loaded some cans on the bike and took them back to Nee Soon. I then borrowed a small truck and returned to the factory for a reasonable supply. In some ways it was a mistake, because all we got for afters was pineapple in its various forms, and some of the interest went out of Charlie Rankin's cooking. Before leaving the canning factory I committed one last act of vandalism. I pulled from the bottom of each stack a number of cans and had the satisfaction of seeing hundreds of them crash to the ground, many bursting open as they hit the ground – a little bit more of my scorched earth policy.

Hundreds of people were now being killed in the air raids on Singapore, the population of the island having been increased by the thousands of refugees from Malaya, pushed there by the threat from the advancing Japanese. Whenever and wherever the enemy planes dropped their bombs there was bound to be a target waiting, and for the most part the target was not a military one. On one occasion, just outside the village of Nee Soon, I watched as bombs fell on a large godown type of warehouse in which there were hundreds of refugees. It was carnage, with men, women and children lying dead everywhere. I had taken shelter in a ditch nearby and saw the whole thing, but there was nothing I or anyone else could do to help. The scale, hysteria and language difficulty made it impossible.

On one of my trips with Colonel Napier we visited the Naval Base. The place was deserted. It was as though the workforce had simply gone home for lunch. Everything was intact, including a quantity of torpedoes waiting to be loaded into a vessel, though I was not able to tell if they were armed. I do remember Colonel Napier seething under his breath. The place looked gift-packed for the Japanese.

I thought of my own efforts at implementing a scorched earth policy on my way down country and wondered what was going to happen here. We finally left the base rather quickly having been caught in a fierce air raid.

I had never really considered, except in passing, the possibility of being captured and taken prisoner. The possibility of being killed, yes, but surrender, no. I had no idea what other men thought about the way things were going, but I began to feel that we would very soon be in a situation where we would be required to fight to the last man, though it never did become a topic of conversation. As far as I was concerned, the matter was taken out of my hands in a way I did not anticipate.

I was delivering dispatches, thinking that my position was reasonably satisfactory since the possibility of being shot at had been reduced. The Japanese were still on the mainland, and riding the motor bike around the outskirts of Singapore was not particularly dangerous. Also there was very little chance of finding myself on the wrong side of the battle lines. However, as I was riding through a plantation there was a loud explosion. I parted company with my motor cycle, and went flying through the air. I was quite unable to understand what had happened for some time. On recovering my senses, and discovering I was still alive, I realised I must have been caught in an air raid or perhaps a shelling from the mainland.

When all had settled down I could only walk with great difficulty. My left foot felt quite dead. I managed to mount my bike and get myself back to Nee Soon where it was suspected I had broken my ankle. I was told I would have to go into hospital and, in due course, I was delivered to the General Hospital in the city. I was given a wash, various injections and a medical examination and put to bed. Fortunately time proved my ankle was not broken as we had thought, and in a matter of a couple of days I was hobbling around with the aid of a stick. When I asked if I could return to my unit I was told, "In a couple of days."

It was obvious the medical facilities of the General were stretched to the limit and that the staff were having an up-hill struggle. As I was considered to be 'walking wounded', it was necessary that I should give all the help I could wherever it was needed. A Merchant Seaman and I became friends and made ourselves ward orderlies and general dogsbodies. We carried and served food, washed patients, dressed simple wounds and consoled crying children. We carried and fetched wherever we were needed, including patients to the operating theatre, even holding down fractious patients whilst they were being operated on – a most unsavoury job.

The water shortage in the hospital was most acute and the toilets had ceased to work, so baths and showers were out of the question. For drinking water I made regular trips on to the roof of the building to collect rainwater from a number of tanks. After the water had been boiled then cooled in the refrigerator it was taken round to the patients. Cooking was definitely not a forte of mine but in the hospital I served up the most massive stews to both patients and staff, using whatever tinned goods were available.

My Merchant Navy friend and I had another very unpleasant task to perform. As patients died, both civilian and military, we helped dispose of the bodies as soon as possible, and for this purpose a number of large trenches had been dug in the grounds. At first we carried the bodies out as soon as they had been pronounced dead by one of the doctors, since the sheer lack of space, with people lying all over the floor of each ward and even two deep down each side of the corridor, made quick disposal imperative.

However, in the last few hours of the war it was only safe to remove the dead during the hours of darkness, since during daylight we were shot at by snipers. There were snipers all over the island, and we were told that a few Japanese had managed to infiltrate, or had been there all the time, causing a great deal of chaos. This meant that one of the short passages leading into the grounds of the hospital had to be turned into a mortuary, and it was here the bodies were placed until we could safely take them outside.

On my return to Singapore in 1983 I discovered, from the memorial placed near the graves, that over 300 people had been buried in those grounds.

By now the war was very close indeed. We were getting reports from new patients who were being admitted every few minutes.

The author and his wife visiting the site of the mass grave.

49

The hospital was vastly overcrowded and it was obvious conditions were deteriorating to the point of being unmanageable. The nursing staff were working around the clock, and although their labours were quite incredible there really was no way they could hope to remain on top of the situation.

On one occasion my naval friend and I were asked if we would mind helping to hold down a fractious patient who was having a leg amputated. During the operation the theatre sister must have seen how green I had turned and she continually enquired if I was alright. It was one thing to see mangled limbs on the battlefield. It is a different experience to see them removed in front of one's eyes.

Finally the day came when the shelling and the shooting stopped and we were told Singapore had fallen to the Japanese. We had capitulated, we were no longer a fighting force but prisoners of war. The silence was almost as bad as the noise had been. Then, within a few hours, the hospital authorities were told that all patients and staff would have to evacuate the building and we had no more than twenty-four hours to clear the place. All equipment and drugs were to be left, nothing whatsoever was to be taken out of the building other than the patients. Eventually a Japanese officer arrived to inspect the hospital. A lone figure, complete with long dangling sword, he made his way along the main corridor past the end of each ward making no attempt to speak to anyone, just looking to his left and right, bowing now and again, and smiling all the time.

The following day we prepared to evacuate the building. Instructions had been given regarding the destination of various categories of patient, and as one of the walking-wounded I would have to go out and find my unit. The next few hours were spent bandaging selected patients in places where they were not wounded, and inside the bandages we hid scalpels, needles, drugs, syringes and anything else we could hide. Each patient was told what we were doing, and why. Their instructions were to explain to the medical authorities, wherever they might finish up, what we had done.

Eventually I too had to leave. I walked out of the hospital with the aim of finding my friends of the 80th Anti Tank Signal Section. I had no idea where to start. There were hundreds of people milling around, all of them, like me, trying to find their way to somewhere. My only possessions were the clothes I stood up in, a few personal items, a packet of twenty Gold Flake cigarettes, and for some reason or other, an army greatcoat in a sandbag sack. Things were looking rather bleak. As I walked around the city I was stunned by the extent of the carnage.

There were bodies in almost every street, nearly all, from what I could make out, were civilians. Many had been beheaded and the heads stuck on poles nearby. In some cases they had been tied to trees and bayoneted. What their crimes were I had no idea. I was aware of the vulnerability of my own position, a lone soldier walking through the streets of a city that had been occupied by the enemy in the past twenty-four hours. I was unarmed, and it was obvious the Japanese had been having one of their field days. I was now seeing with my own eyes the culture of the race that had made me a prisoner. I now began to consider what on earth the future held for me, and my friends.

I asked questions of various individuals who looked as though they might know something. Did any of them know what was happening to people like me? Where should I go? Where was I supposed to be? Two groups of Chinese civilians, roped together, passed me. Their guards prodding at them with their bayonets. It wasn't difficult to imagine what their fate was going to be.

A European male civilian finally told me that he thought all troops were being gathered together somewhere in Changi, he suggested I should head out that way. I started walking in that direction. After a short time I got a lift in a military truck full of troops. They also were heading for Changi.

⌐┤⌐ EPILOGUE ONE ┤⌐┤

Defeat cries out for explanation;
Whereas success, like charity, covers a multitude of sins.

Mahan

In the years since the war I have asked, and been asked, many times, "How did the Japanese achieve such a measure of success in the early stages of the war?"

When advancing an opinion some have suggested that since the Allied forces outnumbered the forces of the Japanese by a considerable margin, the Allies should not have relinquished control of Malaya and Singapore. These same authorities on numbers, for some reason or other, never included any statistics to show the relative scale of men and equipment of the two forces.

Then there is the school of thought that extols the superior fighting qualities of the Japanese – their refusal to surrender and willingness to die rather than be captured. This particular trait is also provided by some as an excuse for the way they treated their military prisoners. "Well of course, they had no time for us, since we were the lowest of the low because we surrendered." There are those with a vague knowledge of Japanese history who talk about the *Samurai*, the 18th century mercenary, that existed amongst the Japanese. There are undoubtedly a great many illusions about the Japanese military. For instance, that each man is bursting with this *Samurai* Spirit and is ready to sacrifice his life, not because he has to, but because he enjoys it. As I saw it the Japanese military were just human beings – though some would question that statement – with the same problems and desires of soldiers of other nations. They were far from being the supermen who embodied a medieval code of honour, or loyalty – an attribute which existed only in the imagination of writers who specialize in the deeds of history. Brave, yes, but I venture to suggest it would be safe to say that more Japanese soldiers died crying out for their mother than did those who died with the Emperor's name on their lips.

They were mainly forced recruits, enrolled from the villages and towns of Japan, their peace-time occupations similar in many ways to the occupations of any conscripted army in times of war. Their anxieties were for their families and they were as eager to return to their homes as any member of other military forces serving in a foreign land.

The *Samurai* Spirit of the average Japanese is on a par with the stories of King Arthur and his Knights. One might just as well begin to apply the Western chivalry and knightly deeds of Sir Lancelot to the character and ability of the British soldier. In fact the code of the *Samurai* did not even go so far in the matter of chivalry as did that of the medieval Knight, especially in matters such as the protection of the weak and courtesy towards the fair sex. There is the idea, as prevalent as it is vague, that the Japanese soldier was guided in his actions by an ancient and lofty code of chivalry called *Bushido*. But it is as well to recall that the late Basil Hall Chamberlain, formerly Professor Emeritus of Japanese Philology in the Imperial University in Tokyo, drew attention to the fact that "the very word Bushido appears in no dictionary, native or foreign, before the year 1900. Chivalrous individuals existed of course in Japan as in all countries at every period; but *Bushido*, as an institution or a code of rules, is a new invention." The accounts given of it, he wrote, had been fabricated for foreign consumption, as part of the propaganda of what he called "the new Japanese religion of loyalty and patriotism." In more modern terms the Emperor-centred system, *kokutai*, a National Entity.

The Japanese are nothing if not clever, and their cleverness has been abundantly shown by their success in duping foreigners about their all-pervading high-mindedness in exploiting foreign sentimentality about their beautiful country and its institutions. We should understand that those who controlled Japan before the war for the "Greater East Asia Co-prosperity Sphere" were totalitarian fanatics guided less by their exalted principles than by a ruthless ambition for their race.

The history of the average *Samurai* tells us he had little compunction about which way he dealt with an enemy. Even cold blooded murder would serve if that was the only way of avenging one's honour. The world of the *Samurai* extended no further than the boundary of his own *Shogun*'s domain. To the ordinary *Samurai* an Imperial order would not have been law: he recognised no law above that of his daimyo, or lord of the Province. The person responsible for paying and feeding him.

Speaking generally, the Japanese soldier was treated in a rather paternalistic fashion, as if he were a-child or a half-wit. This was brought home to me even before I began studying the Japanese after the war. And a measure of this was very evident in the prison camps where these would-be 20th century *Samurai* were our guards.

Discipline was very harsh for the Japanese soldier, and based on fear. The soldier was taught, one might even say brainwashed to a very high degree, into obeying without thinking. When this sort of thinking, or non-thinking, was applied in battle he soon discovered that he might just as well advance and by so doing take a chance on not being killed, because if he attempted to go back he certainly would be.

The handing out of corporal punishment to lower ranks was most certainly not confined to non-commissioned ranks. It seemed to be the norm that physical violence could be committed on anyone, even in public view.

One gets the idea that as a people they are not particularly stable. They certainly seem to be subject to moods of extreme violence. Self-control was not something I would attribute as being part of their make-up. One has only to read history to discover that even in the life of the modern politicians these extremes are shown quite clearly. Suicide – and I do not confuse suicide with *seppuku* or *hara-kiri* – among the young, as well as among the older generation, has always been quite common in the history of the Japanese.

Another reason given for the defeat of the British in the early part of the war with Japan was the lack of training for war in the terrain to be encountered in places like Malaya. It was certainly true that in such matters the Allied forces were very green indeed, apart from a very few exceptions. Certainly the 11th Indian Division, and others who came into the battle area after them, had little or no time to be trained in real jungle fighting. On the other hand, the Japanese had experienced the benefit of a training ground in Formosa for many years. They had also been at war in China from the early 1930s, and China was, without any doubt, her killing ground and main war training area.

The operations carried out in Malaya in particular had already been practised and honed in the jungles of French Indo-China, made possible by the co-operation of the Vichy government who were in control prior to the actual attack on the mainland in 1941.

It must also be remembered that at no time in Japan's history of war has she ever actually declared her intentions beforehand. In the case of Manchuria this was taken, as it was put at the time, "from the inside out". A so called incident was staged on the Japanese-owned railway near Mukden, and a further incident in 1937 was the start of the so called war against China, though it is never referred to as such by the Japanese; it is still called The China Incident.

The invasion of the island of Batan, north of Luzon, which took place at dawn on 8 December 1941 was the start of the invasion of the Phillipines.

In the case of Hong Kong, at 9 a.m. also on 8 December 1941, the Japanese Air Force attacked and destroyed what Allied air force there was, though it didn't amount to very much – three torpedo bombers and two amphibian planes. Their ground forces attacked across the border between China and Hong Kong and Kowloon. No warnings were given and no declaration of war was made.

The Japanese forces moved into Thailand without any resistance. Early that same morning they landed at Kota Baru, Northern Malaya, and around noon of the same day the Japanese Air Force bombed Singapore without any warning or declaration of war. At the same time the infamous and now well documented attack on Pearl Harbour took place, during which the American Pacific Fleet was virtually destroyed. Again, no declaration of war. In fact, at the precise moment the attack on Pearl Harbour took place the Japanese Ambassador was still engaged in talks with his opposite number in the United States.

The foregoing sets out to highlight some of the ways in which Japan, by her very deviousness, managed to strike a number of blows which helped to cripple her enemies from the start. When one considers just how well prepared Japan was for the war in the Far East, it has to be said that the Allies were equally as far removed from being ready. In fact, one has the impression that they were apparently so unaware it bordered on the criminal.

On 8 December 1941 *H.M.S. Repulse* and *H.M.S. Prince of Wales* were both sunk, not because of any inefficiency on the part of her Captain and crew, but because of a lack of information and of air cover. Thus, within hours of the war against Japan starting, the whole of the Allies sea power was destroyed.

There was, in fact, no effective air striking, or defence air force, in Malaya or Singapore right from the start. At the outbreak of the war with Japan the strength of the Royal Air Force was, in total, 141 operationally serviceable aircraft, made up as follows:

43 Brewster Buffalo fighters, slow machines whose performance at height was very poor indeed, while at the same time the two fuselage guns on these machines had a fault on the interrupter gear;

One Squadron of Blenheim night fighters;

Two Squadrons of Blenheim bombers, which suffered from a lack of flying range;

Two Squadrons of Vickers Vildebeeste torpedo bombers which had been declared obsolete in 1940, having a top speed of only 100 miles per hour.

Two Squadrons of Hudson Reconnaissance planes neither of which however were up to strength.

And finally three Catalina Flying Boats.

There was a shortage of spare parts for all these planes, to the point where, in 1941, flying training had to be curtailed.

There were no transport aircraft, no long-range bombers, no dive bombers, no army co-operation aircraft and no photo-reconnaissance aircraft.

On the ground there were no tanks or armoured cars, though there were a few bren-gun carriers. There were also a few anti-aircraft guns, though these were mainly of the fixed defence type. Of the fixed defences in Singapore, they were just that, fixed.

The now very well known 15" guns were fixed to defend the approach to Keppel Harbour, while one covered the Naval Base. There were also some 9.2 and 6" batteries, all with the same line of defence.

There was an active indifference amongst the senior commanders on the question of fixed defences, the reason, given by General Percival, and repeated by Major-General Woodburn Kirby, was that "fixed defences are bad for morale of both the troops and the civilian population." And so, in spite of the lesson that must have been evident from the beach defences that were erected in Great Britain, the beaches of Singapore and Malaya were virtually unprotected. Road blocks against tanks were very few and far between, with virtually no pillboxes in the southern areas. As Winston Churchill said, when told of the lack of defences for the island of Singapore, "It was like launching a battleship without a bottom."

The final statistics on the campaign in Malaya are concerned with the number of troops involved on both sides – numbers which were to be verified after hostilities had ceased.

Allied troops immediately prior to the outbreak of war numbered 80,000 men. Of these a considerable number were, of course, administrative personel.

The total strength of front line Japanese troops engaged in the battles of Malaya and Singapore by 8 February 1942 was 110,660. They had 168 pieces of artillery, 150 tanks, and 354 aircraft plus 180 naval air force support. The total number of operational air strength supporting the army amounted to about 560 aircraft, of which some 180 were fighters.

There was at this time no proper civil defence organisation, and no air raid precaution system in Malaya, Singapore or Hong Kong.

So, one could go on for a long time about the lack of preparedness in

Malaya and Singapore, but others have filled pages in this sphere of the war much better than I could ever hope to do. All I have tried to do is to show why the Japanese had such an advantage in the first few months of the war in the Pacific.

Moreover, Japan was really fighting a war on one front only, the China Incident now having been more or less taken care of. In contrast the Allies were fighting battles on all possible fronts in Europe and the Middle East. Japan was not unaware of this added bonus when making the decision to "Strike South" in order to obtain the raw materials she so badly needed, to say nothing of the potential territorial gains.

PART TWO

I'll Die Tomorrow

CHAPTER SEVEN

Without freedom, no one really has a name.

———————————— Milton Acorda ————————————

When I eventually found my unit they were occupying the Naval Cadet barracks in Changi. I was surprised by the welcome they gave me. Although I had been in hospital I did not expect to be treated as though I had returned from the dead. But that is exactly what my colleagues thought, and only then did I discover how fortunate I had been. Everyone had assumed that I had been taken to the Alexandra Military hospital, and not to the city's civilian General hospital. The Japanese, I was now told, had over-run the area around the Alexandra hospital on 13 February, they had killed everyone in sight, doctors, nurses and patients. Some patients were actually on the operating table when they were bayoneted. I have often wondered whether it was fate, coincidence, or simply ignorance that had led the driver to choose the civilian and not the military hospital. In my wanderings through the bloody streets of Singapore and now through the account I was given of the butchery in the Alexandra Hospital, I was certainly relieved to have found myself among friends once more.

After a few days in limbo in the Naval barracks we were moved to Changi Jail. Built of steel and concrete, it looked to me like a very permanent place of incarceration. As we passed through the entrance doors there were various attempts to find humour in the situation, and more than one wit cried out in mock anguish, "I didn't do it, I was framed". The previous inmates had either been moved or released; it was certainly empty when we moved in. My own unit was housed in a large room which had been used as the prison laundry, a concrete barn of a room. The cold hard floor was our bedspace.

The morale of many of us, certainly among the men I knew, was not too high at this time. To be taken prisoner was a hard knock to take, but the uncertain future at the hands of the Japanese was something about which we could only speculate, their attitude and temperament being an unknown factor to us at this time. We were now beginning to have an inkling of what it was like to be permanently hungry. Whilst our meals in the last few weeks of the war may not have been regular, at least we had enough to keep us satisfied. Now we were down to scratch meals, and it was beginning to tell.

An incident at this time probably sums up the personal effect that dented morale, uncertainty about the future and plain hunger were beginning to have on us. It also had its comic dimension and perhaps it can serve as one of those barrack-room pieces of advice, along the lines of How Not To Win A Military Decoration.

It started when one of my Signals NCOs, Sergeant Dougie Suttee, a pleasant and inoffensive man, asked me to carry out a routine task – one of those inconsequential little jobs that, under the normal circumstances of army life would have been done without thinking twice about it, however grudging. But in a defeated and demoralized condition I refused and, like the proverbial molehill, this soon grew out of all proportion. Doug and I got into a row. The Battery Sergeant Major, Harry Dubock, was then brought in. Harry was one of the best, and under normal circumstances I wouldn't have considered falling out with him, but on this occasion he got very little change out of me.

Harry used to spit whenever he got excited, in particular when he used the word "fucking", which came out as "pucking". Because things got a little heated he used the word many times, and with his face very close to mine, I got a shower of spittle. I suggested he shouldn't spit at me and that he should also moderate his language. Harry was almost speechless. He sent for Lieutenant McKnight, my own Signals officer. I really couldn't object to what he had to say. Personal irritation and cheek amounted to insubordination, and I was told so. When Lieutenant McKnight finished I was dismissed, I turned and walked away towards the door of the laundry building.

It was just then that Mr Mcknight called after me for a final word, and as we walked out into the exercise yard he said, "For your information you were going to be awarded some sort of decoration for what you have done in this campaign. Now, in view of what has just happened, you can consider it all off."

Those precise words, and my reply have remained with me. "Sir," I said, "if that is the only way you, an officer, can get your own back on me, a Signalman, you know exactly what you can do with your decoration."

Lieutenant McKnight and I were together as prisoners until August 1943 when he left for Shirakowa and we never did speak again to each other. I last saw him as we disembarked from the boat at Liverpool dock in 1945. True to his word, I never received a decoration.

Changi jail was very overcrowded and very claustrophobic but thankfully our stay there was not overlong. It was in fact only a few weeks later that we were moved once again, this time to the area around the *padang*, a sportsfield opposite Selarang Barracks in Changi. This gave us rather more room in which to move about, plus the fact that we were out in the open air, literally so. I spent the first few weeks sleeping once more on a concrete floor, in what had been a military motor-transport shed covered by a tin roof. Later, however, we had the benefit of more weather-proof accommodation by moving into a wooden barrack building.

Our status had become somewhat bizarre, though I have no doubt the officers in charge felt it was all for the best because we now reverted to our function as an army unit. Part One Orders were published, promotions were handed out, and there was, in effect, a Company Office. We were a Regimental Unit once more; so much so that someone suggested we should apply to go on leave. The return to drill parades, marching up and down with the R.S.M. barking out his orders, was perhaps the most conspicuous sign that we should observe outward gestures of normality – it was like going back to my first few weeks in the service. We also had fitness exercises and a modicum of P.T. But without doubt the most rigorous reminder that we were still under military discipline happened when the findings of a Court Martial were declared. It was also one of the most absurd episodes I experienced in my prisoner of war life.

Gunner Appleton, Happy to us, had been tried on a charge of desertion in the face of the enemy. This arose because he supposedly deserted his post on an anti-tank gun somewhere up-country when the Japanese broke through in the area of his gun emplacement. His defence was that far from leaving his gun he had attempted to defend the position by manning a Bren gun. When he was eventually forced to leave he made his way to the coast, finally obtaining a lift by means of some form of sea-going vessel, to Singapore where he stayed until capitulation.

After the trial and verdict we were paraded in the form of a three sided square and Happy was brought to the fourth side of the square where his offence, and sentence, were read out by an officer. In my heart I was certain that even if Happy was guilty there should have been a few other people up there with him, some of them occupying rather more senior positions than he. We listened in silence as the officer read out his sentence: a term of confinement to the Field Punishment Barracks that had been set up in Changi. A prison within a prison, as it were. The Field Punishment Barracks was in an area known as Temple Hill, and a sergeant and I were given the duty of escorting Happy to his place of detention. That was when he told me his version.

At Alor Star, said Happy, the position, had become quite untenable and he, like everybody else, had got out. Once in Singapore he reported to a branch of the Military Police to tell them who he was and what had happened. They, of course, were quite unable to find his unit for him and suggested he should serve with them until such time as he managed to locate them. Some time passed in this sensible military arrangement until one day, unknown to him, he was recognised and reported. The trouble was that he was unable to produce any evidence to prove his story and he had lost all connections with the Military Police.

When we arrived at the Field Punishment Barracks at Temple Hill, the sergeant explained to the Military Police why Happy was being brought to them and they began to question him. It transpired that he was still under some sort of medical treatment, a point that had been overlooked during the sentencing. The receiving officer refused to take him in.

There was a slight pause. Then Happy, obviously relieved at his escape, said, "For Christ's sake, let's get out of here." We left at the double. The notoriety of Temple Hill was only too well known. There were stories that men inside the place had actually eaten flies to try to catch dysentery to get out. Though unable to vouch for that particular story what I do know is that its reputation was enough to prompt someone to write a song about the place called "Hear The Ringing of the Bells At Temple Hill". The barracks themselves were built around what appeared to be two sets of vehicle garages, with two equal blocks of about eight or ten garages with accommodation over. These backed onto a small hill and had been surrounded with a barbed wire palisade. It had the appearance of an emergency glasshouse. I don't know who first thought of the idea, or who was responsible for putting it into practice, but as far as I was concerned it was, under the circumstances, an abomination.

We delivered Happy back to the unit. What happened to him I have no idea, though I did hear that his army paybook was found and that, as he had said all along, it verified he was being paid by the Military Police in Singapore. I also heard that, whilst he was technically released, he was refused a document to prove he was innocent of the desertion charges brought against him. I only hope he survived the next three years after his Court Martial.

At this stage, I had been a prisoner for about three months and food hadn't really been all that bad. Many of the warehouses in Singapore contained a fair amount of European food and we had not been much of a drain on the resources of the Japanese. That is not to say we weren't feeling hungry; we were, though it was later that we began to recognise the difference between hunger and starvation.

The Japanese were responsible for the issuing of rations according to the numbers in each unit, and the food was then processed and distributed by our own catering staff. The messing system – officers, senior NCOs, and other ranks – was re-introduced and, given the shortage of rations, there were inevitable rumblings about who was getting what. Were the officers, who were in charge of the food, getting more than their fair share? Was the rationing system correct? And so on. In order to meet these, and other criticisms, a communal mess committee was formed. We were learning very quickly that nothing supercedes the priority placed on food.

There were various ways of augmenting the rations issued by the Japanese, and every avenue was explored. Foraging parties began to go out to scavenge whatever could be found. The easiest food supplement was the ubiquitous coconut, though with so many hungry men in such a small area, even these began to get scarce, and any that were found went into the communal pot.

It was during one of these foraging expeditions I was first introduced to one of the most delicious of foods, known locally as Millionaire's Cabbage. It is the top two or three feet of the trunk of a coconut tree – a rich, thick, strandy white substance, which, when boiled, looks like ordinary cabbage. But, even allowing for the situation when anything might have tasted good, I remain convinced that this highly nutritious food was by far the best thing I have ever tasted. Under normal circumstances it is almost, if not actually, a criminal act to cut down a healthy coconut tree, and not something a local person would look on too kindly. The tree, of course would not bear any further fruit.

Coconuts formed a large part of our diet and provided us with some variety to our meals. We chipped and fried them. Oil could be obtained by pulping the nut and squeezing the juice out into a container. It served not only as cooking fat but also as fuel for illumination. A lamp was made from an empty can with a piece of rag sticking out through the lid. The light was very useful for many after-dark activities, and an absolute prerequisite to get in on the one and only game of Monopoly that existed in our part of the camp. This game was so popular it was played outside at night and to be a participant meant one had to provide a light, and even then only after serving time in the queue.

Prisoners who had any worthwhile possessions could enter the bartering market which grew up around the camp, the retailers being the local people who brought their wares to the wire. Anyone fortunate enough to have goods, or money, to supplement their food situation could do some sort of deal, though it would be true to say that the greatest profit went to the person bringing the food. It really was a seller's market. Having neither goods nor money, the only way in which I could supplement my food ration was through stealing. The opportunity presented itself whenever I took part in one of the working parties the Japanese required in Singapore – hard work, but sometimes worthwhile.

There was one occasion when a group of us stole food from a market stall in the town and the shopkeeper, having seen us, complained to the Japanese guard in charge. To our very great surprise he completely disregarded the complaint, walked back to the stall and took food to give to us. He gave us to understand later that he was a rice grower in Japan and wanted us to know that he knew what it was like to be hungry. We didn't meet many of his sort in the years ahead. That day we acquired a great deal of food to take back to camp. I can't really say that it worried us that we were stealing from the local traders because a lot of the goods we stole were in fact marked with a military, or NAAFI mark. The stuff had already been stolen once.

A much prized and valuable food was Marmite. It was said to contain a great deal of vitamin B and B1, and the lack of these particular vitamins was, by all accounts, the basis of much of our sickness, in particular dermatitis of the scrotum, or as it was better known, "itchy balls". A perfectly true story is told about this complaint. One of our men who suffered in this way was advised by the Medical Officer to get his hands on some Marmite as a means of alleviating it. He did manage to obtain a jar, but instead of eating it, he proceeded to smear it on the affected parts. Far from being cured, of course, the pain got worse.

In many ways the Japanese generally left us to our own devices. We were lumped together at one end of the island in a series of vaguely defined camps and buildings and were required to go on working parties, mostly to clear bombed areas and general debris. We were aware we were being used as propaganda by the Japanese who filmed us on various occasions, since as victors they were at liberty to use us in that way. For our part, as long as we could get near the shops and the docks now and again to continue our Fagin-like activities, the working parties served our purpose quite well.

The main work in Singapore was in the Bukit Timor area near the golf course, here the Japanese had a large permanent working party building a shrine to their dead. I'm pleased to say I never did work on that particular project, though some of the stories that went round were really the talk of Changi: of how the prisoners were outwitting the Japanese, partly for the fun of it, and also in order to get money to buy food. One such story, and I do not doubt the authenticity of it, concerned

66

the driver of a steam roller. A very saleable commodity in the town was petrol and anyone who could steal it was on to a good thing. The driver of the steam roller regularly drew a quota of petrol each day on the strength of needing it to run his machine and needless to say he sold the petrol every day to a willing buyer.

Most of the time the Japanese left us alone in Changi, though there were times when they showed us just how ruthless they could be – the Selarang Incident being a case in point.

The Japanese had issued a form which read: "I, the undersigned, hereby solemnly swear on my honour that I will not, under any circumstances, attempt to escape." Based on the military convention that a prisoner of war would attempt to escape if he had the opportunity we naturally had to refuse to sign. The Japanese, however, did not recognise this line of thinking, and at mid-day on 31 August ordered that by 5 p.m. that evening all prisoners should be assembled within the area bounded by Selarang Barracks.

Selarang Barracks, 1942.

The exodus from the various areas within Changi involved some 17,000 British and Australian soldiers. We were allowed to take with us only those items we could carry. About this exercise it has been said that, "The concentration of such a large body of troops within the perimeter of Selarang Barracks was calculated as probably the highest concentration of human beings since the Black Hole of Calcutta." For several days we faced severe problems of sanitation and water supplies. A make-shift hospital had to be arranged and provision for a cemetery within the barrack square.

A cooking area had to be allowed for and latrines had to be dug. There were two water taps available for the whole of the 17,000 men. The heat in the day was almost unbearable, and at night we were lucky if we could find a space in which to lie down. And still we held out.

It was during this episode that certain senior officers were gathered up and taken away in a truck. It was later that we heard they had been made to witness the execution of a number of prisoners who had attempted to escape. When the news of the executions got around there was a great deal of tension among the prisoners, it was possible that this tension communicated itself to the Japanese because a number of mounted machine guns made appeared on the edge of the square. However, it was obvious to us all that we would have stood very little chance against the armed guards, so that muttering and mumbling was as far as we got – though it was a further insight as to the diabolical nature of the enemy.

Finally, the Japanese used their ultimate weapon. They threatened to bring into the area the men who were in hospital. In particular, they specified the diphtheria cases. It became obvious to our senior officers that, if the Japanese carried out their threat, there would have been nothing to prevent an epidemic which would wipe out all the prisoners. So, on the advice of the Medical Officers, we were given the order to sign the "no escape" document. We all realised that the method of obtaining our signatures would absolve us from any disciplinary action when we got home. Not until we had all signed were we allowed to return to our various locations.

It wasn't only the Japanese who could threaten life and limb. Another threat came from the turncoats who formed the so called "Free Indian Army". These were men of the regular Indian Army and civilians who, rather than be prisoners, agreed to become part of an organisation set up by the Japanese to patrol the areas around the prisoner of war camps. They were armed and wore uniforms and, although they had no real military standing as far as their bosses were concerned, they made it quite clear that we were supposed to treat them as members of the Japanese forces and salute them at all times. This caused its own set of problems.

One man who was moving from one part of Changi to another on his way to the hospital failed to salute a truck load of the Indian renegades. They stopped the truck and two of them proceeded to beat him up. Their excuse was that he failed to salute them. The man in question had only

68

one arm, and under the other arm was the bedding he was carrying to the hospital.

This was far from being an isolated incident. I was caught myself a few days later while attending the hospital to visit a friend. I was carrying a banner with certain Japanese characters written on it which was supposed to provide me with free passage within a restricted area. I was well on my way to the hospital when I was stopped by a member of The Free Indian Army. He began to question me in Hindustani but my knowledge of his language was very limited indeed, though I did know that "*na mallam*" meant "I don't understand".

"*Na mallam?*" he cried out, and promptly hit me across the ear. He then went into a loud verbal torrent which I listened to for about five seconds before I took off.

On occasions Changi appeared almost normal. I was part of a cricket eleven representing the 80th Anti Tank against an Australian Eleven from the other side of the road. We had the playing-field, they had some of the equipment. Would we accept a challenge from them? We did and over they came. The Australians won the toss and put us in to bat. From our point of view the details weren't worth remembering – we were all out for eleven. They went in to bat and their opening batsmen scored 110 not out. We were devastated. It was not until after the game that we were formally introduced to their opening batsmen, the same pair who had been wicket keeper and bowler in our magnificent score of eleven. Barnett and Chipperfield two of Australia's Test Team. There never was a return match.

When the Japanese began sorting out groups to leave the island none of us knew just where we were going. All the Japanese would say was that the conditions would be better and there would be more food. Because of a bout of dengue fever it meant I was separated from many of my friends who went to work on the Burma railway project, though at the time they were unaware of their destination.

It was only a matter of time however before being ordered to pack and leave for an unknown place. The Japanese went to a great deal of trouble to give us a medical, though in view of what happened afterwards I never could understand why they bothered. On 25 October 1942 eleven hundred of us were taken by truck to the docks in Singapore. On the way we drove past the big church in the city, where a civilian reverend was standing on the steps of the church welcoming people as they went in. It all seemed rather incongruous to me at the time, though it indelibly fixed the day of my departure as a Sunday.

While we were waiting to board ship a number of us took the opportunity to reconnoitre the area. This proved to be very productive

69

and we were able to steal some food from a store we found in one of the warehouses on the dock-side. It was not without its dangers, but we thought it was well worth the risk. My own haul was a couple of jars of Marmite and a tin of milk.

After some delay we were instructed to board what looked like a cargo ship, though it proved to have been converted to a Japanese troop-ship, the *England Maru* – a most ironic touch. Once on board we were required to strip and, like sheep going through a sheep dip, had to immerse ourselves in a long wooden trough full of hot water and disinfectant. Following on from this we were very quickly herded below decks into a number of holds. It seemed to me at the time that we were well below the water line and that was the nearest thing to being aboard an African slave ship.

The two holds above us were occupied by a number of Japanese troops who were being moved either to another theatre of war or to Japan. Every evening, standing around the edge of their hold, they went through a repertoire of martial singing that, as the journey progressed, became more and more strident to our ears.

Our hold, in the bowels of the ship, was furnished on three sides with a series of wooden stages, like large shelves, with a space of three or four feet between each shelf. This meant that we had to be seated in a cross-legged fashion and when we lay down the space between each body was almost non-existent. The only entrance to the hold was by a vertical ladder, and with so many men suffering from dysentery – or more simply the 'squits' – going up the ladder behind somebody was a risky business. Great care had to be taken to hold a tight sphincter when climbing.

We were not allowed on deck until the ship was well out at sea, and then only for fifteen minutes. This was to be the routine during the next few weeks, just a quarter of an hour each day in the fresh air, the rest of the time consigned to the stinking holds below. Part of this small but invaluable daily break on deck could be used for a visit to the very primitive toilets, which were really nothing more than a large box arrangement with a hole in the base, the whole thing being suspended over the side of the ship. Without doubt it was the most frightening way of going to the toilet I have ever known. But the alternative facilities were buckets in each hold. When they were full they had to be lifted out on the end of a rope, and one unsteady pull meant the contents finishing up on the floor of the hold. A panic-stricken spell in the deck toilets was preferable to a floor strewn with faeces.

For the next few days the ship battered its way through the South China Sea, pitching and rolling in a most alarming way. We listened to the ancient plates and timbers creaking around us and, at times, mused on the irony that this ship in which we were travelling to an unknown destination had been built, many years before, on the banks of the Clyde. As each day progressed conditions in the hold got worse and worse. At times the stench was almost overpowering, and to add to the general misery more and more men were going down with dysentery. The part of the accommodation that had been set aside as a sick bay was totally inadequate.

I think it was during this voyage I really learned to overcome any squeamishness I might still have had. With my shoulder against a bulkhead, and one leg braced against an upright to counter the rolling of the ship, I sat eating one of our twice daily portions of boiled rice while at the same time watching a man nearby who was obviously in the throes of dysentery. With his backside on a latrine bucket he was vomiting from his other end into a container, and quite often missing it. At the next roll of the ship he pitched forward, spilling the contents of both containers, and went crashing face downward onto the deck. I put down my rice, wiped up the spillage as best as I could, and helped him back onto the bucket before returning to my meal. My sensibilities had been numbed to the point where I could now eat anything, anywhere.

The paucity of the rations took on a new dimension on board ship, but in a sense the obsession over food began to lessen, for there were now other problems to concern ourselves with: illness, sea sickness, and the future. I was, at the time, like other men to whom I spoke, prepared to accept the acute shortage of food as a temporary situation. There were, after all, over a thousand prisoners on board plus several hundred Japanese troops and the ship's crew. It was a fairly small ship and rations were bound to be scarce. The problem, I reasoned, would end when we arrived at our destination. The one thing that never entered my head was that our future was one of sheer starvation, in some cases to the point of death.

There were deaths on board ship. Just how many I don't know, for almost as soon as the men died their bodies were buried at sea. I suppose I should have been a little more apprehensive, even frightened, but it was only with hindsight that I was made aware that Japanese ships carrying prisoners of war were actually being attacked by American submarines. There were no markings to indicate what the cargo was made up of and, in any case, it was also a Japanese troop-carrier. No doubt that was all part of the Japanese strategy. A number of such ships, the *Lisbon Maru*, the *Ryuku Maru*, the *Zyonyu Maru* and the *Maros Maru* among them were attacked, and sunk, with many hundreds of prisoners on board. My sublime naivety raises the question of what we knew, or did not know at the time, and what were just optimistic or pessimistic imaginings.

None of us knew where we were being taken or for what purpose. Not for us the joys of a secret radio, of picking up something our captors didn't know. The state of the outside world was a closed book. Had I even had the wit to think of a secret radio, I'm damned if I knew where it could have been kept, our baggage was far from being private, and such a luxury would have been considered most dangerous.

While in Singapore, during the first few months as prisoners, the phrase "bore-hole news" was coined, an expression indicating that the news being bandied about was not necessarily true. The source of such news would have originated in conversations between men who were sitting on the toilet, built over a bore-hole, who had nothing else to do except think up items of news that might make life happier for the people who wanted to believe it. In reality, from now on, we were only going to get the news the Japanese wanted us to have.

So the *England Maru* ploughed on, taking us nearer and nearer to Kinkaseki and the copper mine. The full reality of daily life down the mine could not be foreseen on that vivid first day when we landed on Formosa in November 1942, as we came up for air out of the crowded hold of such an ill-named ship, smelling a new land, parading through the streets to begin the long, exhausting, and for some, lethal march up through the mountains to our new home.

Not until we got to Kinkaseki did we learn what the Japanese intentions were, that we were to work in a copper mine. We were to work "diligently". "Work diligently," we were to be told continuously, "and there will be food." It was simply a piece of information, a command issued from a Camp Commandant through an interpreter. There was no way we could have even guessed that this place, to which 523 men had been arbitrarily dispatched, was to become notorious as the epitome of a slave camp, and was to be known as such over the whole of the island. A place where, as men died, or as men became too ill to work, they were replaced by others sent in from other camps so that they too could die.

I suppose, however, the first inkling of reality began to take shape, in both mind and body as we stood there in that playground for local children. Receiving instructions from the uniformed man in charge. All of us I think – I know it was true for myself – were beginning to learn that tomorrow is another day. All that matters for now is getting through this one, acclimatizing oneself to pain, discomfort, and deprivation, steeling oneself to live as far as one was able, to ignore what tomorrow may bring, and just to live one day at a time.

CHAPTER EIGHT

When a man has pity on all living creatures then only is he noble.

———— Buddha ————

The camp at Kinkaseki was in an ideal location, that is, from the point of view of the Japanese: tucked away in a decidedly inhospitable landscape with two sides of the camp overlooking a deep and perilous gorge, the third hemmed in by the steep slope of a mountain, and on the fourth a high wire fence. The whole of the site was contained in a natural bowl in the landscape, and it was covered, invariably, in rain and cloud.

The camp at Kinkaseki

Within this bowl, on a plateau of flat ground, were a number of wooden huts, four of them serving as sleeping quarters for prisoners. Others consisted of stores, lavatories and a communal bath house. Above, on the slope of the hill, a single storey building served as accommodation

73

for the hospital and medical quarters. Even further up the hill a long low building was the office and living quarters for the Japanese Camp Commandant. From this vantage point he was able to survey the whole enclosure, including the guards' quarters which lay outside the main area. The camp entrance was secured by a guardroom, manned at all times by the Japanese. The general configuration and security measures at Kinkaseki did not conform to the popular conception of a prisoner of war camp, with miles of barbed wire and high watch towers at each corner. There were no searchlights, machine guns or patrolling dogs.

But anyone who might be led to believe that from this absence of external paraphernalia escape was a genuine possibility should think again. We were on an island. Just over a hundred miles or so to the west was the mainland of China, where the Japanese were already in control. About five hundred miles to the north were the islands of Japan. On the south and western side there was nothing till the Phillipines, again under Japanese control; a few thousand miles on the other side of the Pacific, were the shores of the U.S.A.

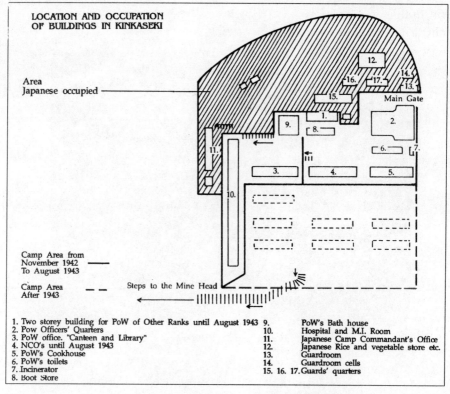

LOCATION AND OCCUPATION
OF BUILDINGS IN KINKASEKI

Area
Japanese occupied

Main Gate

Camp Area from
November 1942
To August 1943

Camp Area
After 1943

Steps to the Mine Head

1. Two storey building for PoW of Other Ranks until August 1943
2. Pow Officers' Quarters
3. PoW office. "Canteen and Library"
4. NCO's until August 1943
5. PoW's Cookhouse
6. PoW's toilets
7. Incinerator
8. Boot Store
9. PoW's Bath house
10. Hospital and M.I. Room
11. Japanese Camp Commandant's Office
12. Japanese Rice and vegetable store etc.
13. Guardroom
14. Guardroom cells
15. 16. 17. Guards' quarters

Location and Occupation of Buildings in Kinkaseki.

74

More effectively, we were under constant supervision day and night. We were also counted formally about ten times a day. Even if one did decide to leave the camp, where was there to go? The northern part of the island had a most inhospitable climate. What would we find to eat? We were Europeans, ignorant about the flora and fauna of Formosa. But perhaps the most telling thing was that there was virtually no chance of any of us hoping to merge with the local population. As Europeans we stood out in sharp contrast against a sea of Oriental features. And in any case, we were completely unaware as to where the loyalties of the locals were directed.

Finally, we spent most of our days below the ground in the mine, and we were all starved, ill, and completely exhausted for most of the time. There was not a man amongst us who could have survived even a day or two on the run, trying to keep clear of the inevitable wholesale search. Any thought of escape from Kinkaseki could be no more than a thought stillborn, added to which was the certain knowledge that death, not solitary confinement for a few days – or some other such European punishment – would inevitably follow capture. In all probability other prisoners would also be executed as accessories, since the guard system known as *fushinban* would automatically include them.

During the first few days in Kinkaseki the patterns were set, although it wasn't until 22 September that the first working parties went down the mine. Already quite a number of men were far too sick for anything but hospital. According to the brief Official Account of life in the camp compiled for record purposes by our own administrative officers, at least ten men died in the first few days, partly as a result of the arduous journey from the harbour at Kiirun. Dozens of men were still very ill with dysentery, a legacy from conditions on board ship. The severe change in climate from tropical Singapore to a place which, during the winter, could be quite cold and invariably very wet, took its toll on our constitutions.

Personal items had been confiscated on entering Kinkaseki, including books, pens, pencils, diaries, knives and any other sharp instruments. However, I had managed to conceal a small diary. Another item we were deprived of was footwear. Boots had to be handed over, and in return each prisoner was issued with a pair of wooden sandals, known by the Japanese as *geta*. At the beginning they took a lot of getting used to, and when wet became quite treacherous because one's feet continuously slipped off them. This lack of proper footwear was another major deterrent to any thoughts of escape.

Very soon after arrival the Japanese took a photograph of each prisoner holding a placard in front of his chest displaying his individual camp number. Mine was 466. A record was also made of each man's fingerprints. From now on we were to grow accustomed to the guttural request from the guards, "*Nambanga?*" – What is your number?

In the beginning work was confined to the camp. When the guards wanted a job done they walked into one of the huts, pointed to the number of men they wanted and took them off. The work wasn't particularly arduous, but it was a full time job to try and keep out of the way of the guards in order to avoid conflict.

Among the guards there were three distinct types. At the head was Lieutenant Wakiyama, the Camp Commandant. His role was the same as any Commanding Officer in any unit, and though we didn't see him every day he was always about somewhere. I never heard him speak a word of English, though all of us shared the feeling that he was quite capable of doing so. The Second in Command, Lieutenant Kozi Tamaki, made himself much more obvious to us. He had a reasonable smattering of English and a great deal of authority to go with it. Other junior officers were Lieutenant Nobuo Suzuki, Lieutenant Iwawo Tahara and Lieutenant Yoshijiro Oita. Of the non-commissioned ranks, Sergeant Major Tatsuo Furuo played the part of Sergeant Major in any army. There were also a number of Sergeants, one of whom was the Guard Commander and he had a number of junior N.C.O.s and other ranks under him. There appeared to be regular changes in the numbers and personnel of this particular section of the staff.

The remainder of the Japanese were the permanent staff attached to the medical side of the administration, though the amount of medical knowledge among them was very limited indeed. In fact one might go so far as to say it was non-existent. Finally, there were a number of men who, whilst they were wearing Japanese uniforms, did not appear to have any standing at all. We discovered that they were in fact Formosans who had been drafted into the Japanese army. Once we got to know them, and their position in the life of the camp they were referred to as Runabouts, a title that summed up their purpose in the service of their masters. They held no rank as such and were never to be able to rise to any position above that of private.

None of the Runabouts were gifted with very much intelligence, nor did they look as if they would ever be engaged in a combat capacity except in an emergency. Their uniforms were rather decrepit, and the rifles they carried, complete with fixed bayonets, seemed too big for their small stature. They were undoubtedly a product of a mixture of Chinese/Formosan and Japanese during the period of Japanese rule in Formosa. They certainly went to great lengths to please their masters, and one of the ways in which they thought they could curry favour was in their treatment towards us as prisoners. They had the right to beat us and this they did at the least provocation. They were like dangerous children attempting to ape their dangerous parents. Each one was soon given a nickname according to his particular appearance or other characteristic.

Shortly after we settled in the camp, Lieutenant Wakiyama, issued an injunction: we were required to learn the Japanese language at the rate of six words a day. He did not specify which six, or for that matter who was to teach us. Of the 523 prisoners I believe that only Lieut. Brown spoke any Japanese at all. As far as we were concerned our captors were still very much a part of the mysterious East, a race of people about whom we knew very little. Apart from Lieut. Brown the officers, usually from a background of wider education, were no better off than were the rest of us. And here we were, in daily confrontation with about a hundred Japanese who were equally as unaware of our language and customs. For the sake of survival it was obviously imperative that we should know something about them. I do not know where or when I first heard it, but the phrase that was to prove to be a great truth very often during those years was, "In order to beat your enemy you must first learn his language."

It was going to be difficult, but at least it paid us to learn to count in Japanese – *ichi, ni, san, shi, go, roku, shichi, hachi, ku, ju* – the numbers one to ten, and so on up to the hundreds became fixed in my brain, there they have remained. As has my camp number – yon roku roku. There were many other words which I was destined to remember, words which gave a degree of security as I worked down the mine – words of self-preservation.

The Japanese introduced a system which really amounted to us guarding ourselves, known as *fushinban*, or night watch. From lights out until reveille there would be a prisoner in each squad responsible for the movements of fellow prisoners. The guard was carried out in one hour shifts, so that, having done an hour from, say, 9 p.m. to 10 p.m. you would then make sure that the person sleeping next to you was awake – and on his feet – before you went to bed. He, in turn, would then do an hour and wake the next man, and so it went on through the night.

At various times throughout the night a Japanese guard, accompanied by a couple of Runabouts, made a tour of the huts to take a roll call. When they entered the hut the prisoner on guard at the moment had to report, in Japanese, the following information. "*Dai ippan*" – Number one squad; "*Sohei nijuni mei*" – total twenty-two men; "*Chico san mei*" – absent three men; "*Ichi mei byoki*" – one man sick in

77

hospital; "*Ni mei benjo*" – two men lavatory; "*Genzei ichi kyu mei*" – present nineteen men; "*Ima ijoarimasen*" – nothing more to report.

Interior of hut at camp at Kinkaseki.

On a board, just inside the door of the hut, the man on guard had to put the camp number of the man who was at the toilets. When the guards entered they would check the board and ask how long the prisoner had been away. There would be a short waiting time, after which one of the Runabouts would be sent to fetch him back. Until the man was seen and accounted for the hut check was incomplete; the men in the hospital would have been checked before the roll call started. There was never any variance in the system. It was never, to my knowledge, passed over lightly. The guards would know, at any hour of the day or night, exactly where each prisoner was. If ever there was any doubt regarding the count the guard would wake all the men in the hut and they would have to get on their feet to be counted properly. As far as they were concerned, dummy heads and rolled up blankets just didn't work.

The same thing would happen if the guard came into the hut and there was no *fushinban* on duty. The whole of the squad would be awakened and questioned until the man who was supposed to be on guard was found. He then got a beating. Sometimes all the inmates of the hut were beaten. It all depended how the questioning went.

All the foregoing made escape in the night impossible, or at best, offered no more than a thirty minute start for a potential escaper. Therefore, it was obvious that should a prisoner ever have managed to escape it would soon be discovered and then at least two people were going to get it, quite literally, in the neck. One was the prisoner who was supposed to be on guard at the time and the other was the Squad *Hanchoe*, not to mention the man who escaped.

Hanchoe was the name for the leader or foreman each squad had appointed. He was the prisoner through whom orders came from above, either from our own officers, or from the Japanese Commander. Very often the squad *hanchoe* took the can back when anything went wrong. Someone trying to escape would have been classed as something going very wrong. Being a *hanchoe* was not a privilege.

The senior British officer in Kinkaseki was Colonel W.E.S.Napier, the C.O. of the 80th Anti-Tank Regiment. Soon after our arrival in the camp he was required to appoint officers for certain posts designated by the Japanese for administrative duties. Major J.F.Crossley became the Personnel Administrator, a really front line and difficult job. He was required to negotiate directly with the Japanese on all matters. For what it is worth, I thought he did it extremely well. Captain J.E.R.Franke was Commodity officer, Lieut. H.A.Hudson Canteen officer, Lieut. R.W.Hellyer the officer responsible for accounts, and Major I.C.Pedley the librarian. Some of these titles were, in part, quite spurious. The Commodities Officer, for example, seemed to be responsible for nothing more than issuing light bulbs. The so called canteen was most certainly not what it was meant to portray. Now and again, and it literally was now and again, there would be an issue of cigarettes. When that happened the cry of "Reek up!" would echo round the camp. It was supposed to be some sort of pay for our work down the mine and probably worked out at one cigarette per week. There was also the occasional issue of small rice cakes. Taken over the year it meant about one rice cake a month.

The librarian did his best but the only books in existence were the ones the Japanese confiscated when we entered the camp. I do remember reading three books, *The Socialist Sixth of The World*, *The Sun is My Undoing* and *The Seven Pillars of Wisdom*. It surprised me that some of our men had actually carried these books round in their knapsacks all the way to Kinkaseki. So, though the occupational titles were grand at least it gave some sort of order in the camp, and each officer did his best to stand between the Japanese and ourselves, very often to their own discomfort.

Wakiyama's reign as Camp Commandant at Kinkaseki was short and stormy. As a Japanese he seemed more unstable than most, both in his dealing with us and with his own men. Indeed, the element of fear which was always a prevailing feature of camp life was much more pronounced during the time Wakiyama was there. A very strong rumour went round after his sudden disappearance that he had committed suicide. We liked to think it was true. In the records of the War Crimes Trials his name is mentioned, but nothing more. Nobody seems to have the knowledge as to what happened to him, and all references are in the past tense. He was succeeded by Captain Yaychachi Immamura. For a few weeks things seemed to improve, though that might have been an illusion. What was not an illusion were the constant daily beatings which the Japanese dished out throughout the long period of camp life, whoever the man at the top was.

It is difficult, unless seen, to appreciate what is covered by the general term beating. I write only of my own personal experience, from the receiving end, and from what I saw happen to other prisoners. The surprising thing is that the Japanese guards did not seem to use the full-blooded punch with the closed fist, the sort of blow one would see used by people in a boxing ring. For some reason it was not part of their repertoire. Instead they used the slap across the face, delivered with the palm of the hand. They used it very effectively – by no means a soft slap – and for the smallest misdemeanour, real or imagined. I do not mean to infer that they were not capable of knocking someone out. Far from it. A beating could mean a series of blows to the head or face with the hands, but more often than not a weapon was used. This could be anything from a rifle to a bamboo stick or pole. The poles were part of the equipment they used in their sport of *Kendo*. When practising they, of course, were wearing some form of protection. In our case we were totally unprotected and we were obliged to stand and take it.

Physical violence was with us all the time at Kinkaseki. We were victims right from the start and it is fitting to quote a letter sent as early as 22 February 1943 from the Personnel Administrator, Major Crossley, to the Camp Commander:

"The present state of the men in this camp is one of nervous tension, for no one knows at what moment he will be knocked off his feet, or for what. I submit that if it is intention of the Nippon Army to continue this treatment then all prisoners will become mentally unbalanced within the next few months.

"Another typical example has occurred whilst I am typing this letter. The Commander of the guard walked into the office and, with the butt of his rifle, knocked me straight off the typewriter and almost through the window of the office. I now request that you will investigate the above instances (examples of beatings) and ensure that we may at least be treated as human beings."

There have been many accounts dwelling on the brutality and

violence in Japanese prisoner of war camps. It is impossible to write about them and leave out the brutality. Likewise, the story of the camp at Kinkaseki would be incomplete without a record detailing the inhumanities of the Japanese. It was an essential part of the ruthless regime we were now under, and it started from the very first day.

The Official Account records several examples:

On the long march from Zeiho, the station where we detrained on the first day after leaving the ship, Private J. Jordan, a man who was very sick indeed, even on the ship, was constantly beaten all the way from the station to the camp. He was unable, even with help from his friends, to keep up the pace. Jordan never recovered and he died in February.

At the end of December, after only a few days in camp, a sick officer was beaten up by, of all people, the Japanese Medical Sergeant, known to us as Sanitary Sid, a man who was to gain one of the worst reputations for brutality at Kinkaseki.

Men were beaten-up simply because they were singing. On another occasion guards came round the camp and attacked all the sick men.

One particularly brutal beating took place on 8 February 1943. Eight soldiers entered the officers' billet and made straight for Captain Sewell. The attack lasted an hour, with each soldier taking it in turn, and they finished up with an attack by rifle butts. The Official Account of this beating ends by saying 'he was in a very bad way.' There was an interesting sequel to the beating of Captain Sewell. A protest was made to the Commandant, seeking an explanation for the gratuitous violence inflicted on him, and as a result the guards responsible were made to apologise. They were then lined up and in a most ceremonious way struck across the face by a number of their comrades. This was the only time when a protestation brought such an end result.

The guards had various tricks which they employed in order to provide themselves with entertainment during the long hours of guard duty. One of their favourites was for two or three of them to make an unannounced charge into a hut. As there was a door at each end of the building it wasn't possible to be on our feet and bowing in two directions at the same time. Some, if not all, the members of that particular squad were then beaten up for not saluting one or other of the guards.

That was exactly what happened on 19 February 1943, when an identical raid was made and five prisoners were attacked for lying down. These men had been working in the mine all day and the Commandant's instructions were that men who had been working could lie down after supper. It still didn't prevent the beatings. As the years went on and the beatings became the order of the day I began to treat the whole thing as a boxing lesson. I learned to roll with the punch, not too obviously, but enough to take some of the sting out of the blow. I suppose that in many ways I didn't help myself when taking a beating by refusing to go down. It was noticeable that if one fell to the ground sometimes the beating was only half as bad as it was when a measure of dumb insolence, as it was known in the British army, came into play. I suspect that many of my beatings were extended for that reason.

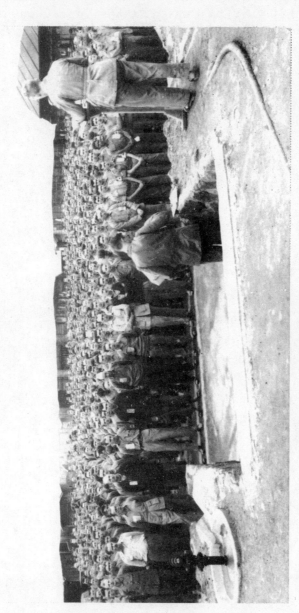

Religious service. A photograph taken by the Japanese for propaganda purposes, the background is masked so that the location of the camp could not be determined. The men are wearing clothes "for special occasions". 1943.

CHAPTER NINE

Out of suffering have emerged the strongest souls;
the most massive characters are seared with scars.

———————————————— E.H.Chapin ————————————————

Christmas Day 1942 was as bleak a Christmas as one could imagine: dull grey skies, a hostile miserable landscape, and a compound full of starving men whose greatest hope was to live long enough to see the end of the war and to return to their homes, families and sanity. We were being watched over by a group of sadistic monsters who, however tradition might describe them as being a gentle-natured people, whose religion had taught them that all creatures, great and small, were to be respected, saw fit not to include us in that category. Towards us these people showed no hint of compassion. They represented a people who spent about a third of their life bowing their heads to each other as a mark of respect, and, no doubt, pretending butter wouldn't melt in their mouth.

Our Christmas dinner in 1942 consisted of a small amount of boiled rice and a piece of pickled turnip.

An advance party went down the mine on 22 December 1942. The reports they brought back were not too horrific. Most of the men said in fact that it was preferable to being under the eagle eyes of the camp guards all day.

A week later it was my turn, along with the remainder of the prisoners who were classed as fit for work. In a curious way I was looking forward to the experience. I had never been down a mine, though I had heard enough stories about the coal mines in the days of my youth in Lancashire to feel a small degree of apprehension. But, like the other men, I also thought it would provide some relief from the constant attention of the guards.

To prepare us for the enforced labour we were issued with a variety of clothing and equipment: a shirt and a pair of shorts of a most ghastly green, giving the impression, both by texture and colour, they had been made from grass, and that was about how substantial they felt. For footwear we were given a pair of fabric split-toed boots with rubber soles. They seemed to be in general use among the lower ranks of the Japanese and we soon gave them the name "tabbies", a form of their correct Japanese name *jika tabi*. The general impression of the whole outfit was that they didn't seem to be substantial enough to last very long at all in a mine environment.

We were also provided with a safety helmet. This was made from compressed cardboard and its life could also be reckoned in weeks rather than months. In fact it turned out just that way. The helmet lasted no more than a few wettings, either from the water in the mine or the rain outside, and as an element of safety wear was worse than useless – indeed, we were more likely to put our heads in jeopardy by giving too much credence to the safety aspect of the helmet. It certainly failed to protect us from falling rocks and low tunnels. The rubber-soled tabbies outlasted the other clothing, but even then it wasn't too long before most of us were wearing just the soles tied on with string. Generally speaking within a year we were all working quite naked and barefooted, or at best wearing nothing more than a G-string.

Undoubtedly the most important accessory of all was the miners lamp. Made from steel and brass and fuelled by carbide, it was reminiscent of the vehicle lighting used by motorists and motor cyclists before the advent of the dynamo. The lower part of the lamp contained the carbide and the upper part the water; an adjustable screw controlled the amount of water allowed to come into contact with the carbide, whereupon, all things being equal, the result was an ignitible gas which was forced out through a burner in the upper part of the lamp. I suspected these were fairly old, but they still appeared to be quite serviceable. There was a complete absence of combustible gas in the mine, consequently it was quite safe to use a naked flame. Although the lamps required a fair degree of maintenance it was a small price to pay for such an invaluable piece of equipment. Apart from providing illumination, the lamp also had its uses when it came to warning us of the lack of oxygen in certain working areas. A flickering, guttering lamp was an indispensable warning signal.

The final item was just about as valuable as the lamp, though some may have considered it much more important. Known to us as a "bento box" it was in fact a portable luncheon box made of wood. About five inches long, three or four inches across, and about one and a half to two inches deep, it had a sliding lid much the same as a child's pencil box. To transport it to and from the mine we secured it with a piece of string and fastened it to our waist. Containing our mid-day meal of rice and the occasional slice of pickled turnip, or, as we knew it, "yellow peril", it was collected each morning at the same time as our breakfast rice. A modicum of excitement was experienced each time since now and again there might even be a piece of dried fish as an extra delicacy.

One test of character was to avoid eating the contents whilst the first hunger of the day was being felt. Many did succumb and had to manage the rest of the day without food. On top of that penance there was also a chance that if one of the guards became aware of a prematurely emptied bento box he would feel the regulations had been broken, therefore some form of punishment was in order.

The first day down the mine was cold and wet. As usual reveille was about 6 a.m. The men responsible for fetching the food served out the morning rice and brought the bento boxes for the people going down the mine that day. Then, immediately after breakfast, we paraded for what was to become the pattern for many months to come. The guards screamed and shouted. A rifle butt in the small of the back urged the more tardy of us onto the parade ground. We numbered and re-numbered, partly because the guards seemed to be incapable of counting a few men, but also because we were still far from fluent in our ability to number easily in Japanese, especially in the early hours of the morning.

It was on these morning work parades we began to get to know some of the Runabouts a little better. They appeared quite incapable of understanding a simple order, often making a mess of the most simple action. I soon came to the conclusion, however, that their fluster was not so much from simple-mindedness but the result of a deep fear of their Japanese overlords. Consequently the more the Japanese shouted the more of a mess they got into.

One character soon became known to us as Lampo, since his sole task on parade each morning was to go round screaming "Lampo, lampo", having undoubtedly been given instructions to make sure the prisoners had mine lamps with them before they left the camp. It was quite harmless as far as we were concerned, but first thing in the morning it got on our nerves, especially as we were hardly likely to leave without one of the most important items of the day.

We left the camp in single file, the man in front being the one with the lowest camp number. Unless he was off sick that man was Jasper Adams, Prisoner Number One. We followed on behind, with a couple of guards in front and the remainder spread out at intervals along the column.

Our route took us past the guardroom and on up the side of the hill which towered over the camp. The summit was on a section of hillside not visible from the camp but from there, beyond a wide stretch of barren terrain, we could see the ocean spread out before us, grey in appearance, and reminiscent of the English Channel on a winter's day.

There were days when the sea contained strands of colouring, browns and greens, as though a painter's palette had been washed in it. This was caused by the spoil from the mine having been dumped on the shore line. It lent the view an appearance totally out of character with the surrounding drab moonscape.

The route down the hillside to the mine,
as it was in 1983, after the 'steps' had disintegrated.

The beginning of the descent to the mine-head was one of those infernal tricks that nature, abetted by man, added to the torture of our daily existence under the Japanese. It was a long winding route of rough stone steps built into the side of the hill. Not being uniformly spaced, each step of a different height or width to the previous one, it was impossible to maintain any sort of rhythm. Each step had to be negotiated as an individual exercise.

Someone had counted these steps. The Official Account gives the number as 1186, though this is not considered to be the definitive number. These were of course only the external steps. There were a few hundred more inside the mine that were required to be negotiated each day.

The 1186 steps from the mine, up the hillside to the camp.

The minehead consisted of a conglomeration of tin sheds in various stages of decay, and the whole area was a mass of narrow-gauge railway lines on which rested a variety of bogey trucks. Each morning there was a great deal of activity, with civilian men and women workers arriving at the minehead. There were also a number of formalities to be observed before we entered the mine proper. Naturally we were counted, at least twice, once by the guards who had accompanied us to the mine, and then by the civilian members of the mining staff. When each faction was satisfied that they were handing over and receiving the same number of prisoners, and that no one had miraculously escape into the Formosan mountains, we were led towards the mine entrance.

Mine Entrance.

Just before entering the tunnel each squad was ordered to halt, turn to the right, and bow in the direction of a shrine built into the wall. The purpose of which, so we were given to understand, was to protect all miners in their working hours below the ground. Once these formalities were observed the order was given to proceed in single file. It was a walk-in mine, despite the winding gear and cage, the principle use of which was for conveying the full and empty bogeys into and out of the mine.

Entrance to the mine. Workman bowing in the direction of the shrine.

Mine entrance from inside the mine.

In the main tunnel there were a number of electric lights, but these were not of sufficient intensity to enable us to see well. We walked on a series of boards laid fore and aft between the rails and supported by the railway sleepers. Many of these boards were loose and in some cases lacked support at one end; often when the man in front stepped on the end of a loose board, the back end came up just in time to catch the shins of the person behind him. Alternatively, it could happen that a board shifted so much that the follower stepped onto thin air. Therefore, warning cries of "Plank!" and "Hole!" echoed along the column in the semi-darkness. There were also angry Anglo-Saxon cries of "Fucking hell!" when somebody missed his footing and spreadeagled himself on the rails, very often causing a minor injury. Such hazards certainly enlivened the process of going to work.

The Boards leading into the mine.

Although the walk-in seemed to go on forever it was, in reality, about three quarters of a mile before we turned off and began to descend a further series of rough steps bringing us to the first of the working levels.

Descending steps inside the mine.

It was on this level I was to work for the next two and a half years.

The lighting improved slightly as we were led into a main tunnel about five hundred yards long finishing at a crossroads formed by other tunnels of minor importance. This main tunnel was about nine or ten feet wide, supported at intervals in the normal way with a web of wooden props. These provided a headroom of about eight feet. To the right of the crossroads was the lift shaft containing the cage which was driven by the mechanism we had seen at the surface.

To the left of the crossroads, which was where we were directed, was a short tunnel some six or seven feet wide by about six feet high and about twenty feet long with fixed benches along its length. This was known as the *mishi*, or luncheon room. It was in this tunnel we prepared for work, removing our clothing and lighting the carbide lamps that Lampo had made sure we had with us before we left the camp.

There followed a number of instructions from our civilian overseers, delivered in a mixture of very broken English/Japanese, the gist of which was to the effect that we should take great care of our mine lamp, and how it was to be used and maintained. Finally we were paraded in the main tunnel where orders were given as to what we were expected to accomplish in the course of the day.

We were then assigned to various areas known as holes, referred to in future by its number. These holes were located at the end of each of the side tunnels leading off the main roadway. At the end of each blind tunnel we ascended a ladder leading into the actual workings.

It was complete Stygian blackness, hard to get used to and, at first, quite frightening. We soon realised what all the fuss was about regarding the carrying of a working lamp. If it went out we were in trouble.

One of the working holes.

Each working hole contained the ore which, in the early days, was drilled and blasted by civilian workers. Our job as unskilled, slave labour, was to collect the ore and throw it into the chute built alongside the ladder which had provided our access. From the bottom of the chute the material was loaded into bogeys, these were then pushed along the main tunnel to the crossroads. Here they were checked by a civilian, usually a young woman, and credited to the appropriate numbered work-place. The checking process formed part of the system in as much as it enabled the civilian overseers, or *hanchoes*, to know how hard each batch of prisoners was working. At the start of the day the prisoners in each hole were allocated a quota of bogeys which had to be completed.

Each bogey held about three quarters of a ton, on the first day there were three of us in one hole and our quota was set at one bogey each. This didn't provide us with any problems. The working area was reasonably dry, and it was warm. It was also dark, and the only access into the hole was via the ladder near the chute so we were very quickly aware when anyone was approaching.

Bogey Man loading Bogey under chute.

How naive we were in those first few days, under the impression that life had suddenly become very kind. We could relax after our quota was completed and there wasn't a camp guard in sight. At lunch time a *hanchoe* came round all the holes and called up the ladder *yasumi*, an indication that it was time to rest. Leaving our quiet dark hiding place we returned to the *mishi* room where we had left our outer clothing that morning. For about thirty minutes we had the pleasure of each other's company, swapping stories about the morning's work and eating cold boiled rice from our bento boxes. Then, our short break over, we were packed off back to work again until the time came to go back to camp when once more the cries of "*Yasumi!*" would echo round the work holes. After a wash at one of the wooden water troughs in the main tunnel we dressed in the *mishi* room and were escorted out of the mine.

Once at the mine entrance we were met by some of the camp guards and were put through the counting routine a few times before moving off to the camp. On that first day I discovered what it was like to climb a total of over two thousand steps out of the mine and back up the side of

94

the hill. I certainly hadn't been working very hard but by the time I arrived in the camp I was beginning to feel the strain.

The day hadn't been too bad at all, at least that was what we told the people who hadn't been down the mine, and some felt we had had the best of the deal. They had been harassed all day by guards who had nothing else to do. Most of us therefore came to the conclusion that the best place to be was down the mine.

Such euphoria was to be short lived. As the days passed, and we were made aware of the requirements of the mine *hanchoes*, so we discovered the real world of our Japanese bosses. Where we had been filling a quota of two or three bogeys per man in the early days they were soon demanding around five or six, and eventually the figure was to be increased to twelve or thirteen a man. Climbing the steps at the end of the day began to take on a new meaning, and, as the demands on our work production increased, so the nature of the *hanchoes* became more and more inhuman. Beatings from people we had nicknamed Frying Pan and Pan Face became more and more vicious, reaching the point of being quite sadistic in many cases, even more so from their immediate bosses, The Ghost and The Eagle.

Generally speaking the names we gave to the *hanchoes* came from their appearance, or what they did. The Ghost and The Shadow were two bar *hanchoes*, the sergeants of the mine hierarchy, they earned their nicknames from the uncanny way they had of suddenly appearing as if from nowhere, creeping up behind us as we were working in a hole. They obviously knew their way around since they were capable of putting out their lamps and moving around in the dark in an attempt to catch us sitting down on the job. Those unfortunate enough to be caught were given a clubbing with the hammer.

A *hanchoe*'s hammer was a formidable weapon. It consisted of a very small steel head on the end of a three foot long slim handle. Its real purpose was much the same as the hammer used by a wheel tapper on the railways. The purpose being that when a hanging rock was struck the sound given out served to prove whether such rock was dangerous or otherwise. At no time did I see a *hanchoe* using his hammer for that purpose. Almost without exception the *hanchoes* on the first floor had, at some time or other, beaten a prisoner with his hammer, in some cases to the point where the prisoner became unconscious, and there were many times when the beating only just stopped short of killing. So now the mine was no longer a place of refuge from the camp.

Most prisoners were engaged in what was known as chunkle and basket work. For this a wooden-shafted pull-hoe was used, the head shaped like the spade insignia on a pack of cards. The basket, a handwoven affair, about eighteen inches square with a back to it about four inches high, was placed on the ground and the ore scraped into it. The contents were then thrown into the chute. It was a monotonous job but required a degree of attention because almost without exception the floor was uneven and the lighting insufficient. When engaged on this work each man moved anything from nine to fifteen tons in a day. Such labour would have tried the strength of a fit, well fed man. For prisoners in bad health, dying from starvation, it was not surprising that climbing the steps at the end of the day was the final straw.

Coupled with all the problems of trying to fulfil an impossible quota there were other hardships that could befall an unlucky prisoner. One of these was a blocked chute. This was a malfunction that in most cases was outside the control of the man in the hole, being simply the way in which the ore got packed inside the chute. The usual method of clearing it was to prod the blockage with a bar through gaps between the logs on the side of the chute. But if that failed the other alternatives were to tackle the problem from above or below, both equally dangerous. From below you stood a chance of having several tons of rock falling on you, whilst tackling it from above meant getting caught up in the suddenly moving rock. This particular hazard did in fact result in many broken limbs as the months passed.

The other great folly was to allow a wheelbarrow to fall down the chute. In some holes, where the ore was a long way from the chute, a wheelbarrow was made available. Heavy and clumsy though they were, it was better than making innumerable trips to the chute with a basket. When a man got tired it was very easy to lose control at the top of the chute and the job of retrieving a heavy barrow required the efforts of three or four men, and even then it was no easy task. Should the *hanchoe* appear on the scene at such an inopportune moment one was also punished for wasting time – precious time which was not allowed for in the handing out of daily quotas. Yet it was very often the difference between reaching a quota and falling short of it.

All the holes had their own characteristics. Some were quite small and, in the beginning of their construction, the roof could be just a matter of three or four feet from the floor. Such places were quite claustrophobic as well as being even more dangerous and extremely difficult places in which to work. At the other end of the scale there were holes with the spaciousness of a cathedral with a high vaulted ceiling. The danger in these places came from the collapse of the whole or part of the roof, when even a small rockfall could cause quite serious injuries.

The Main Tunnel.

A major collapse could, and did, cause death. Sometimes there would be a brief warning, like the falling of a few small pieces, then it was usually possible to get out in time. More often than not a fall would happen without any warning.

It was supposed to be the job of the *hanchoes* to attend to the safety of the mine, but in practice it was left to the prisoners to make every effort, first thing in the morning, to check the roof and walls and bring down any potentially unsafe rock left hanging from the blasting the night before. However, in spite of all our precautions, men were still injured or killed.

The danger was due in part to the fact that, unlike a coal mine where the face is worked, in our case the raw material was obtained in the copper mine by blasting it from the roof; in other words we worked upwards with the roof unsupported. Another idiosyncrasy from one hole to another was the variability in temperature. Some were so hot as to preclude any possibility of working for more than a few minutes at a time, while some were so cold that the only way to keep warm was in fact to work. In other holes the air was so bad that a few minutes continuous work was all that was possible. In such holes the first indication of any problems was a realisation that the the flame of the lamp was getting smaller, and it was at that point it was advisable to get out of the hole before complete darkness descended; any attempt to wander around without a light made falling down a chute a real possibility.

That was the fate of a friend of mine, "Mac" McLoughlin. He fell down a chute and broke his leg in a couple of places and I had to get him out on my own. He was one of the lucky ones. Gunner Millership, who did the same thing, broke his neck and died.

Another problem in many of the holes was the acid water which continuously dripped from the roof and, dependent on the temperature, would burn the skin, or at best cause a nasty rash. But by far the worst effect was when the acid got into the eyes. This could cause a temporary blindness which could last for many hours, or even days. One solution was to get to a water butt as soon as possible and immerse one's head in the water.

On each level there were one or two prisoners designated as hammer men, though not the same as the *hanchoe* with his hammer. These were simply men whose job was to go from hole to hole breaking the larger pieces of rock in order that it could be put into the chute without causing a blockage. The hammer they used was most unusual. The head was standard looking enough and weighed about five or six pounds. It was attached to a shaft through a hole which was no more than half an inch in diameter. The shaft itself was almost like a blackthorn twig, about two and a half feet long and willowy as a wand. To use it effectively required a technique quite different from that of a normal sledge hammer.

Then there were the prisoners who emptied the chutes, the bogey men. Their job was to find empty bogeys, fill them and push each one to the crossroads for transporting to the head of the mine. They were also responsible for each load being credited to the appropriate hole. A good bogey man could be very useful to the chunkle and basket men since there were various ways of filling a bogey with something other than ore. Old wooden props for example took up a great deal of space. There was, however, just one rule: don't get caught, the rewards could be quite bruising.

"Light work for sick prisoners".

Each job had its problems, for the bogey man they started when a fully-loaded bogey came off the rails. As each load weighed about three quarters of a ton, it could take four or five men to get it back on the rails. A passing *hanchoe* would fail to see the bad rail which caused the problem, he would consider it had been done on purpose and bring his hammer into action. After all, every *hanchoe* knew that bogey pushing was, as they said, "light work for sick prisoners."

Eventually another job was created which was not evident when we first went into the mine: "*Brickie brickie mei.*" This was a term used by the *hanchoe*, though we knew it as drilling. Long Tom, so called because he was rather taller than the average Formosan, was the drilling *hanchoe* and was, as far as I was concerned, nowhere near as vicious as the others. During the time I worked with him I never once saw him strike a prisoner. Certainly he never struck me.

I became a driller a few months after going to work in the mine and I was still drilling when the mine closed. I suppose in some ways it was like being a dispatch rider, I was almost a free agent. For the most part I was working quite alone. Each morning I was given a quota of work and Long Tom would visit me about three times during the day, though I could be bothered just as much by other *hanchoes* who were passing my way. My task was to drill from six to ten holes a day, each one some two to three metres in depth, in a given area and in a predetermined pattern. The machines were fairly heavy, made of cast iron and weighing about 60 pounds and were powered by compressed air supplied by an air line into each hole. The drill bits came in lengths of one to three metres.

The action of the drill was both a hammering and a rotating movement, and at times required all one's strength and attention to keep it under control. Certainly the job was no sinecure. Like the chunkle and basket men, what I was able to produce depended on whatever factors came into play each day, with some days being easier than others.

I started from scratch, finding out the hard way the sort of thing that could go wrong. Probably the biggest fault, and the most difficult to overcome, was when a drill became stuck in a partly drilled hole, caused as a rule by drilling too long without clearing the spoil. When such calamities happened it really was extremely difficult to free the drill bit. Frustration would then set in. If, at times like that, it was Long Tom who came along, he would help free the drill. If, however, it was one of the chunkle and basket *hanchoes*, his answer, as always, was to lay about with his hammer. Getting a drill stuck was the sort of mistake one tried not to make too often.

Some work holes were much more difficult than others. At times it meant spending long periods lying on the floor and drilling. In others one could be perched high on a pile of spoil trying to maintain a balance with a machine that seemed to have a mind of its own and was making every effort to throw the operator to the floor.

Prior to our taking over, the drilling had been carried out by some of the civilian workers, usually during the night when we were away from the mine. These people were known to us as Black Sappers because of their black trousers and jackets. It was our understanding that they were men who had been brought from mainland China and were almost prisoners themselves. They were obliged to occupy specific parts of the area and, so we were given to understand, were not permitted to move about as freely as were other villagers. They were identified by a name patch on their clothing.

There were two Black Sappers in particular I came to know quite well, or at least as well as one can be expected to know another person when there is no common language. Known to us as Stropper Joe and Shanghai Lil, they were both strong, well-built young men. But best of all they were very helpful indeed in my education as a driller. Should I ever run into trouble with a machine fault or a drill bit that had stuck, an approach to either of them would get me out of trouble in no time at all.

Prisoner working a Stropper drill.

Stropper got his name from the type of drilling machine in which he specialized. The name we gave to the machine may well not be technically correct but to me it will always remain a Stropper drill. The

100

basic configuration was the same as the hand drill but with two essential differences. In use it was affixed to a stand wedged between the floor and the roof but, unlike the hand drill, water was forced through the centre of the drilling bit to help clear the hole. Although it was a much easier machine to operate it had the disadvantage in that it was extremely heavy to move from location to location, and also very difficult to set up in some of the holes. Stropper Joe taught me to use the machine, though for him transporting it was infinitely easier than for me.

One of the crimes in drilling was to use a drill bit for anything other than the purpose for which it was intended. Some men used them as levers to free blocked chutes, put derailed bogeys back onto the rails, or for levering out any large hanging rock that appeared to be dangerous. All these activities could bend the bit out of true, making it useless for drilling until it had been straightened. Because they had to have attention it was possible for the authorities to become aware of the misuse, again with the inevitable result.

The noise and vibration involved in the job of drilling also caused problems. In the process of drilling it was impossible to be aware of the early warning signs of an impending roof collapse, and at the same time it was those very vibrations which could instigate a fall. One such fall killed one man who was working behind me as chunkle and basket man, and in that accident I received a large gash on my upper arm. A further danger was the accidental extinguishing of one's lamp, finding a way to the chute, and the ladder which provided the way out of the hole without falling down it could then be extremely difficult. All these were matters which one had to experience in order to be aware of as each day progressed.

Before long, however, a new job was added to that of just drilling the holes. The mine management decided that each driller should also lay the charges and do our own blasting, the operation normally carried out by civilian workers after we had left the mine.

We were not told the reason for the change, but I had to admit I found the idea quite exciting. The dangers I hadn't considered. It meant we were now to be entrusted with gelignite, fuses and detonators. And there were various possible ramifications to this new turn of events. To place such material in the hands of prisoners of war seemed a very strange thing to do, especially as we had full control over its disposal. What difference was it going to make if I put two sticks or three sticks of gelignite in a hole? How was anyone going to know if I used only five out of the six detonators I had been given?

The possibilities of our new-found power were discussed at great length. We could take the blasting material back to camp and blow the whole lot to Kingdom-come.

But then where would we be? Where were we to go after our glorious breakout? I had no doubt that prisoners in Europe could have made good use of explosives, but it was not for us. Still, there was the possibility of sabotaging the Japanese war effort. Why should we use all the explosives to produce ore? The less ore we produced the less we assisted the Japanese. The answer to that was easy. If we didn't blast out sufficient ore the chunkle and basket men would be unable to produce their bogey quota and would be punished accordingly. It was a vicious circle and we finally came to the conclusion we would have to blast as instructed.

In my own case the only small victory I gained was to hide the occasional stick of gelignite, along with a detonator or two, under a load of ore in a bogey going out of the mine, though this was only where the ore was plentiful, and who knows what the odd detonator might do here and there, somewhere within the workings outside the mine. Conversely if I thought the circumstances were right I would say I had drilled seven holes instead of six; I could then collect the extra material and dump it. That way I was still in the war.

My blasting days came to an end in January 1945 following the death of Len Cullop, a friend of mine. We had worked together in the mine since his arrival in Kinkaseki from Number Two camp at Taichu in November 1943. I was responsible for teaching him the rudiments of drilling and many times we had helped each other out. On the day Len was killed we were drilling in adjacent holes. When we had finished we collected our blasting materials from Long Tom and returned to our work-place. This meant we started laying our charges at about the same time.

The preparation for blasting was carried out by placing two or three sticks of gelignite into each of the drilled holes, it was then tamped down to the back of the hole with a wooden pole. After treating all the holes in this way a detonator was inserted into the final stick of gelignite, each stick was gently placed in its hole and carefully pushed home. The fuse length for each drilled hole was timed for about three minutes, though we used to slow down the burning rate by putting a small cut about two inches from the start of each fuse, this gave us a few more seconds to get out.

I was paying attention to what I was doing and had almost finished placing the detonators into the six holes when I heard what I thought was an explosion. I consciously thought to myself that Len seemed to have got on very well to have placed all his charges, lit them and then got out. I carried on with what I was doing and, having lit the fuses, went down the ladder and waited near the bottom counting the blasts. This was a normal precaution. It wasn't wise to go back into a hole immediately after blasting. For one thing the place would be full of smoke. For another, and more important reason, I liked to make sure there were not going to be any delayed explosions. I went to one of the water tubs and swilled myself down. After a while I became concerned at not seeing Len. I really thought he was going to be at the water tank since his charges had gone off before I had finished.

When I finally I went to look for him I found him on the ground at the foot of the ladder leading into the hole where he had been working. His lamp was near him but not lit. My first thought was that he had fallen down the ladder, though I was to discover he was hurt much more seriously.

He told me, before they came to carry him away, that he had been caught in the blast of his own charges. Whether it was because he had been too slow in getting out of the hole, a premature explosion caused by a bad fuse, a badly placed detonator or a piece of faulty gelignite I have no way of knowing. Len died, as the Official Accounts states, on October 1, 1945, and the cause of his death was given as "Shock following internal haemmorrhage caused by a penetrating wound injuring the liver (explosion in mine)." His death resulted in the *hanchoe* taking over the job of blasting again. I couldn't really say I was sorry to lose the job.

As a driller working alone there were times when I was tempted to take a rest. On one memorable occasion I thought I had the perfect excuse.

The compressed air which powered the drill suddenly failed, a frequent fault and one which we as prisoners could do nothing about. I sat down to take a well earned rest. There was total silence and almost complete darkness. My vigilance relaxed. My sixth sense was switched off.

Suddenly, and without any warning The Eagle was standing in front of me.

"*Yasumi ka?*" – "Why are you resting?"

Being quite sure of my ground, I replied with the truth. "Kuki nai *hanchoe*." – "No air, *hanchoe*."

To me that sounded as good a reason for not drilling as one could possibly have, but not to him.

"*Kuki nai ka, dame.*" – "No air? That reason isn't any good." He started to lay into me with his hammer.

That day was the nearest I ever came to retaliating. Whilst the blows and his ranting descended on me I worked it all out. Just by picking up a drill bit which was close to hand, I could fell him with one blow. I would then beat him to a pulp and hide his body under the rocks in the hole. They would never find him.

All this went through my mind as I parried some of the blows from his hammer. I was very close to reaching for the drill bit. But then I realised the other *hanchoes* knew I was working in this particular hole. It wouldn't take a genius to put two and two together, and I also would be dead.

I don't suppose The Eagle ever realised just how close he was that day to ending up as part of the mine. With a reasonable chance of being undetected I don't think I would have hesitated as long as I did. Later, I spent hours going over it in my mind and working out the pros and cons of killing him and disposing of the body. In my mind I did it a thousand times.

One offence in the mine which was not condoned by either side was that of using a working hole as a toilet. It was forgivable by us if a man had the squits and had been unable to get to the ladder in time, but otherwise not. The smell seemed to quadruple in the atmosphere of the still and unventilated air of a hole. The correct course of action was to get down into the main tunnel, then use the channel of water which ran down one side, to be washed away outside the mine somewhere.

Whilst there were civilian men, like the Black Sappers, working in the mine, there were also a number of women. What manner of work they did I had no idea, except for the ones who, now and again, were responsible for checking the bogeys into the cage at the crossroads. Our only contact with these women was in competing on occasions for the use of the water tubs. Whilst we were quite naked they at least wore a sort of white chemise. They must have found us somewhat amusing since their giggles echoed the length of the tunnel.

CHAPTER
TEN

The tyrant is nothing but a slave turned inside out.

————— Herbert Spencer, 23 January 1943 —————

"Men who had not worked well in the mine (men who failed to fill their quota) were made to run up and down a hill and were beaten as they ran. During the evening, in pouring rain, fifteen men, all sick, and mostly from the hospital, were lined up and ordered to take off their shirts, made to carry out physical exercises and were beaten. The reason for this was that they failed to have their identification photographs taken. Gunner Black and Lance Corporal Paterson never recovered from this and died in the camp later."

So records the Official Account; the medical account says they died from Malnutrition Oedema.

Before Lieutenant Wakiyama, the Camp Commandant up to September 1943, disappeared overnight from Kinkaseki, thirty-five prisoners under his care had died. In August of 1943 another 123 prisoners had to be removed from Kinkaseki because, even under the demanding standards of the Japanese, they were too sick to work in the mine any longer and were therefore a liability.

This meant that of the original 523 men who entered Kinkaseki there were only 365 remaining by the time Wakiyama went.

The causes of death were recorded in medical language: diphtheria, dysentery, encephalitis, malnutrition oedema, heart failure, and so on. In addition there were the mine accidents, though in truth the word accident does not really apply. There was Gunner Millership's fractured skull, Gunner Sweeney's multiple crushing injuries, and before 1943 was out there were to be many more deaths in the mine.

The background to the loss of life, which cannot be so simply stated on a death certificate, but which formed part of the crucial physical and mental deterioration, even to the loss of alertness down the mine, was due to the system of constant brutal treatment.

The preceding notes were taken from the Official Account, and, whilst the Official Account cannot pretend to cover in depth the cruelties that went on, it at least serves to exemplify some of the tortures practised in Kinkaseki,

"The Hill" consisted of forty to fifty steps leading from the square to the level of the hospital ward, and then on up to the offices of the Japanese Camp Commandant. The punishment, when a prisoner was considered not to be "diligent" enough at his work, was that he was made to run up and down these steps until he collapsed. As a rule it didn't take very long for this to happen. One has to consider the man had already done a day's work, had climbed hundreds of steps to get to the camp, and was a very sick man before he started his punishment. He was certainly very much undernourished. Only a sadist could put a man through such torture as a result of a report from a mine *hanchoe*.

In this way the Japanese were in fact working against themselves, for the worse they treated the prisoners the less they had. On the other hand many of us were quickly coming to the conclusion that this was their intention all along – to kill us all off.

There were many other forms of punishment. A favourite with the guards was to make a prisoner stand outside the guardroom with a heavy object held at arm's length, or above the head. Each time he dropped the weight, or he himself fell to the ground, he was kicked and beaten and made to get to his feet again, whereupon the punishment was continued. This seems to be a rather unofficial punishment, in other words it was not in sight or sound of the Commander's office, though I doubted if that would have made a great deal of difference.

Further punishments are recorded in the Official Account for 28 January 1943: "Seven men of the dysentery ward were caught by the Camp Commander (Lieut. Wakiyama) playing cards. They were sentenced to be handcuffed together (two couples and a three) for a period of three days. One of the men, Gunner Pestell, who was seriously ill at the time, died three weeks later."

There was no doubt that Pestell's death was a direct result of this particular punishment. Whilst on the surface it might well not sound a very onerous form of punishment, that of simple handcuffing, when the full implications are considered it becomes something of a nightmarish experience. In the first place all the men concerned were already suffering from dysentery, a very debilitating disease, and the Commander was aware of this when he sentenced them. Each man would have to go to the lavatory as many as twenty or more times a day and night. This would mean that neither man was able to get any rest. But even if neither man needed to rise during the night to attend to his needs, the mere act of restless sleep would be sufficient to disturb the other. Under the circumstances it was a diabolical form of punishment.

Detention in a small cell near the guardroom was known to the Japanese as the *eiso*. To us it was the ice-box, and it was a place every man did his best to keep clear of. It was a bare room about eight feet square. In one corner of the room was a hole. Below the hole, and therefore outside, was a bucket to be used as a toilet. A prisoner would only be allowed to bring his blankets from the billet and nothing else, and, while serving his sentence, would usually be made to work around the camp and all the time under close control of one of the guards. When not working or sleeping he was required to sit in one particular part of the room, not in the normal way, but with his legs underneath the body and squatting back on his heels. That way, after a very short time, the whole of the lower limbs would go quite dead. At no time was a prisoner allowed to sit in any other position, or to lean against the walls of the room. He had also to be in a position in the room where he could be seen by a guard when he looked through a peep-hole in the door. Food consisted of one small rice ball and a cup of water each mealtime. Any deviation from the rules would bring down the wrath of the guards at any time of the day or night.

Once again, such treatment was an act of sadism. One has only to remember the state of the health of every man in camp, yet being sick didn't save a man from the ice-box.

One prisoner who experienced a few days in the ice box was Gunner Bill Myson, though his particular story had an element of humour to it. He was a rather simple type of man and good natured, but in my opinion should never have been in any of the services at all. Even the Japanese considered he should not go down the mine and gave him just odd jobs to do round the camp. I think he had been sweeping the area around the square when he stopped for a break and placed his broom against the wall of a nearby hut. Unfortunately he chose to prop it near the large painted map of the world the Japanese had erected. The areas and countries on the map were coloured a bright, rising sun red, where the Japanese had acquired holdings, whilst those coloured in pink were the Allied possessions.

It was a propaganda map but the ironic twist was that the longer the map stayed where it was, with the sun shining on it, the rising sun red slowly turned to pink. A final embellishment was a number of nails with Japanese flags hanging from them to indicate their successes during the war.

As Bill prepared to continue his sweeping duties Lieutenant Wakiyama entered the camp. Bill placed his broom back against the hut and prepared to salute him. The broom slipped to the ground taking with it one of the flags in the area around the Phillipines. The

Commandant went berserk, as only Wakiyama could, and he set about poor Bill.

When he grew tired of laying into him he called a parade of all the prisoners in the camp who were not down the mine. They were ordered to turn towards the map and salute. Following that, each British officer was singled out and ordered to march up to the map, salute, take a pace back, salute again then return to the parade. The assembled prisoners were then treated to a long harangue about the glories of Nippon and its armed forces. Myson was finally marched off to the guardroom.

That evening when we returned from the mine the whole camp was paraded yet again. Bill was brought before us and his offence was read out in great detail before being sentenced to ten days in the ice box.

Quite a number of people spent time in the ice box, but in Bill's case there was an interesting sequel to the whole thing. At the time of his offence he had been sleeping in a hut designated the *kikuri* ward. This was the isolation building and was intended to take the overflow of dysentery patients. However, while Bill was doing his time in jail this hut had been emptied of all men, the windows taken out, and the whole place hosed down. The interior of the building hadn't really dried out and it presented an even more bleak appearance than usual.

Bill was released from the guardroom just before the evening roll call and, without saying anything to anyone, had gone to his original sleeping place. Even though there weren't any windows or doors, and it was empty and cold, Bill bedded himself down. When the guards came to his squad for roll-call they were, according to them, one man short. The squad *hanchoe* repeatedly argued that all men had been accounted for, the guards said they hadn't.

Things were beginning to get rather heated and no one knew quite what the answer was. Suddenly one of the Runabouts came into the hut with Bill in tow. He had found him fast asleep in the now empty isolation hut. The unusual thing was that the guards found the whole episode quite funny. There was, for once, laughter all round.

It was not only prisoners who came in for ill treatment and punishment; animals also suffered. On our arrival back from the mine one particular evening there was the usual parade and counting before we were due to be dismissed. But, on this particular day it would seem that several of the cockerels belonging to the Japanese had apparently scored some black marks. We were kept on parade in order that we could be made aware of their wrong doings.

Wakiyama, through Pops the interpreter, went into great detail about how two of the cockerels had run amok and chased some ducks around the Japanese compound. For this they were to be punished:

sentenced to three days standing on one leg, the other leg tied to a wooden stake.

There was another occasion when a stray dog wandered into the camp. We had no objection, but the Japanese felt it was an intrusion and should be punished. The animal was sentenced to have one rear leg fastened up underneath the stomach for a few days. It disappeared after a short while. I often wondered if we had eaten it.

Gunner Myson's accidental sabotage of the Japanese Empire occurred at a time when our officers found themselves in the front line. On 25 February, 1943, a group of them were ordered to prepare for work at the minehead, and on the following day ten of them actually came with the rest of the workforce. For the first time they were at least acquiring a first hand experience of the steps down the side of the mountain. They were not being forced to work down the mine but on the surface on sluicing operations where copper was recovered from the slag. Once they discovered the actual nature of the work they came to the conclusion it was directly aiding the Japanese war effort. For them it was in contravention of Military regulations.

The following letter was sent to the Commandant:

Dear Sir,

All officers, with the exception of those unfit, have now had an opportunity of working on the Copper Sluicing Tanks at the mine. They have now unanimously decided that this type of work is a direct aid to a nation at war with King and Country and cannot therefore be carried out by officers holding the King's Commission.

It is a well known fact that the Code of Honour of Officers of the Imperial Nipponese Army to their Emperor and Country is of the highest standard and we feel sure they would not, under any circumstances, deliberately do anything in the nature of forcing British Officers to break their Code of Honour and their Oath of Allegiance to to their King and Country.

The regulations expressly forbidding officers to do this type of work is contained in our manual of Military Law which I understand is in your possession.

We all appreciate the thoughtfulness of the Camp Commander in providing us with this work on the grounds of Health and we much regret the trouble that has been caused as we fully realise the difficulties under present circumstances.

The letter was signed by Lieutenant Colonel W.E.S.Napier and Lieutenant Colonel J.F.H. Fasson on 2 March 1943. It was obviously a very difficult letter to write and was intended to soft-soap Wakiyama. In the event, though, it obviously failed. It was returned later in the day by the Japanese interpreter who said that all officers who agreed with the contents should also sign. As a result the following letter was substituted.

Sir,

We the undersigned having fully considered the work of sluicing copper at the mine, are agreed that it is of such a nature that it contravenes the Regulations set out in the Manual of Military Law for British Officers holding the King's Commission, therefore, under these circumstances we are unable to continue this type of work.

This letter was signed by all thirty officers in the camp and re-submitted.

Lieutenant Wakiyama then played another card. He said he didn't understand what was meant by "direct aid". A very lengthy letter was then sent to him laying out chapter and verse of the appropriate regulations while at the same time examples were given of the type of work that would be acceptable. The examples given were: gardening for extra food for PoW personnel, camp cemetery, poultry farming for PoW personnel and administration within the camp.

This did not meet with the approval of Wakiyama and he ordered all officers to parade. He said it was tantamount to a declaration of war and ordered that all officers would work in the camp on jobs like emptying latrines and so on. He then made the following statement and sentence, having read out all thirty names:

These officers have declined insincerely the propositions made courteously by the Nippon army and furthermore have submitted paper full of insolence and openly expressed their intention not to co-operate with Nippon Army.

On account of such discourteousness and disobedience on their part they are sentenced to be imprisoned indefinitely until they show repentance.

The officers were then searched and placed in a completely empty billet with guards on the inside. The food was two riceballs per meal and a little hot water, similar to the treatment in the ice box. That happened on 3 March 1943. On 7 March the Japanese interpreter conveyed a message that they should submit a letter of apology. The following letter was sent:

> *The officers agree to the working conditions as shown in the Treaty regulating the work to be done by officer PoW.*
>
> *We wish to add our apologise for any discourtesies and misunderstandings which have occurred.*

This letter was signed by Major G.B.Sanderson who was now Squad Chief, Colonel Fasson having been relieved of his post by the Commandant.

The result of this latest letter was that the officers were considered once more to have insulted the Nippon army and their rations were cut to one rice ball. Some of the officers were becoming quite ill.

On 10 March the interpreter gave Major Sanderson a typed letter which he said should be submitted to the Commandant. He inferred that if this letter were sent all would be well and the officers would not be made to work in contravention of their regulations. It was obviously meant to be some sort of face-saver, so under the circumstances, and since every word of the letter was written by the Japanese themselves, the officers could not be held to account. The letter was as follows:

> *To The Commander,*
>
> *We are indebted to the Commander as he has accepted our request pleasantly and gave work to 10 Officers to begin with when we voluntarily applied for it. However, all of us have contended the work as it gives direct aid to the country now at war with our country and submitted it to the Nippon Officer in charge. He suggested us to stop work on the following day so that we can fully discuss the matter, and at the same time he required us to make definite reply on the day till 15 hours on whether we stop or to continue it. We have replied him to continue the work.*
>
> *On 2nd. inst. we have again reported him to stop work, this we now see showing ourselves totally lacking consciousness and insulting Nippon and her soldiers.*
>
> *We are ashamed for what we have conferred and decided on the 2nd. inst. and feel sorry for Nippon, Nippon Army and the Commander and exposed our blunder to our N.C.O. and men. We are entirely refraining from the work since and*

recollecting the teaching Commander gave us. We must restore our honour and worrying how we could do so.

We attribute all mistakes in the past to our fault and would request the Commander to clean slate this unpleasant incident and allow us to resume work at earliest opportunity.

This was, however, not the end of the situation, as in spite of the fact that the letter had obviously been written on the express orders of Wakiyama, he still felt it necessary to reply to his own letter:

Perusing the letter wrote to me by your officers I find all

1. *of them consider the work in the copper sluicing their main point and expect to be released as term of exchange in resuming the work there.*

2. *Commander of the camp heard very often of your work on so "called voluntary basis" and knows very well how it is sloven and irresponsible, he did not imprison you to enforce you to work, in overlooking the stipulation of International Law.*

3. *In refusing to work you gave some false legal points as excuse and I gave you an explanation on the International Law because your dubious principle will bring you nothing but contempt of other party, therefore requiring you an introspection, remember, I do not mean to demand you to work.*

4. *Commander of this camp extremely hates your thought itself indicating as not to "co-operate in industrial activity in enemy country" you entirely forget a favour by which your lives in the Battle field have been narrowly saved from danger, and still maintain hostile attitude if you so can determine that this camp is also the same as Battle field and we Nippon army will treat you with same feeling as yours.*

The Official Account reports at this point that the only ground gained was a reduction in the hot water ration. It was very obvious that Wakiyama had no intention of releasing the officers. He had created a Japanese incident and could find no way out of it which would allow him to come up smelling of roses. No further letters were submitted at this point.

On 17 March the Commandant interviewed each British officer individually, which took until 20 March. Each officer was required to write on a piece of paper his willingness to work. To the outsider it became obvious that Wakiyama was riding a tiger and he had no idea how to get off. The signed papers, indicating that each officer was willing to work were Wakiyama's evidence when he had to report the matter to his superiors.

However, the saga continued. The officers had been on very low rations of rice and water since 3 March, and then late in the afternoon of 20 March Wakiyama entered the hut where they were serving their sentence. Standing on a chair he said he was still not satisfied, as some of the statements made by the officers at their interrogation did not agree. At this point Colonel Napier realised someone had to break the impasse at which they seemed to have arrived, so he stepped forward and told Wakiyama that he accepted full responsibility for what had happened.

The Camp Commander realised he was being given the opportunity to dismount from the tiger. He at once sentenced Colonel Napier to a further five days imprisonment, Colonel Fasson to a further three days while the remainder were released.

Even then Wakiyama was unable to let the matter drop. His face had to be saved in the most public way possible. He caused the following notice to be displayed on the camp notice board:

29 Officers, Prisoners of War.
While being imprisoned on account of disobedience are released today as they have shown remarkable repentance.

Lieutenant Colonel Fasson.
While being placed in an important role as liasion officer concerning petition made by all officers O.O.W. for their work. he neglected to convey the wishes of the Nippon Army to them causing the incident enlarged unnecessarily. For such reason he is sentenced to be imprisoned for three days.

Lieutenant Colonel Napier.
For reason he has made a false statement against the enquiry of the Camp Commander he is sentenced to be imprisoned for five days.
20th March, 18 Year of SHOWA. *

---

* 18th year of Hirohito's reign. *Showa* means "enlightened peace".

The Prison Rules were then printed on a large sheet of paper and hung on the wall of the hut.

1. *TO OBSERVE STRICTLY IN THE ROOM.*

2. *No smoking allowed.*

3. *Must keep quiet.*

4. *No exercise allowed.*

5. *No reading allowed.*

6. *No one except* **Shushin** *[Red Medical Card] is allowed to lie down till lights out.*

7. *It is not allowed to lean back to the wall.*

8. *It is allowed to posses only handkerchief and waste paper.*

9. *No one is allowed to go out of billet except when ordered by Nippon Army or those with permission to work outside.*

So ended that particular round between our officers and the Camp Commandant. I must say I felt very sorry for them each day as we passed their hut on our way to work. The rations we received as being normal were bad enough. Their sixteen days or so of extreme starvation did very little for their state of health. The incident highlighted the obvious difficulties of communication. Lieutenant Brown, who had some knowledge of Japanese, did not arrive in Kinkaseki until later in the year. Also it showed the immense gulf between the British and the Japanese mentalities.

It appeared to me that the myth of the Japanese army working like a well-oiled machine was in fact just that – a myth. The minute something happened which was out of the ordinary, when a doubt was raised, these so called superior beings were out of their depth.

CHAPTER ELEVEN

*To my mind it is unfortunate that no evidence was forthcoming
from any of the PoW doctors or medical orderlies who must have
been in continual contact with the accused; their testimony, if
available, would have undoubtedly strengthened the prosecutions
case with reference in particular to the alleged withholding of
drugs by the accused and the reduced ration for sick prisoners by
Sergeant Tashiro, the evidence might possibly have resulted in
deservedly severer sentences.*

———— Lt. Colonel D.A.Wright. AJAG. Land Forces, Judge Advocate. ————

Sergeant Taranosuke Tashiro, or as we knew him, Sanitary Sid, the
senior Japanese Medical Officer, was a brutal thug of a man who, more
than any other of the Japanese at Kinkaseki, could, and should, have
been indicted on countless charges of murder.

The purges carried out in the camp hospital were all at his
instigation, though at times he was assisted by others, a cadre that
made up the so called Japanese medical staff. Their styling and
knowledge should not be confused with our own medical staff trained in
the doctoring and nursing of sick men.

Such skills did not appear to be a requirement of the Japanese in
such a post. Each morning Sanitary Sid started his rounds by visiting
the hospital where his idea of examining a patient was, quite literally,
by testing whether a man could stand up to a beating or not. I would not
suggest he went around beating each and every patient, some were
obviously ill enough for even him to see it, but generally speaking it
seemed to be his test. Being ill, or being declared ill, by our own
competent doctor was not enough for Sanitary Sid.

On 29 May 1943, Sanitary Sid paraded all the sick men and sent
ninety per cent of them to work, though earlier, on 20 May it was noted
in the Official Account that, as a result of an all-out drive to get men to
work, less than fifty per cent were fit enough to walk there. The camp
records show the periodic removal from the camp of prisoners who were
considered too sick, even by Japanese standards, not in their tens, but
in hundreds. These men were being replaced by prisoners from other
less taxing camps on the island.

Extreme sickness in Kinkaseki was an ever present part of the vicious circle in which we were caught. Conditions and food were never such as to allow any man to become anywhere near what might even remotely considered as fit and ready for work, and there was no doubt that each and every man in Kinkaseki, at any given time in normal life, would have been considered a suitable case for a long stay in hospital. Even on a good day.

Our Medical Officer, Captain P.G.Seed, was in the direct firing line of Sanitary Sid's rages, often taking a beating because he choose to try and protect the men he knew were in need of protection. By about July 1943 Captain Seed became increasingly desperate about the methods being used to determine whether men were fit for work or not. He felt compelled to write to the Commandant about one particular man, Sergeant Baker. As a result of the letter the Japanese officer in charge of the work detail allowed Baker to be admitted to hospital.

Sergeant Tashiro's reaction on seeing Baker in hospital was, according to the Official Account, "to become crazy with rage." Sergeant Baker was ordered out of hospital by Sanitary Sid who then went looking for Captain Seed. When he found him he beat him up.

A system, introduced by the Japanese, of classifying prisoners who were sick was supposed to solve the problems of who should be doing what, who should be at work and who was allowed to lie down. Under this system, apart from the men who were admitted to hospital, a sick man was issued with a card of a particular colour and this had to be displayed at all times. A Red Card permitted sick men to lie down during the day. Their own word for this state was *shushin*, which in British army terms would be the equivalent of bed down.

There was also a White Card which, while it conceded that a man was too sick to go down the mine, meant that he could be employed around the camp. Another victim for Tashiro, who felt he should be the final arbiter of who was fit to go down the mine and who was not, and he did so. It was useless to argue that this was the Official decree; to attempt to do so was to incur his violence. The card system was under threat from the start because it was never a solution to the problem of the really sick men who were not permitted to go to hospital.

I was fortunate in as much as I only came up against Sanitary Sid once. I had injured my left eye whilst working in the mine. At the time I thought I had simply got some grit in it, but all efforts to remove it failed. It became increasingly inflamed, and by the end of the day I was quite unable to see. When I reported to our Medical Officer in camp there was nothing he could do for me until the inflammation had been reduced and I spent most of that evening bathing the eye in cold water.

The following day I was on my first sick parade since entering Kinkaseki, and Captain Seed was quite adamant that I should stay in camp for a day. It proved to be a most unfortunate decision because, after everyone had left for the mine, Tashiro called a parade of all sick men, and I got a bashing for not going to work.

Later that day Captain Seed, with the aid of a pair of tweezers. removed two minute pieces of stone which had become embedded on the eye. For some months afterwards he told me he could still see the scars left by the particles. I went to work next day, even though my eye was as painful as could be, and I was almost feeling my way around.

The most common form of illness was dysentery. This debilitating complaint caused considerable suffering as well as inconvenience. A man with the squits – the mild, debilitating but seldom fatal form of dysentery – could be going to the lavatory as many as twenty, or even thirty, times a day and the need to go would strike without warning at any time.

In the case of dysentery the outward symptoms were the same, but inwardly it was the most excruciating bowel pain that could be experienced. As it was expressed many times: "Except for the lining of my stomach there is nothing left to pass." The burning sensation in the bowels and the anus could last for days, causing considerable pain and loss of valuable recuperating sleep. It was possible to watch men literally fade away before death finally came. Not everyone who suffered from dysentery died. Had that been the case we would all have been dead in the first few months.

The only drug available for treating this particular disease, was charcoal powder. It was perhaps the panacea for most of the ills which left you spending the day and the night crouched over a hole in the floor. Concocted by Captain Seed, he would hand them out, knowing in his heart that he was supplying nothing more than a placebo. But if it gave the recipient a little bit of heart, then so be it.

The first fatality in Kinkaseki was Lance Corporal J.Griffiths who died of diphtheria. When Captain Seed diagnosed the illness the day after we arrived in the camp the Japanese medical staff ran out of the building. So much for their dedication to their profession.

My own illnesses as a prisoner were to come much later, though of course there were times when I felt so bad I just wanted to lie down and die. Diagnosed illnesses were many and various, the better known being dysentery, malaria, beri-beri and a severe dose of the squits.

There were also the everyday type of problems like boils, ulcers, and gashes that looked as though they were going to turn to gangrene. Treatment for wounds such as these which were caused in the mine was quite inadequate. We used everything we had that could be torn up into bandaging, and these were used over and over again. One treatment for a wound which had become a pus-laden mess was to bind it up and let it heal in its own pus. The alternative was for Captain Seed to clear out the wound with the handle of a spoon which had first been sterilized in a flame; effective, but so very painful.

Boils were commonplace. The worst session I experienced was a batch of six on my right hip, just where the waist-band of my trousers had been rubbing. When I went to see the Medical officer he considered them ripe for treatment, a treatment which was certainly culled from the medical mists of time.

He placed a small quantity of spirit in a glass jar which he then ignited. Whilst it was still burning he upended the vessel and placed it over the worst of the boils, first making sure the edges of the glass made good contact with the surrounding skin. The end result was a bit of witch doctor magic. Though I appreciated the scientific principle behind his actions because, following the law I had been taught in my early science lessons that "nature abhors a vacuum", something had to take the place of the air which was being exhausted by the flame. The skin, the flesh and the contents of the boil rose into the jar. When the suction was sufficient the boil burst, and the puss and poison were sucked out. A simple remedy, very painful and very effective.

As I was being treated a Japanese guard came into the medical room suffering from the same affliction. He thought the treatment I was having was highly amusing and laughed the whole way through, but when his turn came he refused to suffer the vacuum treatment.

His boil was on the thigh and, after examining it, Captain Seed decided on a different form of treatment. Without a word he made a quick pass with his hand and the deed was almost done using half a razor blade. The guard almost went through the roof with a warrior-like cry of pain. The subsequent squeezing of the boil must also have been quite excruciating, I didn't wait to see the final outcome.

Some men suffered from a complaint which attacked the end of the finger, a very painful eruption which eventually rotted away not only the flesh but also the bone. In medical terms it was a whitlow and the only form of treatment was to root away in the end of the finger with a pair of tweezers and remove all the bits of bone. To the recipient it must have been nothing short of absolute agony. But then, as a sufferer, what other choice did he have?

When I had a raging toothache the only treatment available was to have the thing extracted, without anaesthetics. There was very little with which to ease pain, even in the hospital where pain and death were a common occurrence. As early as 1943 Captain Seed was writing to the Commandant pointing out how many men had died in the first three months in Kinkaseki, and was forecasting deaths of enormous proportions unless something was done about the situation.

The Japanese authorities themselves provided very little in the way of drugs. The initial supply brought from Singapore was quickly exhausted, and all that was available was a small amount which our own officers were allowed to purchase, though I have no notion of how this worked. Any Red Cross supplies that came into the camp were confiscated by the Japanese, not only the food but items which could have been used by the M.O. All was kept under lock and key.

A year and two months later, in May 1944, when we had had a change of Commandant, the situation was certainly no better. At a conference of the Japanese and our officers it was pointed out that the hospital was desperately short of drugs and equipment, but the appeal had little effect, apart from the fact that about a month after the meeting and the provision of a list of requirements the only item supplied was a quantity of what we called bug powder.

Not once during our time at Kinkaseki was a Red Cross representative permitted to visit the camp. In severe cases, when surgery was required, the Japanese allowed prisoners to be taken to the nearby Nippon Mining Company hospital. Early in 1943 one man, the victim of a bad mining accident, had to be taken to the hospital to have a leg amputated. Such concession of having treatment at the mining hospital, however, could never be relied upon. On 15 June, 1943, Sergeant Davies, who was suffering from acute appendicitis, was refused treatment by the Japanese. It was only after a prolonged argument that he was transferred for what was to prove a successful operation by a civilian doctor at the hospital. The Japanese in the camp were trying to insist that the operation should be carried out by our own medical staff. I certainly wouldn't have given him much of a chance considering the total lack of anaesthetics and the broken razor-blade type of surgery he would have had to have undergone.

Nevertheless, many miracles were accomplished almost every day by the medical staff headed originally by Captain Seed, and later by Major Ben Wheeler, not just minor matters like boils and whitlows, but medical expertise which ranked as major tests for both doctor and patient.

It was certainly not within the scope of my knowledge to have been aware of everything that went on in the medical rooms, or the hospital itself. However, I did know of men like "Mac" Mcloughlin, the man I extricated from a chute after a mining accident with a broken leg. He owes his mobility today to people like Major Wheeler.

But there were moments of humour, even with that most debilitating of illnesses, dysentery. Jasper Adams, a tall and, even under normal circumstances, lean man with long thin legs, the leader of the parade out of the camp each morning, was suffering to such an extent that it was running down the back of his legs as he stood on parade, a most humiliating thing to happen to anyone. A wag who was standing behind him said, "Hey, Jasper, you're shitting yourself."

Jasper replied in the most hurtful of voices, "I can't fucking help it! What's the point of trying to stop it? It just fucking happens." By the time we reached the top of the hill leading out of the camp, Jasper was well to the rear of the parade. Even the guards were walking in front of him.

The first episode involving Bill Myson happened not too long after we first arrived in Kinkaseki. We were still in the two-storey building, sleeping on the floor with no passage down the centre. Bill's bed space was at the far end of the squad, quite some distance from the exit door of the building. Under normal circumstances this was no problem, but Bill had the squits, which meant that during the night, when he wanted to visit the toilets, he had to step over each of the sleeping men. The inevitable happened. As he stepped across each of the sleepers he deposited on each one a measure of his problem. Bill didn't think to mention it, even if it had crossed his mind, as he made his way out of the hut in the darkness. The result wasn't found until the affected people awoke.

But that wasn't the end of Bill's misfortunes. Because he wasn't working down the mine one of his jobs was to bring the rice from the cookhouse each morning. Between the hut and the cookhouse was a small track which, because of the muddy conditions, had been covered in ashes. On the way back from the cookhouse Bill slipped off his wooden clogs and went base over apex on the cinder track, so did the bucket of boiled rice. Bill's remedy was to simply scrape it all back into the bucket and say nothing when he came into the hut.

The rice was served and a discussion soon started in an attempt to find out what the new ingredient was. Taste buds were put to work and there were wild guesses from various quarters, some quite exotic. It was not until someone thought to ask Bill if any comments had been made by the cooks when they were issuing the rice that the truth came out. By that time most of us had eaten our cinder-flavoured breakfast rice.

Both Jasper Adams and Bill Myson were in the first party of forty-seven sick to leave Kinkaseki in August 1943 to go to a camp in Shirakowa, on the island of Formosa. The records show that Jasper died in Shirakowa. Bill, I presume, made it back to the U.K.

At this time Sanitary Sid gave an order that all the sick men in camp had to kill fifty flies a day. It was in itself a reasonably good idea, since flies were one of the major ways of spreading dysentery. Such an undertaking could only be for our own good and anything which helped to reduce the spread of disease was welcomed.

However, Tashiro had one more trick up his sleeve which would allow him to indulge in his pastime of prisoner-bashing. When each man considered he had filled his quota of dead insects he had to report, complete with the bodies, to the medical sergeant. As they brought their killings to him Sanitary Sid then went carefully through the routine of counting them and woe betide any man who was even one fly short. He not only confiscated the flies the men had already caught but then required them to start all over again and produce another fifty dead flies. As a bonus Tashiro handed out a couple of smacks across the face. It was quite common to see men counting their dead flies over and over again before finally reporting their quota. In many cases the not-so-sick men also helped out any man who was really sick and to whom even fly hunting would have been beyond his capabilities.

During the first year in Kinkaseki illness and death became a part of everyday experience. There were times when it was quite frightening to see how quickly the health of a man could deteriorate. One day he would be there in the squad billet or walking around the camp and, as far as the eye could ascertain, he would seem to be in reasonable physical condition. A day or two later he could be seen to be wasting away and the next thing was that he would be taken to hospital. Within a short time we would hear he was dead.

A mental or physical breakdown? Or was it simply the lack of the desire to live? Who can say? In many ways I thought myself most fortunate. I often thought I had rather less to worry about than some prisoners, and perhaps that increased my chances of survival. Also I was comparatively young, having reached my 21st birthday barely a month after arriving in Kinkaseki.

My personal anxieties were restricted, more or less, to worrying about my mother and father, and my sister and brother. I used to think that I was glad it was I who was the prisoner and not my younger brother. Other prisoners had wives and children back home, in cities perhaps which were the target of German bombing, and such worries were bound to have had an effect. To face their own immediate problems, and to be unaware of what was happening at home, must have produced a state of mind that was not to be envied.

Many of us had friends in the camp, men we had known from the time we left the U.K. and who had shared our experiences before the war started in Malaya. When these friends were in hospital, or had been hurt down the mine, it was as if a member of the family had been affected. One friend of mine, Jim Boughey, died in February 1943 in Kinkaseki. The medical report said "malnutrition oedema with heart failure". Jim and I had some great times together on our travels from Scotland to Malaya and it caused me a great deal of sorrow when he died.

Deaths were beginning to become quite regular and a routine had to be devised when it came to disposing of the bodies. A cemetery had been started on the hillside near the village, and each time a burial party was required it would, as far as possible, be formed from within the man's own squad. His body would be prepared by our own medical staff and left in the bath house until such time as a party was appointed. Only on very rare occasions did the Japanese show any respect for our dead. When they did it was for someone who had been killed in the mine rather than anyone who had died from studied neglect. A great outward show would be made, with large baskets of fruit and flowers supplied by the mining company, all laid out in great display. But the minute they had finished taking their propaganda photographs of a senior Japanese officer making his obsequious, hypocritical bow towards the offerings to the dead, the fruit and flowers were taken away, no doubt to fill the bellies of the guards themselves; it was certainly never passed on to us.

A display of 'Food for the dead'.
The central panel says: "Jyun shoku sha no Rei" "The Soul of Martyrs".

Apart from such occasions they showed scant respect for our dead. I went on only one burial party, that of Jimmy Boughey. Six prisoners were required to carry the body which was contained in a box so flimsy we wondered if it would last out the journey to the cemetery. All the while, the body, stripped of any clothing, moved from one side of the coffin to the other as we man-handled it up the steep slope to its last resting place. All the while we were pushed and prodded with the usual cries of "Speedo, speedo," from the guards.

After what seemed like hours we reached an area on the side of the hill which had been levelled out, and as we began to scrape a hole it became obvious there was only the thinnest of top soil. It was almost bare rock, and for this reason only the bare minimum of a hole was made. A short burial service was conducted by the British officer accompanying the party, not much more than "Ashes to ashes and dust to dust." A covering of soil, and a rough cross placed at the head completed the ceremony, to the accompaniment of the same grunts of "Speedo" from the guards.

Such a crude ceremony might seem a callous attitude towards death, but it was certainly not intended to be so. Speaking for myself, it was a physical ordeal to stagger over the rough ground with the weight of a body on my shoulder and the irreverence of the guards which seemed multiplied on occasions like these. I found myself thinking that whatever I may have felt for the person when he was alive my sympathies were with those of us who were still alive. There was precious little to spare to waste on the dead. In the battle to survive it was the living who needed whatever sympathy was available. Shed tears for the man you had buried, by all means, but his troubles were now over, they couldn't hurt him anymore. He was at rest.

For the remainder of us the struggle was to continue, and we had no idea how long it might be before we would be carried, with much pushing and pulling, up the side of the hill. Tomorrow was another day.

CHAPTER
TWELVE

*If Japan had won we would be using slave labour to build bigger
pyramids than the pharaohs.*
Instead we are erecting new factories with American bulldozers.

A Japanese newspaper man in 1948, reporting
his findings on the streets of Tokyo.

The true picture of what it was like to work in the mine cannot be too far removed from the poet Dante's vision of *The Inferno*. An underground pit of caves, tunnels and crevices, a world of utter darkness, illuminated only by the pale flickering of carbide lamps, where desperate souls hacked, scraped and filled trucks with sweat pouring down their naked bodies, over uncannily protruding rib cages, shoulders and thigh bones. And behind them, like the agents of Mephistopheles, the *hanchoes* with their hammers, forcing their charges on to ever more impossible labours.

Apart from the absence of the fiery furnace the comparison is not so far fetched. While in the beginning the mine might have offered a means of escape from the rigours of life in the camp our outlook soon changed. As the weeks and months passed by we began to see that the initial experience of mine work with its holiday-camp atmosphere, filling one or two bogeys a day, getting the task done and then finding some quiet corner in which to rest while waiting for the call of "*Yasumi!*" was a pipe dream.

The tempo soon increased, and before long we were being worked to the limit and beyond. Daily quotas were being increased to ridiculous proportions and all the time we were getting weaker and weaker. It was useless to try to argue against the insane demands, because that only brought on more and more beatings and tortuous punishments from the *hanchoes*.

Every day now the ritual was played out. We would parade outside the rest-room and the quotas against each hole would be checked. Culprits would be questioned by Frying Pan and Pan Face. There would be a great deal of shouting from both of them as they worked themselves into a rage. Finally certain numbers would be called out and the

125

beatings would begin. The severity was enormous and many men collapsed under the blows. The rest of us, the ones who were to escape punishment, were obliged to stand by helplessly. The men who had been beaten senseless would then have to be helped back to camp up those hundreds of steps.

The final valediction of Dante himself.

Yes, we had been living in a fools' paradise. We had failed to get to know our enemies and we soon learned that this particular hell had all kinds of agonies and tortures. It really was many faceted. As Dante's version contained various circles, each one designed for a different type of sinner, so the Kinkaseki copper mine had its own variations.

There were the hot holes, where the temperature reached astounding levels. There were wet holes, where the water trickled down from the roof and walls, the dissolved acid burning into the skin and the eyes. There were the holes that were both hot and wet, when the acid water which trickled into the eyes really did burn.

There was even the torture in the early days of arriving at lunch time for the midday rice to find that cockroaches had invaded the wooden lunch box and were soiling, or devouring, part of our most precious meal. We learned some of the devil's tricks, in this case by making sure before leaving that the bento was securely fastened and wrapped in the rags we called our outer clothing. Even then it didn't always work, but the visit of the cockroaches didn't prevent us eating what they had left.

Then to turn the diabolical screw even further there were other little devices. As well as increasing the work quota the *hanchoes* also reduced the number of men working in each hole. This was real Machiavellian thinking. With more men in the hole the work load could be shared when one or two men were not feeling up to the mark. Where there were only two men in a hole there wasn't a great deal of sharing that could be done, each man had to work, and it was at times like this when the accidents were more likely to happen.

One of the attributes of hell is perhaps that time stands still, damnation is eternal, and thankfully the comparison was not entirely accurate. Even while slaving in our subterranean ant's nest I always harboured the simple prospect of the midday break. The return to camp to tuck into another portion of rice. Then the heaven of a night's sleep.

However, in one sense, time did take on an abnormal, unearthly quality. It is difficult now to put across exactly how it began to lose meaning. One day blurring into the next, a pure matter of survival, and the thought of next week, next month, losing all significance. If I did think of anything further than today or tomorrow, it was a kind of make-believe. My life was becoming crushingly routine, if that is the right word for a daily fare of beating, starvation, illness and work.

In retrospect therefore it is easy to see that events which occurred early on in camp life, like the first deaths, the first beatings, or a crisis such as the officers' rebellion, stuck in the memory. The brutality was novel, because of its extremity, and it is true that the Japanese lost no time in those first few months in showing us who was boss. But even after that the treatment didn't ease off. They were still beating us just as viciously as ever two years later. In fact it would be true to say it got even worse; certainly the rations did.

Did our senses become conditioned after a while to such things? Were our first lurid fears gradually diminished by repetition? No, that would not be entirely true. For always, underneath, we were still sickened by the treatment; every physical assault aroused some residue of disgust, and every callous, unnecessary death a hatred for them and a compassion for the victim. We were certainly not becoming brutalised by brutality. In any case, we had a bond between us. Whilst we may not have known our enemy, we at least knew who he was, that fact was never in doubt.

Time grew indistinct, I had a vague sense of what season it was, perhaps even which month. But even that used to pale into insignificance. After all, what did time mean, what importance could it have to a life devoted to survival?

I noticed whether it was a colder time of the year, or a warmer one, but beyond that seasons didn't count for much. It always seemed to be raining.

The Official Account, kept by one of the officers, has a basic sequence of events, but even that, after the first few months, lapsed into cursory observations, as though the writers were also affected by the real loss of time. For a prisoner like myself, down the mine each day, the whole experience took on an even more blurred quality as far as accurate dating and marking the passage of time was concerned.

As we came out of the mine we were required to face the shrine. This monument, decorated with orange leaf, was built into the wall just before the entrance. We made obeisance with the words "*sai kei rei*" but we also uttered our own little entreaty to whatever Gods were listening: "a tin of bully-beef and a packet of fags, please."

It was invariably wishful thinking, for only the daily ration of boiled rice awaited us. As for cigarettes, Kinkaseki was the ideal place to break the habit. But answers to our prayers did sometimes occur, and the first we would know of it was towards the end of the long climb back to camp. At the top of the mountain and during the short walk down the other side we could see the parade ground of the camp below us. On the rare occasions when our luck was in one of the prisoners who had not been down the mine would be standing in the middle of the camp and would occasionally wave his arms. We knew then that something out of the ordinary awaited us. Had the Japanese decided to issue a little something from the hoard of Red Cross supplies they had tucked away? A tin of bully between two of us, something to go into the communal stew perhaps, and a few cigarettes?

We were all aware they had received these supplies. The parcels had been seen. But how much was issued to us, and how much they kept for themselves it was impossible to tell. Once, and only once, early in 1945, we hit the jackpot. I remember the scene well, as if it were all the birthdays, and all the Christmases there had ever been, all rolled into one.

We arrived back in camp after the day's work, having had the signal as we approached. But this time it was different, this time it was all the prayers at the mine-head answered in one go. There, on each man's bed-space, was a complete Red Cross parcel. It had been opened but not disturbed, everything was in there.

I sat and opened my parcel; it contained tin upon tin of food, chocolate and cigarettes. It was as if I was in the middle of a communal dream. Before long the the hut was full of the aroma of tobacco smoke. It was as though each man had been given the greatest wish of his life, everyone became more of a human being. It wasn't many seconds before some of the tins were being opened and pieces of chocolate were consumed. The only reason the cigarettes won the race was because it was quicker to light a Lucky Strike or a Chesterfield than to open a tin. The date on the parcels was 1942, so here we were, three years later enjoying our bonus. If the date had been even ten years earlier we would still have enjoyed it, just the thought of some responsible human hand having touched what I was now touching was enough to bring tears to the eyes.

But how different we all are, how we retain our quirks of character even in the most arduous circumstances. After three years of deprivation it was interesting to see how different men adopted totally dissimilar ways of dealing with this treasure. One would have thought we would all have acted like a pack of hungry wolves. Indeed, there was at least one man who did set to with such eagerness that by the time lights-out came everything eatable had gone. Who was to say Charlie Benson was wrong? To use his own words: "I'm not going to leave anything for you bastards to have if anything happens to me." Who could blame him?

By contrast another man was all caution and ate only a small amount before settling down for the night. The following morning I watched him at breakfast. Carefully he opened a small tin of bacon and extracted the piece of greaseproof lining paper. Mixing this with his morning rice he had bacon flavoured rice! Just as carefully he then retrieved the paper, making sure every grain was removed, and he returned it to the tin. This sort of thing went on for days. Long after even the most cautious of us had consumed everything, this man still had food left.

That feast day in 1945 sticks in the memory like a beacon because apart from such happenings there was literally no way of supplementing our daily rations in Kinkaseki, legally or illegally. There was virtually no contact with any of the local populace, apart from the one or two down the mine, and they seemed to be almost as badly off as we were. But even if we could have spoken with any of the members of the village there was nothing with which we could barter. It was out of the question to hope to grab anything which might be lying about in the mine, the area was as barren as it could be.

Just now and again one or two of the more friendly civilian workers slipped the odd item of pickled cucumber to me in the darkness of the mine. Even then it it was a mere trifle.

There was a constant battle between our own officers and the Japanese rations officer to make sure the amounts ordered by the Commandant were in fact handed over. I had no doubts that the rank and file of the Japanese were not above starving us for their own ends.

There is an entry in the Official Account which says "during 1944 the food was not too bad." I have absolutely no recollection of a period when I would have applied that term to the food situation. I can only assume it was meant to apply in a relative sort of way.

Throughout the years in Kinkaseki representations were made by Major Crossley, and the Medical Officers, about the cause of many of the deaths and the illnesses in the camp, and that these could, in many cases, be avoided by supplementing the diet. The deficiencies of fat, protein and vitamin B were the main causes. But nothing ever came of these warnings. It was pointed out in 1944 that the average weight of the prisoners was down from 9.36 stone (59.5 kilos) to 8.81 stone (56 kilos), a drop of just over half a stone in a few weeks.

Although such communications tended to understate the real picture by steering clear of dramatisation, due to the Japanese sensitivity towards any criticism, the Medical Officers and the Major did suggest that not everything was being done to alleviate the problem of food deficiencies.

I was quite unaware of the state of the rations in any other of the camps on the island, being one of the minority who managed to stay the course in Kinkaseki. Certainly, however, rations in the Jungle Camp where I ended up from April 1945 to the end of the war, were a great deal worse than in the mining camp.

What made the food situation worse was the policy of "no work, no food". The amount with which we were issued each day was based on the number of men who were declared fit for work; the sick were, quite literally, supposed to go without. In practice it was not quite as lethal as that because the final distribution of prepared food was in our hands.

Prisoners ill in hospital, or those confined to squad huts for lesser forms of sickness, received the same amount of food. Our behaviour was unquestioning on this – but, because of the system, it was at the expense of everyone else.

Some documented proof of how the Japanese implemented their 'no work, no food' policy can be gained from the Official Account of 1944. A record was kept of how many units of food were issued. It shows that during the months when there were more sick men, and therefore fewer fit for work, there is a generally corresponding decline in the amount of rice doled out. Thus in January, when there were 710 fit men and 75 sick, the rice ration was 625 units. In September, with 623 fit and 133 sick, the ration was down to 575 units.

We did however find ways of sharing the food in a more clandestine manner so that the regulations of the Japanese were not applied.

Supposedly, a canteen purchasing ticket issued to prisoners.
At the time the prisoners were not aware of what the ticket said.

ISSUED Number 107
One Sen Ticket
Taiwan Prison
Wine Purchase Ticket

As a postscript to the question of food the following is an example of Japanese thinking on the matter. The lecture was given by the Orderly Officer, Lieutenant Ichie a member of the Imperial Japanese Army:

"You must stop complaining about your food and losing your weight. You are prisoners because you have lost the war and you are not here for recreation. You should think yourselves lucky your lives are assured in this camp. In the last war the Germans had their rations cut to a third. The people outside this camp are getting very little more than you. I have assessed your food and find you are getting three thousand calories, which is sufficient for human existence. Only yesterday the papers said that rations in Britain had had a further drastic cut.

"Another thing, you are going to the latrines too much while you are working. This is a sign of over feeding, any man caught will have his rations cut."

CHAPTER

THIRTEEN

From 1936 to 1940 are to be the test years. It is almost certain that in the early stages of this period the Military Party will attempt another coup. Political murders are likely to increase, and finally the Party will attempt to acquire complete control.

Sooner or later Japan will penetrate further into China. Eventually she will over-run the whole Republic. It will mean the mightiest war that the world has ever known.

———————— Prof. Taid O'Conroy. The Menace of Japan (1936) ————————

"We by the grace of heaven, Emperor of Japan seated on the throne of a line unbroken for ages eternal, enjoin upon ye, Our loyal and brave subjects:

"We hereby declare war on the United States of America and the British Empire. The men and officers of Our army and navy shall do their utmost in prosecuting the war. Our public servants of various departments shall perform faithfully and diligently their appointed tasks, and all other subjects of Ours shall pursue their respective duties; the entire nation with a united will shall mobilise their total strength so that nothing will miscarry in the attainment of Our war aims.

"To insure the stability of East Asia and to contribute to world peace is the far sighted policy which was formulated by Our Great Illustrious Imperial Grandsire and Our Great Imperial Sire succeeding Him, and which We lay constantly to heart. To cultivate friendship among nations and to enjoy prosperity in common with all nations has always been the guiding principle of Our empires' foreign policy. It has been truly unavoidable and far from Our wishes that Our empire has now been brought to cross swords with America and Britain. More than four years have passed since China, failing to comprehend the true intentions of Our empire, and recklessly courting trouble, disturbed the peace of East Asia and compelled Our empire to take up arms. Although there has been re-established the National Government of China, with which Japan has affected neighbourly intercourse and co-operation, the regime which has survived at Chungking, relying on American and British protection, still continues its fratricidal opposition. Eager for the realisation of their inordinate ambition to dominate the Orient, both America and Britain, giving support to the Chungking regime, have aggravated the disturbances in East Asia. Moreover, these two powers, inducing other countries to follow suit, increased military preparations on all sides of Our empire to challenge Us. They have obstructed by every means our peaceful commerce, and finally resorted to a direct severance of economic relations, menacing gravely the existence of Our empire. Patiently We have waited and long have We endured, in the hope that Our government might retrieve the situation in peace. But our adversaries showing not the least spirit of conciliation, have unduly delayed a settlement; and in the meantime they have intensified the economic and political pressures to compel thereby Our empire to submission. This trend of affairs would, if left unchecked, not only nullify Our empire's attempts of many years for the sake of stabilisation of East Asia, but also endanger the very existence of Our nation. The situation being such as it is, Our empire for its existence and self-defence has no other recourse but to appeal to arms and to crush every obstacle in its path. The Hallowed spirits of Our Imperial Ancestors guarding us from above, we rely upon the loyalty and courage of Our subjects in Our confident expectation that the task bequeathed by Our forefathers will be carried forward, and that the sources of evil will be speedlily eradicated and an enduring peace immutability established in East Asia, preserving thereby the glory of Our empire."

Thus the Imperial Rescript of Emperor Hirohito, normally taking no more than a few minutes to read, was given to the world as a fit and proper reason for plunging the whole of the Orient into war.

To speak those same words, accepting some slight rhetorical drama in the voice, takes perhaps six or seven minutes. But here the tones were of unabashed reverence, with a deliberate pause between each phrase to allow the words, like a litany, to hang in the air. How long did it take? Fifteen minutes, twenty minutes? Double that, because it had to be carefully translated into English.

We were kept standing on the parade square in the pouring rain. It became almost impossible to remain on our feet because it had been hours since our last taste of food and, after having finished a day's work in the mine, we had just about managed to drag our weary bodies up hundreds of steps to get back into the camp. Some of the men had to be supported by others hardly able to support themselves, and everyone was remaining on his feet by will power alone. Not a word must be spoken, the silence complete. A declaration of war, signed and sealed by the God Emperor himself and read out to all prisoners on the

8th of each month. A day designated as Imperial Rescript Proclamation Day – *Taisho Hotaibi*.

We awaited the appearance of the Japanese Commandant. As he came down the steps from his office high above the camp, in his best military uniform, jackboots highly polished, his left hand pushing down on the hilt of his sword to prevent it clanking on the steps behind him, he was aware of the sense of theatre as five hundred or more pairs of eyes and ears await his performance.

Behind him followed the squat figure of "Pops", the Japanese interpreter, rather less impressive in appearance. He was handicapped by having to hold a small lectern above his head with both hands. On this was the camp's copy of *The Rescript*, a document which, at all times, except when actually being read, must be in a position higher than the people gathered around. Because both of Pop's hands were busy he was unable to bear down on the hilt of his sword in the fashion of Captain Immamura, and we stood in silence hoping, as we looked at his short stumpy legs, that they and the sword which trailed behind him would get mixed up. That way the lectern and its biblical cargo would be launched, with desperately flailing limbs, upon the head of the Commandant a few paces below him. He in turn would break his neck in a too rapid descent of the steps which were used to punish half dead prisoners.

Vain wishes. Time after time they both made it safely to the bottom of the steps. Time after time we failed to understand what it was all about. Pops was not the best of interpreters, and we were cold, tired and hungry. We were usually past all hope of concentration. We knew when it was finished, because we were given an order to turn half right which brought us facing the east and the location of the rising sun. The order was then given to salute, and with a bow and a shout of "*Sei keri*" the God figure of Emperor Hirohito was acknowledge. Now we might be free to go and eat our frugal ration of cold rice.

The reading of the rescript was invariably followed by a speech about how well the war was going, Japanese style. It was impossible to take in all that was being said. But we were aware it was hardly worth listening to, being composed of nothing but blatant propaganda. However, we did listen sometimes, like a child that is prepared to listen to a parent reading a well thumbed comic, in the hopes perhaps that there might just be something there that was missed out last time. We might also be given a clue as to how things really were going in the world outside. The Japanese mentality, as I had noticed many times, thought of a rigorous, almost ordained plan. If the plan showed certain failures or discrepancies – such as the war not going their way – we might just detect certain readjustments.

In June 1944 Captain Immamura gave the following address which he also saw fit to have written down and translated for our benefit. At the time we had absolutely no idea of what was happening in Europe or the Pacific. Neither did we have any idea how much correct information Immamura himself was in possession of. It was interesting to note, however, that within a month of this speech the first American air raids started over Formosa.

"I will give you a few advices:

"Of late some prisoners of war are apt to violate the rules and regulations in the mine following impudent attitude to the mine *hanchoes* or not fulfilling your work allotted to you by the mine *hanchoes*.

"Should such an attitude originate in presumption that your country is leading in the war and it will soon be over in the Allies victory it is a great mistake.

"Originally I do not want to speak of the war because it only helps to stir up your peaceful mind in the camp life, but I am afraid you will happen to misact under the misunderstanding and so I will refer to it. At present in Europe and Asia the decisive battle is being fought and has come to decisive stage, no one except God can forecast how it will develop. You must not think either Great Nippon or Germany will be easily defeated, this in fact has been approved by both Churchill and Roosevelt.

"At any rate in the present war Great Nippon and Germany will fight to the last man even if these countries fall in temporary disadvantage. U.S.A. and Britain cannot win in near future, therefore if you think the war would turn out unfavourably for us in this decisive stage of the battle it should take a considerably long time until the war will come to an end. As long as the last Nippon man survives we will not give victory to the Allies. When the whole Nippon nation disappears from this world the Allies can only gain the war. So even if the war would develop as you wish your life as a prisoner of war will continue a pretty long time, i.e. a few more years.

"But it is out of the question when U.S.A. and Britain will give up the war, losing the fight in this decisive period. From this point of view I am paying deep consideration of how I return you fit and well to your own land. Moreover I have endeavoured how to make your life comfortable and peaceful by issuing as good ration as possible in my power. Thus mentally and physically we have been treating you well but it is not because the Axis countries are losing the war. Such a thought is very dangerous for you. In harmony with our kind treatment you must reward us by discharging your allotted work and also obeying faithfully to our instructions. That is the only way you will be treated friendly in this camp, that will be also the way you can lead a peaceful and comfortable life and thus you will able to go home safely.

"I believe it is the will of God and also the duty of men."

What on earth were we to make of such an incredible speech? Was he trying to say, in a very roundabout way that things were not really going very well for them? I was unable to accept that the Japanese were really going to fight to the last man. Armies have been saying such things since time immemorial, and not too many have nations carried out such a vainglorious exercise.

"*Presento*" parades were held at approximately monthly intervals and as a rule they were preceded by some other excuse for a parade, like the reading of the rescript. This meant we could be standing for an extended period of anything from an hour and a half to two hours.

The mine *hanchoes* had a system of determining a man's working qualities over a period of a couple of weeks. Should the *hanchoe* profess to be happy about a particular man's output he would be awarded a *maru*. A circle was marked against his number and the results were passed to his bosses, who in turn passed the information on to the Camp Commander.

On a *presento* night we were paraded after work and would, as on the nights of the Imperial Rescript reading, await the pleasure of Immamura. Down the steps he would come in his usual theatrical way, with Pops bringing up the rear. First of all there would be whatever harangue he had arranged for us and then eventually Pops would announce:

"Big *presento*. When number is called sing *hai* in a loud voice."

Whoever was the recipient was required to run forward and stand to attention in front of Immamura. He would make a pronouncement in Japanese and Pops would translate: "I gif you one piece bled." He would then hand over a slice of bread. The receiver then bowed and returned to his place in the parade.

The items for the *presento* were supplied by the Nippon Mining Company, and could consist of "one piece banana", or "one piece nu-peece", the latter being a bottle of some form of sweet drink. There were probably about seven or eight men to receive manna in this way. In

137

many cases, and if it was appropriate, it very often went to the hospital.

There was no doubt that the real purpose of the *presento* was to cause jealousy among us, but as far as I was concerned, if that was the case, it failed.

Very often the *presento* parades contained another element and finished in a rather different way, the purpose of which was to hand out punishments, also suggested by the mine *hanchoes*.

Identification numbers would be called out and those unfortunate enough were required to acknowledge with the usual *hai* and go to the front of the parade. There they would be screamed at by the Second in Command, probably Lieutenant Tamaki, using a mixture of Japanese and English. In all probability he would also hand out a few slaps across the face and then announce the punishment. This could take the form of running up and down the hill or carrying out some onerous duties within the camp before the transgressor was allowed to have his supper.

At other times they would be sent to the guardroom where the guards had their own particular brands of punishment. In all these cases the unfortunate prisoner had failed to carry out his quota because of some illness and such punishments in the camp often finished him off.

Whilst we had no real way of obtaining news, there were one or two people in the mine who maybe tried to pass news on to us. However, because of the language difficulty, and it should be remembered the people talking to us were probably speaking in their particular version of the Formosan/Chinese language, such attempts could not be taken seriously.

Within the camp there were guards who also liked to think they were passing on news items, but again, whatever they said had to be tempered with a little common sense. One of these so-called sources was a Runabout we called "The Christian". To prove his standing he would enter the hut humming snatches of his own version of Christmas carols. However, just like the other guards, he lost few opportunities of bashing us about.

His actions in providing odd bits of information were obviously designed to boost himself in our eyes, but a major incident in the Autumn of 1943 brought him up short. The affair arose out of a mixture of The Christian's vanity, and an equal measure of naivety in one of our own men, Gunner Daly. Like a few others in the camp, Daly had been keeping a diary of some sort. In this he recorded the latest so called news fed to him by various people like The Christian. It was a very dangerous practice and we knew, without being given notice in writing, that if we were caught the punishment would be very severe. If, however, it was to be done, then the greatest care had to be taken with the results of such notes. Daly's note-book, or whatever it was he kept his snipets in, apparently got wet, and to dry it out he put it on the sill of an open window of the hut. A passing guard found the book and took it off to his superiors. Within a very short time Daly was in the ice box and Major Crossley had been summoned to the office of the Commandant.

The diary contained references to "Frying Pan", "The Christian", "The Count" and others. These terms meant nothing to the Japanese, though perhaps they thought they were code names of some sort, probably of a highly secret nature. Such thinking was not entirely implausible, and they could hardly be blamed for thinking that way. The guards descended on the huts and conducted a search for seditious literature. The names in Daly's book puzzled them and they questioned Major Crossley vigorously.

"Who was Frying Pan, who was Christian, who was The Count?"

Sensing something was wrong Crossley thought quickly. "Ah yes," he said, "all prisoners are Christians, that is their religion. As for frying pan, that was just a form of cooking pot." Whatever the listeners thought of the Major there was no way they could disprove his words.

"And the Count?"

"Well now, that is a high rank amongst the aristocracy of England."

Probably to the mounting annoyance and bewilderment of his interrogator he was released. At once the word was spread around the camp, keep mum and offer the same sort of answers.

The Japanese completely mishandled the situation. Daly was released from the ice box and was of course made aware of the situation at once. He was told that whatever happened he must keep his mouth shut. Within a few minutes he was arrested again, but it was too late. Had Immamura questioned Daly first there was very little doubt he would have given the game away. So it was a very near thing for Daly and the people whose names were in the book.

I couldn't imagine what Daly had written in his diary about Frying Pan, since it was very difficult to believe it could have been items of news he was handing out. As for The Christian he was punished by the prisoners for some time afterwards. Whenever he attempted to get stroppy with us it only needed the word "Christian" to be said in a louder than usual voice and he would panic.

"No, no," he would mutter, "no call Christian." He would then dish out the cigarettes.

The owner of the nickname The Count was Lieutenant Suzuki. He was better dressed than the average Japanese officer, his uniform appeared to be much smarter and his boots were always very highly polished. What was written about him I had no idea, so we were unable to exercise the same blackmail over him as we did over The Christian, and he was posted away from Kinkaseki in October of 1943.

Real news was very scarce indeed in Kinkaseki. Of course men used to return from the mine having talked with one of the locals working on the same floor and felt duty bound to spread whatever news had been given that day. Either through misunderstanding, or misinterpreting what had passed between them, it was very seldom anything worthwhile came out of it. Most of us were disinclined to treat such items of news with any degree of seriousness. We had learnt our lesson a long time ago about "The Yanks being here any day now."

After the war, one ex-prisoner, a man who should have known better, was the instigator of a story that he, after "stealing a dictionary from one of the Japanese offices, was able to read the news sheets put out by the Japanese for consumption by the mine workers." On various grounds the story has to be treated with a certain amount of caution. In the first place anything issued by the Japanese as news sheets, even to the local population, could hardly be taken as credible, since they were hardly going to put out any information which showed them in a bad light. Secondly, in order to read a Japanese dictionary one would have to have a wide knowledge of the symbols of *hiragana*, unless it was written in the romanised form. And why would they require that?

For the interested student it might be as well to quote a piece here from a book by Basil Hall Chamberlain, *Japanese Things*, on the writing and language of the Japanese.

"To read a Japanese newspaper for instance some 3,500 characters must be reasonably well known, plus 96 phonetic symbols similar to shorthand. Each ideogram has three or four different pronunciations and may be written in five distinctive writing styles. At the same time one must bear in mind that the fundamental rule of Japanese syntax is most complicated by European standards. The adjective or genitive precedes the noun which it defines, the adverb precedes the verb, and explanatory or dependent clauses precede the principle clause. The object likewise precedes the verb. The predicative verb or adjective of each clause is placed at the end of that clause, the predictive verb or adjective of the main clause rounding off the entire sentence. This makes a familiar conversation extremely long and complicated. Japanese verbs are highly flexible and bear a complex linguistic work load."

A language with such a peculiar grammar, its uncertain affinities and its ancient literature is difficult enough, but one is then confronted with a double task. Having deciphered the ideograms, be they *Katakana* or *Hiragana*, one has then to find the English translation for each resulting Romanised word or phrase; a Herculean task for anyone. Even more so in the case of someone who has had to work down the mine all day, and with only a few tired hours to himself in the evening. At no time did I ever see, or hear about, a news sheet put out by the Japanese. The propaganda newspaper printed in English and distributed in the camp was strictly for our benefit, as were the impossible feats of heroism committed by Japanese, such stories being mentioned elsewhere. However, I can conceive of no good reason why they should produce any sort of news sheet for consumption by the native population, except that it be for the same reason as the English printed version. I am afraid Sergeant Jack Edwards took upon himself a mantle which was only in his own imagination.

The fact remains, unlike many prisoner of war camps, both in Europe and to a limited extent, in the Far East, we had no means of obtaining really verifiable up-to-date news of the progress of the war. Either from a written or verbal source. We really were isolated from the world in every sense.

CHAPTER

FOURTEEN

To be vanquished and yet not surrender, that is victory.

—————————————— Josef Pilsudski ——————————————

My health, and the general conditions in the camp, grew worse. Consciously or otherwise, I found myself having to devise ways of getting through each day. I was having to concentrate more and more on husbanding what strength I had and refusing to allow the really black moments to dominate my life.

Under the normal circumstances of being sent to prison the prisoner knows, or at least has a reasonable idea, of the length of time he has to serve. There is a light at the end of the tunnel. A day crossed off the calendar means one day less to serve, and that at least can raise the morale a little. In our case it was just the opposite, there was no light at the end of the tunnel. It was one day more, not one less.

And yet, by various means, we kept going. One way was to raise our voices in song whilst entering and leaving the mine workings. Mirth of any sort was not permitted in the camp, and the hours during which we were working in the mine was hardly the time to waste energy singing. But how could they hope to prevent two or three hundred men from singing when they were walking in single file and in the darkness of the mine?

One of the most moving memories I have, and it still brings tears to my eyes and a distinct stirring inside me whenever I hear it, is *Land of Hope and Glory*. To recall the sound, many years later, of a few hundred starved and exhausted men raising their spirits by singing that song as we walked in the darkness of the mine is quite indescribable. Our rendering of such a nationalistic tune had a dual purpose of course. It was not only to raise our spirits, but also an act of defiance, one of the few we could make, and I don't think even selective beatings would have stopped us.

In many ways the words were rather ironic – "Britons never shall be slaves" – because we all knew that was exactly what we were. Nevertheless, each one of us, despite the necessity of hope, had the feeling that what we were enduring could go on for ever, or until the day we died. But we sang with all our might, and we meant every word of it.

There were also various songs written by prisoners, some not quite so well remembered as others. But one song is and always will be remembered, a song that belongs to no other section of prisoners but the men of Kinkaseki. Every man who was ever in No.1 Camp, Formosa, will remember it. Written by Gunner (Trumpeter) J.M.M. Smith, who, with many other songs to his credit, wrote nothing that meant quite so much to the men of Kinkaseki as did the song *Down the Mine Bonnie Laddie*:

> *There's a song in old Formosa that the Nippons loudly sing,*
>
> *You can hear it every evening, oh they make the welkin ring.*
>
> *And they sing to British soldiers who have travelled from afar,*
>
> *To fight for King and Country, now they're prisoners of war.*
>
> *But they know they'll see their homeland in the future once again,*
>
> *But until then the Nippon men will all be heard to say.*

Chorus

> *Down the mine bonnie laddie, down the mine you'll go.*
>
> *Though your feet are lacerated and you dare not answer 'No'*
>
> *Though the rice is insufficient, and we treat you all like swine,*
>
> *Down the mine bonnie laddie, down the mine.*

> *Now the boys were fairly happy, till one cold and cloudy day,*
>
> *When the 'Buncho Dono' called them out, and he to them did say.*
>
> *Now my lads you'll all be wondering why you're out on this parade.*
>
> *Well, now were going to teach you all the Taiwan serenade.*

> *Down the mine bonnie laddie, down the mine you'll go . . .*

You should see us work with chunkles, and work with baskets too,

Though the method is old-fashioned, to the boys its something new.

So we'll work away with patience to the dawn of freedoms day,

But until then the Nippon men will all be heard to say.

Down the mine bonnie laddie, down the mine you'll go . . .

Perhaps one of the most rewarding aspects of life in Kinkaseki, in the context of keeping up spirits, was the comradeship provided by one's fellow men. Everyone was aware of the need for the other. At the same time it was quite surprising how, after a day in the mine, followed by the killing climb up the steps, we could feel somewhat refreshed through the spartan enjoyments of a bath in muddy, lukewarm water, followed by a bowl of boiled rice. It was all relative of course, but it was sufficient to revive us. And for a few hours before lights-out we would sit around on the wooden platforms which formed our bedspace and enjoy each other's company and chat about home.

Some might think it strange, but the one item of conversation that never did arise was women. Sex was a matter that was very far removed from our minds. Certainly there was no doubt that men thought a great deal about their own particular girlfriend or wife. Unusual for a crowd of young soldiers surely, but as someone said: "If you are dying of thirst the last thing one thinks about is a bit of salt bacon."

For men whose constant obsession was food the prevailing talk was of the joys of roast beef and Yorkshire pudding, of fish and chips, of Cornish pasties and what they should contain, of apple pie and home made cakes, and what part of the British Isles produced the tastiest forms of any particular delicacy. We would sit and talk about such things endlessly. Speculating hour after hour on imaginative ideal menus.

Each man had his own gastronomic delight which almost invariably involved native pride and/or the cooking ability of the woman of the home, be it wife or mother. Some menus were, understandably, quite outrageous and quite impossible for a man to consume – though that may well be disproved in the light of later events.

One of my friends, "Mickey" Rooney, actually kept a record of many of the more fanciful menus, and as far as I am aware, still has them, a lasting record of what the spirit of man latches on to in a desperate situation. My own favoured meal, as I recall, was bacon. Lots of bacon and fried tomatoes.

The permanent quest for food also had its down-to-earth side. Hours were spent considering, in absence, the possible variety of refuse in the swill bins of any military camp in the U.K. Many of us would have given our eye teeth for the contents of the average swill bin of past experience.

This was not entirely fanciful dreaming either. The greatest proportion of camp swill from the Japanese cookhouse, meant to fatten up a small number of pigs they kept, ended up in the stomach of certain prisoners. Gunner Cutler was, for a while, in charge of the five pigs which were Japanese property, and his job was to collect the swill from their cookhouse to feed to them. Cutler would first of all fill his own food container, then, as the swill was being fed to the pigs, other men in-the-know would turn up with various containers. The prisoners didn't get much fatter, but neither did the pigs. In fact they were so hungry they used to eat the woodwork of their pens.

Another main topic of conversation centred around the subject of life after we returned home. For various reasons very few men were going to return to their previous occupation. Each man had greater ambitions for himself. It was always my own intention to remain a soldier, since it was what I had always wanted to do. But being a dispatch rider was not to be part of my future life. I had seen enough of the role both in war and peace to know that there were better things.

There was also, I am pleased to recall, always room for humour. There had to be, as we were all aware of the over-riding need to see the funny side of things when times got really hard. And to that end we were helped, quite unwittingly, by the Japanese themselves. We found a great deal to laugh at, in private, about the way they took themselves so seriously, to the point of being quite ridiculous at times. Some episodes were most reminiscent of Gilbert and Sullivan.

There was also humour in some of their supposed attempts to inform us of what was going on in the world outside in the form of the specially produced English edition of the *Nippon Times*, limited copies of which were distributed around the camp. These were meant for our edification, and presumably for developing humility in the face of such a superior race. The tales told, with full journalistic trappings were simply amazing and put the meagre English St. George, with his paltry Dragon, into undeniable shade. Several of the reports are worth preserving, perhaps as a memorial of some sort.

In one such story the newspaper told how the pilot of a Japanese fighter plane came across an American aircraft. "He knew it was an

American", the story goes on, "because of the size of the pilot's nose." The Nippon hero attacks but unfortunately runs out of ammunition before he can shoot down the enemy. Without hesitation he "drew his ceremonial sword, waved it in the air and with cries of *Banzai* crashed his plane into the American aircraft and brought it down." Presumably, the exploit was preordained, for there were no survivors, or eye-witness accounts.

In another stirring adventure we were once again taken into the skies over the Pacific and yet again the lone Nippon pilot ran out of ammunition. Adversity is a true inventor, and for this occasion the warrior of the Rising Sun remembered his *mishi* box which he had brought with him. Removing his rice balls from the box he hurled them at the enemy, striking the American pilot in the eyes, a temporary blinding which caused the plane to crash. Another statistic for the bulletin board in the square.

Finally, and the one I like the best, was the report about the Nippon pilot who ran out of fuel – this made a change from running out of ammunition – during an encounter. Fortunately he remembered the bottle of *Nupis* – a non-alcoholic cordial – which saves the day. By hastily pouring this concoction into the fuel tank of his aircraft it provides him with sufficient time aloft to shoot down the enemy.

Strangely, the standard of English used in these newspaper articles was quite good and led to some speculation about the identity of the writer, or writers.

Captain Yaychachi Immamura took over as Camp Commandant in December 1943, and though his rule was supposed to be more lenient, according to the Official Account, throughout 1944 Kinkaseki remained a place of misery, illness and death. A look at the death roll shows that twenty-two prisoners had succumbed, four of those from accidents. But that does not reveal the true picture. Throughout the year the really sick and the injured were being shunted off to other camps on the island, camps where the regime and the work were not so demanding. Replacement workers were being brought into the mining camp as the batches of sick men were leaving. These replacements were from the so called fit men from other camps on the island. Many of the men who left Kinkaseki as sick men died in transit or in other camps weeks or months later, unable to fully recover from the effects of the mine. The cumulative deprivations and violence revealed themselves in any case like a tidal wave in the early months of 1945 when a further twenty-one men died in less than three months.

The first American air raids started over Formosa in October 1944. Working in the mine all day I was shut off from any outside activity, but above ground in the camp the noise of some of the air battles could be heard clearly enough, although a precedure had been laid down by the Japanese. Any prisoners in camp at the time of a raid were to go into their billet, pull the blinds over the windows and make no noise.

The air raids could feed hopes. I never doubted we were going to win. I always believed that one day I would be going home. I held on to that, believing it with a quiet sort of fervour, like the Christians I suppose when they were going to be fed to the lions. It wasn't something I thought about in a conscious way, neither did I try to work out how it was going to happen. It was a belief, something I just knew. But if the knowledge of the Allied planes coming over seemed to justify those beliefs then so be it. There was, equally, no sense in falling into the trap of becoming too optimistic. Release wasn't going to happen just like that, the daily evidence was too sobering.

There were diversions. The odd camp concert was now allowed, even if on our part there was a fair amount of mock cheerfulness. Certain 'games' were permitted: the football we played was more like tapping a ball to each other whilst trying not to run around too much. But even these activities were, I am sure, only permitted because of the propaganda value they provided: hence the photographs taken by the Japanese. Card playing was allowed now and again, and there were a few books in the so called camp library.

The rigours of the routine remained, however, and sleep was the only way to obtain any real relief. Even in sleep we were to be troubled. There seemed to have been a large import of fleas into our living space. There were also hundreds of bugs sharing our daily lives. These lived in the cracks of the planking from which the huts were built and to squash them, whether by accident or design, was even worse than having them alive. In death they gave off as foul an odour as I have come across, and when somebody did take the life of a bug there was an outcry from all over the billet. Before retiring each night one of our final tasks was to shake the blanket and then try to get to sleep before the bugs got back into bed. Fleas we dealt with by applying the flame of a carbide lamp to the seams of our clothing, otherwise we had to live with them.

CHAPTER
FIFTEEN

Then we considered what to do if the prisoners resisted
and we decided to place explosives in the tunnel
and blow it up with the prisoners inside.
—————— Captain Yaychachi Immamura. War Crimes Trials 1946.——————

Late in 1944 our daily trips to the mine by the route which took us up and down the hillside was made slightly easier. As the entry in the Official Account for November of that year states: "A new tunnel from the mine leading directly into the camp was opened; this meant that the men could go to work without getting wet or cold."

I remember the tunnel very well, and it was an improvement, though perhaps not quite as beneficial as was suggested. We were still required to climb a considerable number of steps to get from the mine workings and back into the camp; the distance was not really any shorter. However, we were grateful for the shelter the tunnel provided in the cold, wet weather.

Cut into the side of hill which formed one side of the camp perimeter, the lower and the upper end was guarded by vast steel doors. In the Public Records Office at Kew after my release I discovered the real significance of the supposed 'short-cut', and the steel doors.

The following are quotes from evidence presented at the War Crimes Trials, the first an affidavit of one Yu Teneki, an office assistant at Kinkaseki.

While working in the office at Kinkaseki there was an order from Prisoner of War Headquarters directing the disposition, by various methods, of prisoners of war in Branch Camps in case of an invasion of the island of Formosa, or any other real emergency.

One of the methods was death at the discretion of the Camp Commanders on their proposed means of disposing of prisoners in various categories. I saw a file copy of the reply from Captain Immamura, Commander at Kinkaseki. It read as follows:

Report on matters concerning disposition of Prisoners of War with the transition of the situation.

25th August 1944. Camp C.O. Taiwan Camp 1.

To C.O. Taiwan Camps.

Report on subject as follows:

In case of sudden pressure of conditions, as an extreme measure, the escape of prisoners of war has been completely provided for by the erection of a high pressure electric wire (3000 volts) around the perimeter of this camp. In case there is help for it because of the situation the prisoners of war will be confined in shaft (mine) at the camp and on the C.O.'s judgement of the situation Extreme Disposition will be carried out at troop strength. If the Extreme Disposition cannot be carried out inside the camp because of the urgency of the situation disposition will be carried out at troop strength, at the decision of the Camp Commanding officer, in an already selected place where they will be moved. If the Extreme Disposition cannot be carried out because of the consumption of troop strength the Extreme Disposition will be carried out with nitric acid which has already been prepared by the Nippon Mining Company.

I expect the above afterwards will be an international problem and outside the Army Staff, the PoW Camp Staff and one of the highest section of the mining staff, this has been treated as secret.

Then, from a statement of Captain Immamura, the Camp Commandant himself:

In either August or September 1944 we studied a plan as to how to deal with prisoners if the camp was attacked by the Allies. The first plan we decided upon was to place all the prisoners in the tunnel at the entrance of the mine from the camp, although this tunnel was not completed at the time.

Then we considered what to do if the prisoners resisted and we decided to place explosives in the tunnel and blow it up with the prisoners inside. In order to carry out this plan it would have been necessary to place the explosives in position but this was never done as there were about seven hundred prisoners and the explosives were not available.

Another plan ordered by Prisoner Headquarters was that the camp should be moved before the camp was attacked by the Allies. Then we considered what to do if it was attacked suddenly and there was no time to move the prisoners, then it was decided the prisoners could be released, permission for this was given by Prisoner Headquarters.

I consulted with Nakamura of the Mining Company as to whether it was possible to blow up the tunnel or not.

A kind of "final solution" or, as the Japanese rather quaintly and chillingly called it, Extreme Disposition.

As I sat there in the Records Office at Kew I couldn't prevent a slight racing of the heart, a shudder perhaps as to how very close I had been to a rather crude but clinical form of extinction. I tried to imagine how we would have been hurried into our tomb, the guards hustling us as usual with their cries of "Speedo, speedo!" It could have been explosives. Immamura's evidence is not really trustworthy. There was no apparent shortage of gelignite, detonators and fuses, I was still using them down the mine.

This Extreme Disposition certainly fits. After all just what would they have done with us if there had been a sudden air-borne, or sea landing, late in 1944, or early 1945? We were only a mile or so from the coast. All military hands would have been needed to tackle the invaders, we would have been in the way, and the last thing they would have wanted would have been a few hundred vengeful prisoners at their backs, even if those same prisoners were hardly able to stand up.

Fortunately it never happened. Fortunate both for us and the Japanese. Mass executions of that sort would obviously have been an embarassment to them, as is made clear in the general instructions revealed in the statements. They had other ways of destroying us, however. With the forthcoming move to the Jungle Camp the ultimate cruelty of their intentions was made clear.

151

CHAPTER
SIXTEEN

*This slavery is surely of the devil
And only grief and harm can come of it.*

———————————— E. Stopford. ————————————

It was difficult for us to assess how important the copper workings were for the Japanese war effort as they continued to drive us like slaves. One note in the Official Account records how, during the autumn of 1944, a "great speedo drive" was started by the Japanese. The results however were counter-productive, many bogeys were derailed, and some of the pneumatic drills inexplicably packed up. Production was supposed to have hit a low level then, and to crown it all, the mine became flooded following heavy rain, and for a time work had to be suspended on the lower levels.

1945 opened with a speech from Immamura in which he congratulated all the prisoners on reaching the beginning of another year. He told us that more decisive battles were being fought in Europe and Asia, but it did not mean the end of the war was in sight. We must be patient and obey the rules of the Great Nippon Army, continuing our diligent work down the mine.

The year wasn't very old when the rumours started. There was certainly something in the air, I don't know exactly when I heard the beginnings of a shift in the emphasis of work down the mine – time didn't fit into memorable calendar dates – but I suppose it must have been during the second month of the year. We were going to move. The mine was going to close. Speculation was rife.

Eventually we were given a general statement that the mine was worked out. But then again there were other reports about supplies of carbide not being available. The question of security was mentioned as a possible reason, that the mine was in too exposed a position for the Japanese to defend. There were stories that we were too large a number over which to exercise real control and that we were to be split up into smaller groups.

The Official Account's version of the closure of the mine places the date at 9 March 1945. Before that date, however, there were some apparent improvements. The Japanese conceded extra *yasumi* (rest) days, which up to now had been set at two a month, and morning reveille was changed to a later time of 6.30 a.m. These were probably concessions granted in the light of the escalating death rate during January, though other explanations for shortening our working day came readily to mind. It would fit in with the shortage of materials: the less time we were down there the less we would use of whatever it was they were running short of.

All these happenings coincided with a deterioration in my own physical condition. I was obliged to spend a further short time in hospital, being unable to walk after a debilitating attack of dysentery and malaria. This was something which would not have been permitted a short time ago when Sanitary Sid was at the height of his powers.

Our Administrative Officers were becoming very alarmed at the general state of health of all prisoners. So much so that a few weeks earlier both Major Crossley and Major Wheeler had pointed out that at least 150 prisoners were unlikely to last out the winter. Lists of weak men were drawn up on Boxing Day 1944. These were constantly updated throughout January and February. It was not until 21 February 1945 that a party of three officers and 207 men left Kinkaseki for Japan. They were accompanied by Captain Immamura, leaving Lieut. Suzuki in charge. This move did not solve all the problems about what to do with the chronically sick men. There were still quite a few left behind, so further lists were then drawn up.

On 26 February 1945 the Japanese called in a civilian doctor to examine Captain Seed, the Medical Officer who had been with us since our arrival in Kinkaseki. Another officer, Captain Stewart, was also in a very bad way. The civilian doctor having examined both officers then announced, through an interpreter, that they were both suffering from acute malnutrition. No treatment was prescribed, nor were any suggestions made as to how they could be brought back to good health. On 22 March Captain Stewart was moved. Sadly, he died shortly afterwards in the camp at Shirakowa.

Captain Stewart was one of the stretcher cases, some of whom were extremely ill, who left us for other camps. Both of our doctors, Major Wheeler and Captain Seed, went with this party of eighty-eight in all, which meant there were now about 350 men remaining in Kinkaseki. The general health of everyone was now in a parlous state, and our medical care was in the hands of a Medical Corps Corporal and Orderlies. Whatever drugs there had been in the camp had also gone with the sick party.

154

Requests were made about this time for Red Cross representatives to visit the camp, but this was turned down on the grounds that the camp was too inaccessible. We were now, therefore, without doctors or drugs and this situation was not to be remedied until 31 May. It was a period in which one man developed mental trouble and another tuberculosis of the spine. Both were moved to Shirakowa and I have no further knowledge of what happened to them.

What, we all wondered, was in store for the rest of us? It could get worse so I didn't give it much thought. I just hoped my one day at a time philosophy would see me through. Neither were we offered any real clues. The mine had closed, our medical care had been curtailed, the Camp Commandant was away in Japan, and speculation as to the future was quite purposeless.

However, the next surprise did give us something of a pointer: we were issued with our old army boots which had been locked away since 1942. It was goodbye to the *tabis* and the wooden *getas* we had been walking around in for the past few years. We had all got into the habit of looking down at the ground whenever we were moving anywhere on foot so it came as a pleasant shock to be able to look ahead, literally, confident that our feet, now shod in a pair of tough boots, would not bump painfully into some sharp object as we perambulated around the camp. Of course it wasn't all relief to start with, After a few minutes of trying to hobble about in a pair of dried out boots, minus socks to soften the rubbing, I began to feel that it might have been better without them. On the other hand I felt there had to be some reason for their actions, so perhaps it was safer to go along with it. It became a matter of perseverance and wait and see.

A small advance party left Kinkaseki at the end of March, and we who were left were ordered to clear the camp of stores. Over a period of the next few days everything was carried to a warehouse in the village and it was there that the most up-to-date item of news came our way.

Close to where we were dumping the sacks and boxes was a small desk on which there was a newspaper. Two or three of us tried to get our hands on it but were caught in the process and given a slap for our troubles. For some reason or other the civilian standing near the desk made no attempt to remove the paper out of temptation's way. Finally a prisoner by the name of Timlin hit on an idea. He borrowed the shirt I was using to protect my back and shoulders from the rubbing of the sacks and, as he got rid of the load he was carrying, he threw the shirt on top of the newspaper. As he turned away he picked up both the shirt and the paper.

We agreed later that it had been worth all the trouble. Later we were told that the main story announced the entry of Russia into the war against the Japanese. History proved otherwise, but at the time whether the story was true or not we had no way of obtaining confirmation. What really mattered was that we wanted to believe it.

I had now been in the mining camp at Kinkaseki for 814 days, for most of which I had been working underground in the copper mine. My weight was down to about seven stone, from an original eleven stone six pounds. I was tired and I was sick. Malnutrition was causing my bones to stick out like the striking notes on a xylophone and I had ulcers on my body the size of two shilling pieces. My back and arms were covered in sores caused by falling rocks in the mine because the wounds refused to heal. I could hardly walk, having only just recovered temporarily from a dose of dysentery and malaria. But I was still alive to take whatever they had planned for my future.

CHAPTER
SEVENTEEN

I saw their starved lips in the gloom
With horrid warning gaped wide,
And I woke and found me here
On the cold hill-side.

———————————————— Keats. ————————————————

There was no way of knowing what time we left Kinkaseki, or how far we had travelled. After boarding a train the rhythm of the wheels lulled me to sleep, wondering, as I drifted off, what was on the other side of the carriage window, the view from which had been cut off by drawn blinds. Anyway, it was a case of farewell to Kinkaseki, and unanswered speculation on what was going to happen next.

We left the train later in the day at a station without a visible name in a small village that seemed to consist of just one simple dirt road flanked on either side by what appeared to be open-fronted shops standing cheek by jowl with the occasional house. The buildings were of mixed construction, some timber while others were built more substantially of brick, but even so the general impression was of some temporary Wild West frontier town. On the outskirts of the village street we were halted on the bank of a nearby river which ran parallel to the road. Here we were provided with the usual meal of a few hundred grains of cold boiled rice.

We were the fittest survivors of the mining camp, but to any casual observer we must have looked as though we were but a few seconds away from instant collapse. I didn't need a mirror to know what I looked like, since the rest of the prisoners provided this reflection: bones sticking out, all hips and ribs and arms and legs as thin as match-sticks. But there didn't seem to be anyone there to see us, except for two children standing a short distance away and staring at us with the unabashed eyes of youth, holding what seemed to me to be some sort of insect – it was about an inch and a half long and held captive on the end of a length of cotton. Periodically the buzzing captive flew round in a circle, the diameter being proscribed by the length of the cotton. I had an inkling how it felt.

There was no one else in sight. Maybe nobody lived here anymore. The only other witnesses were the guards and they, after a short break, ordered us to return to a building at the other end of the street where a miscellany of sacks and other packages awaited us.

A box, a sack, or other such load was pointed out to each of us as we approached. There was no question of choice. The loads varied, but had one thing in common – they all looked very heavy or very awkward. In my case it was a two-man load of a massive pile of blankets. Jack Brazier and I were delegated to share this load, though Jack was, if anything, even thinner than I, but as he and I had been friends for some years I felt I couldn't share it with anyone better. To help us carry the load we were given a makeshift stretcher. This was simply a sheet of canvas tied between two bamboo poles, each pole about seven or eight feet long. We divided the blankets along the length of the stretcher, picked up the poles and joined the waiting column.

As long as I live this day will survive in its startling clarity. Nothing that ever happens to me will diminish, in any way, the memory of the next hours and what Jack and I went through.

When the column finally moved off we picked up our load of blankets. Very soon other prisoners began to overtake us, possibly because their packages were somewhat easier to handle. The basic trouble with our load was that the bamboo poles were too thick, so it wasn't possible for us to curl our fingers around them in order to achieve a firm grip. The result was that within a few minutes the entire weight of the load was concentrated on the tips of our fingers. Finally one of us gave way and the load was spilt all over the ground.

The street in Shinten in 1983.

To explain the situation to the guard was impossible, he either didn't, or couldn't, understand. After re-placing the blankets we picked up the stretcher and staggered on a few more yards. Each time, as one or the other released his grip, so the other was brought crashing to the ground with the load. We soon learnt to warn each other when we had had enough and there was going to be an impending fall, then, by letting go at the same time, we avoided further bruising.

Meanwhile some of the locals had come onto the streets and, as if by example, provided us with an object lesson on how to cope with heavy loads. This consisted of what we came to know as "the coolie trot", short running steps which seemed to cover more ground, stopping for a short rest then off once more. For Jack and I this form of perambulation didn't seem to work, The poles were inclined to bounce too much which meant we lost our grip much sooner. Every two hundred yards or so the load was falling to the ground, and each time one of the guards would come along and administer a swipe or a kick, but it really didn't make any difference. The load was too much and the technicalities of the whole thing made it impossible for us. All we could do was persevere and ignore the guards.

When we eventually left the residential area of the village we crossed a suspension bridge over the river and came onto a narrow track leading into the hills. The way was very rough and stoney and the going got even harder. I began to wonder how many blankets there were, but decided not to count them; I really didn't want to know. With each fall and reloading operation we got weaker and weaker, the agony aggravated even more by being unaware of the distance we were required to carry them.

We then decided to try a new technique. What we needed were a couple of lengths of rope, though where we were going to get them we had no idea. I explained our need to the guard who, by now, was the only other person around, all the other guards and prisoners being out of sight. Desperately I explained to him that what we wanted was to spread the load across our shoulders by means of a halter tied to each end of the poles. I finally got through to him, so at the next house he went in search of the rope. He came back with were two of lengths of stout string. It wasn't quite what I had in mind but we rigged up a couple of halters and off we went.

The path gradually became steeper and more uneven, and we seemed to be climbing for ever upwards. The string began to cut into my shoulders, which added to the pain, and it wasn't long before we were stumbling around once more. The effect now was even worse. Because of the halter arrangement the warning system no longer worked. When one of us fell the other was dragged to the ground, skinning our hands and knees on the sharp surface of the track. We also began to lose patience with each other. The journey began to turn into an unrelieved nightmare. I don't remember the last few yards of that part of the journey for my heart was pounding and the roaring in my ears blocked out everything.

Finally we suffered our last fall. My personal decision was that it was quite impossible to get to my feet again and so, by unspoken and mutual consent, we both remained motionless where we had fallen. I fought to calm the searing rush of breath to my lungs. The only sound I could hear was the blood pulsating faster and faster through my body and causing everything to appear through a red mist. I had experienced such difficulties at other times, like trying to make it to the top of the steps from the mine, but nothing was ever as bad as this new experience. The outside world was blotted out, I was both unable and unwilling to move. There was nothing else for it, I just had to stay where I was.

The dumped stretcher and the blankets were spilled across the path. Jack, in the same condition as I, was sprawled out a few feet away from me, out cold. The moment was frozen, as if we would stay as we were for ever. I think I must have collapsed from the most desperate form of exhaustion. I had no idea how long it was before I came to and realised with a shock that for the first time in almost three and a half years I was in the middle of nowhere, unattended and with no guard in sight.

Where had they all gone? What did they say before they left? Jack, who had also recovered, was just as dumbfounded as I. We remained where we were and discussed the situation. It was certain that dire punishment would follow. They were bound to return and all hell would be let loose. We also knew we would be forced once more into carrying their bloody blankets. We sat in silence, each working out what the repercussions were likely to be, though I had already decided the blankets could stay where they were, nothing was going to make me pick them up again. I was finished.

There was no way of calculating how long we lay there after dragging ourselves to the side of the path. It was possible that we went to sleep, or passed out again. We saw no one and it was pointless to think that we might take off into the unknown.

My next conscious sight was of three figures coming towards us from the direction in which we had seen the column disappear. As they drew near I could make out one of the guards who had remained with us towards the end, while the third figure was that of Lieutenant Kozi Tamaki, my personal bete noire among the Japanese. I had run foul of him once or twice in the past, and I was to do so again in the future. Right now he was heading towards us with his usual swaggering walk and his hand on the hilt of his sword.

But even now, with retribution just a few yards away, Jack and I agreed they could do what they liked. We were not going to pick up their blankets again. We were also aware that even by failing to get to our feet and acknowledging Tamaki's presence we were committing a cardinal sin. It changed nothing.

There was a defiance in our actions, for we had reached the point where we knew it was impossible to carry on, and rather than grovel in the dust we would go out putting on a last defiant face.

Tamaki reached our side, the two guards behind him. He was muttering something, whether to us or the guards I didn't know, but in any case we made no move. Then, standing almost above us, he indicated the load of blankets to the two guards. They packed them all on the stretcher, hoisted it up and went off up the hill.

Tamaki sternly ordered us to follow him as he strode off. Jack and I staggered to our feet, barely able to walk. The two guards had gone from our sight, so off we went in Tamaki's wake. We knew we weren't out of the woods yet; he was leaving his vengeance until later. This was obviously not the time, nor the place. No matter, the die was cast and my own fatalism was simply reinforced.

As we followed the narrow track I could see the wisdom of not carrying the blankets any further than we had. In places the way was intersected by deep ravines and the only way across was by a crude system of footbridges, nothing better than a roughly made ladder across the gap. Beneath was the swirling river and the rocks. These we traversed on hands and knees, not being prepared to trust our sense of balance.

My last clear recollections were of Tamaki grunting and pushing as I dragged myself on all fours up a slight incline to emerge into a sea of faces.

I awoke the following morning and everything slowly filtered back into my mind; Tamaki, the load, the ravine and Jack. Amazingly retribution did not follow. We had refused to carry their damned blankets, we had disobeyed their orders, and we had insulted the great Nippon Army. Yet nothing happened. How could we ever expect to understand the vagaries of the Japanese mentality?

CHAPTER EIGHTEEN

What reinforcement we may gain from hope,
If not, what resolution from despair.

———————————— Milton. ————————————

The village where we had detrained was Shinten, about ten miles from Kukutsu. It was estimated that the load Jack and I had attempted to carry was about 220lbs, almost the combined weight of the pair of us. The same journey was made again and again in the future but it was never going to be as bad; on the other hand I was never going to get used to it either.

The place in which we were now kept was not a camp as such. There were no perimeter walls or fences and, apart from the mountain track, there wasn't a road either. As far as we could see the only inhabitants were the residents of a few wooden houses scattered around the area. There appeared to be no village as such. The district, known as Kukutsu, was about thirty miles south of Taihoku and located on the mountain range of Taihoku Heights which runs down the centre of the island. We were actually on the edge of what had been a tea plantation, now heavily overgrown. Well away from any coast and very well concealed, it was a reasonably safe place to hide a few hundred prisoners from the ever increasing raids by the American Air Force. We called it "The Jungle Camp".

There were about 350 of us and rather fewer guards than had been in evidence in Kinkaseki. But in spite of the reduction of the guards and a lack of any physical enclosure, the surrounding semi-jungle and the camp's location, plus our own physical state, precluded any suggestion of escape.

Ostensibly, our presence was for the purpose of clearing large areas of land and the planting of sweet potatoes. The Official Account states that the island's Prisoner of War Headquarters in Taihoku had laid down a planting programme, once sufficient land was cleared, for the planting of 16,000 sweet potato plants a day. This was recognised as being a physical impossibility even by the camp's own Japanese officers, but the order had been given and they set out to drive us to the limit, and beyond. Work started on the first day in Kukutsu and it never let up.

The ill-treatment reached new heights and the amount of food was greatly reduced. In the mine at Kinkaseki it had at least been possible, at some risk, to find a dark corner and try to recoup our strength. Here it was out of the question – the guards were behind us twenty-four hours a day.

We were organised into various working groups: the Cultivation Party, the Garden Party, the Tamaki or Construction Party, and finally the Town Party. There were no set numbers or work-loads to these, the Japanese decided where the day's priorities lay and the number of men required to work on any particular project. The largest group was the Cultivation Party, usually consisting of about 150 men. Their job was to clear the land, carry out the digging and plant the runners for the potato crop.

It was hard physical labour, because the former tea plants had run riot and the whole area was covered with a tall coarse sharp-leafed grass.I don't know if it was botanically correct but to us it was known as elephant grass. Growing to a height of about eight or nine feet it was murderous stuff to clear. The tip of each leaf was as sharp as a razor and, as it waved about, it cut our half-naked bodies with a painful slashing motion.

The tool we were using was the heavy hoe-like weapon known as the *changkol* (known to us as a chunkle), the universal horticultural tool of the East. In order to use it to its best effect it had to be lifted above the head and smashed down into the ground with a chopping action, using the strength of the arms and shoulders. Once the land had been cleared of the surface growth we then moved forward in a line, raising our chunkles together and chopping down into the ground, half a pace or so at a time digging as we went. At this time the guards would be walking at the rear of the line waiting to see if any man wasn't putting as much of his back into it as they thought he should. If they judged he was slacking they would lay about with whatever they had in their hands at the time, usually a branch of a tree they had picked up.

Men were continually falling to the ground exhausted. The Japanese answer to this was to order the man's friends to drag him out of the way, prop him up under a tree, and leave him for a few minutes – and a few minutes it was. After that one or other of the guards would go over and beat him back into line. Fortunately the digging lines were a concentrated effort every so often, and after each burst we had to start at the beginning and fine the soil down for planting.

164

There were, however, a few advantages to the camp, advantages which had been denied to us in Kinkaseki, because it was possible to supplement our diet in various ways. We now had access to growing matter, for instance. It was difficult to over estimate the value of things like "Jungle Stew", a boiled hotch-potch of grasses, and the stalk of the plant known as traveller's palm. As we didn't return to the camp during the midday break we made the jungle stew over the fires which had been lit for burning the surface plants we had grubbed out during the morning. It was also possible to supplement the stew with items like wasp grubs, or the odd snake. With the rice ration down to about 300 grams a day, anything was a bonus.

There were times in certain areas when it was possible to feign sickness, or ask to go to the *benjo* (lavatory) and, while in the nearby cover, raid a piece of land which had been cultivated by one of the few locals, and steal a sweet potato to eat raw. The potatoes we were planting were grown unfortunately from ivy-like runners, so there was nothing there for us to eat. Then there was the tea, a real boon. I was given to understand that the plants we were uprooting produced very good quality tea in peace time. We boiled the leaves in a large iron bowl, rather like an overgrown wok, and it certainly made a very refreshing drink.

Working directly in the confines of the camp was the Garden Party. Their job was to cultivate an area specifically for use by the Japanese, similar work to the Cultivation Party but on a much reduced scale. This group was made up from the men who were sick or less fit.

The Tamaki/Construction Party was responsible for building the huts in which we lived. These were constructed of bamboo and roofed with a particular type of grass known as attap. As far as possible I tried to stay away from this one, as Tamaki and I seemed to clash every time I came anywhere near him. I suspected he had overheard something I had said about him once after he had bashed me. His English was quite good at times.

Finally there was the Town Party. Chosen, as far as possible, from among the fitter men of the camp, their job was to walk the ten miles or so into Shinten and collect the various supplies of food and whatever, both for our own use and that of the Japanese. Consisting of anything between thirty and a hundred men, the squad would be accompanied by an appropriate number of guards and a Japanese officer. I worked this party quite often and soon got used to the scenery which, on the first awful trip, I had hardly noticed.

We would leave camp soon after breakfast and walk single file along the track. The way led across various crudely built bridges along the shore line of a lake and then up over a rather hilly area, arriving eventually at the suspension bridge over the wide and fast flowing river which was about two or three hundred feet wide. The bridge provided a little light relief on occasions because a body of men crossing such a suspension bridge would be given the order to "break step", to prevent a rythmic action taking place which could cause the bridge to swing from side to side. For us there was no one to give the order, so we marched across in step, and though the swing of the bridge was quite alarming, it was worth it to see the guards take off to the other end to wait for us. It was in fact a rather dangerous thing that we did because if we had gone into the river there was no way we could have been saved. But we did it because for a few moments it gave us a feeling of being rather superior.

Once across, we turned to the right and followed the dirt road between the shops and houses to the building where the stores were kept. On our arrival at the stores the loads were distributed, most of them being in the form of a sack or basket, depending on the contents. Salt, sugar, rice, dried fruit and so on were the usual contents, though it was obvious the only item we were to see any of was the rice. Once the distribution was complete we were taken to a spot near the river where we sat to eat our midday meal which we had carried to the town in the same way we used to carry it to the mine – in a *bento* box.

Most of the loads were heavy; in fact it was calculated that each man was at times carrying a load greater than his own weight. Once the return journey was started there was only one ten-minute break allowed. However, there had to be some sort of compensation for such hard work. We were actually starving to death. Not just hungry – that was three years ago – we were now literally starving, so that any man in our condition, carrying a load of edible produce on his back was going to ignore the danger and steal.

A man who went on a Town Party made sure he had with him what we refered to as a "niggling spoon". The idea was to make a small hole in the outer leaf covering of the basket into the cargo hidden within. We had to be adept and watchful with one eye constantly on the lookout for the guards, but the rewards were worth it. If one was given a sack to carry this was most unfortunate because it usually contained rice and because, in the main, this was for our own use, there was a rule against stealing it. In any case uncooked rice wasn't much good. There was no way of telling what was in any particular container, other than the rice sacks, and so it was only fair that all should have the opportunity to niggle at an edible load, and to this end we would switch loads with each other. One drawback to this system, but one we all accepted, was that if you were the one carrying an excessively "niggled" load on your arrival back in camp and things went wrong, then you carried

166

your own can and took the beating.

There were further perks to be had on the journey to Shinten. On the way into town the few houses we passed often had a tray outside with pineapple slices or fish drying in the sun and in the town itself, outside the open-fronted shops, there were tables on which the traders put some of their foodstuffs for display. Providing one was prepared to take the risk, a nimble move meant a handful of whatever was available.

This was almost a game at times and certain conditions had to be right before any attempt was made. It must not be clumsy, otherwise the guards would soon catch on. You also had to avoid being seen by the householder or shopkeeper. I admit there were times when I fully expected a cry of "Stop thief!", or whatever one shouts in Chinese or Japanese. After all, a large number of starving men could steal an awful lot of food in just a few seconds.

Despite these little extras, gained at very high risk, the Town Party was a very strenuous day's work and men constantly emulated my first trip from Shinten and collapsed under their load. Each man made himself responsible for easing the burden of any man in distress.

"Today you are going to town and will bring back foodstuffs for you to eat. Your rations are no less than any other Nippon person, and even though you may be hungry it is no excuse to steal. When you steal it brings shame on your country. There is a proverb in our army which says that a soldier must never admit to hunger; even when he is hungry he must smile and pretend his stomach is full.

"The loads you are being asked to carry are very small. Any normal Japanese person will carry as much as three times as you do. Even the cultivation work you are doing is only equal to the work of a Japanese child or old woman."

We had just been addressed by Lieutenant Tamaki, his remarks being directed at the Town Party before we left one morning in July 1945 for another long haul from Shinten. He was obviously aware of the stealing, how could it be otherwise? And, as if to impress upon us the moral weight of his strictures, a few days later he almost drove us into the ground.

The Official Account records that on July 19 one hundred men were dragooned into the Town Party to complete the transport of stores back to the camp. "The march on this day was the grimmest ever," the report says. Speaking personally, as a regular on the town trips, I was never on any other sort. Among the supplies brought back were thirty sacks, each containing four British Red Cross parcels, all dated 1942. Fifteen of us carried two sacks, while the remaining 85 were used to transport Japanese army stores.

Tamaki himself accompanied the party and, the camp diary notes, "It was apparent that he intended to get the maximum out of the prisoners. The loads were heavier than usual and the beatings more severe. Tamaki himself resorting to the walking stick he carried with him. The majority of the men reached the camp in a state of physical exhaustion and almost mentally deranged. This was one of the trips where Tamaki and I clashed once more, and I felt the weight of his stick on the road back.

The Japanese, with their very strange way of behaving, declared the following day the first ever public holiday in the Jungle Camp. It was probable that even they recognised that no one was fit enough to get to his feet, though I couldn't help thinking there was some other, deeper and more insidious reason for their generosity, but at least it may have helped to save my life, yet again.

20 July 1945 was the day when the three year old Red Cross parcels were issued, one parcel between four men.

In the months prior to this it was obvious that the Japanese were taking us below the level of human endurance and existence. Rice rations were at first cut to 350 grams and then further to 250 grams per man per day (350 grams is 12 ounces, 250 grams is slightly over 8 ounces) almost half the level of rice we had in Kinkaseki. A few sweet potatoes were supposed to be included in the diet, but by August 1945 we were all in the throes of extreme starvation.

There was no hospital as such in the Jungle Camp, although the medical team had been increased by the addition of some American Medical Corps prisoners of war. In May 1945 the medical officers had seen that the situation was to become quite impossible unless the main problem, that of food, was given sensible consideration, and to this end a letter was sent on 22 May to the Camp Commandant from Sergeant Bingham, the Assistant Personnel Administrator:

During the last few days the men have worked very hard and long hours, which they understand is necessary to build the camp quickly. However, it is requested that consideration be given to an issue of more food as, on the present rations, most of the men are very weak when they finish work. This may have serious effects on their health in a few days' time. On the present rations the men do not receive as much food as they did before leaving the old camp and are working much harder. Today two men were injured through falling timbers because they were absolutely exhausted.

Tamaki's reply to this letter was to call in Sergeant Bingham and slap him around the face. This was quite moderate for him, being a specialist in the scream and boot method.

Efforts were now made to reinstate the Sick Card system which had afforded some relief at Kinkaseki but had been dropped on the move to the new camp. Our own medical staff tried to limit the number of men off work each day to about sixty, realising that such numbers were as far as they could push the matter. Even so, the Japanese counterparts, including Sanitary Sid, often held their own impromptu parades and frequently sent out men who were really too sick to work.

In order to fill out the picture I quote a few extracts from the entries in the Official Account.

June 6:   *"A day never passes without two or three really brutal beatings and many others of less magnitude."*

June 30:   *"Situation pretty grim. Food very short, very little vegetables. Constant daily beatings and, what is more wearing, the interminable shouting of "Speedo, speedo!" the words used by the Formosan guards to spur the men on to work harder, these are having a disastrous effect on the men's health, both mentally and physically."*

July 7:   *"Black day at cultivation. Commenced work at 7.20; break 9.20 to 9.30; lunch 11.55; recommenced work 13.00; break 15.30 to 15.43; Work finished 18.10. Work party reached camp 18.40. The Sergeant Major (Furo) really went to town. He felled six or seven men. Broom came in for the brunt of his fury, being knocked to the ground five times, and on each occasion he was kicked viciously."*

CHAPTER NINETEEN

The prisoners had a tendency to go too slowly,
I myself hit one or two with a bamboo stick.

———— Captain Yaychachi Immamura. (In evidence to I.M.T.) ————

There has to be a protection mechanism to help one survive, but how long it can last is probably a question of temperament. How can a man cope, for example, with some of the horrors of the front line – seeing people blown to bits, or the bayoneting of innocent civilians without putting up some sort of shutter? How can a man continue going up a road into possible death without some form of inner determination? And how, in the pitch darkness of a mine, does a prisoner prevent himself being overcome by panic and thereby falling down a shaft? What makes one man, despite utter exhaustion and absolute starvation, determine to carry on and survive? What makes the resolve of another eventually dissipate?

Some men have always been more prone to going under. At Kinkaseki it was almost impossible at times to determine when a man who was physically deteriorating before your eyes had mentally given in. The slide towards death was, at times, alarmingly sudden, from apparently relative fitness one day to virtual collapse the next. I am not qualified to give any medical or psychological explanation of the link between mind and body, but there has to be one.

I am also aware that physical conditions can be such that there is always the danger of losing one's mind. At the Jungle Camp the risks were ten times greater than in the mine. The conditions and the violence were more severe.

There was also the added danger of losing control because of too many blows to the head. This happened at the beginning of June 1945 to one prisoner, Corporal J. Flynn. He was out with a party of men cutting down the elephant grass when the Japanese sergeant, Nakajima Hitoshi, ordered them all to be lined up. Those who, in his opinion, had not done sufficient work, were to be beaten by the Formosan Runabouts. Flynn was among those singled out and the guard who dealt with him, known to us as "Nasty Carpenter", used the handle of a sickle to beat him round the head. Flynn fell unconscious and had to be carried back to camp.

When he failed to reappear for the afternoon's work Major Crossley went to investigate. He found Flynn in his hut where he was being held down by two men They explained that Flynn had been raving ever since he came in. Doctors were called to him and they stated he was suffering from manic depression of the brain, caused, no doubt, by the severe blows to the head. Flynn later became even more violent and two medical orderlies had to watch over him.

During the next few days Flynn showed no signs of recovery and started wandering aimlessly round the camp. Tamaki called for Major Crossley and the Medical Officer, Captain Schneider, and between the blows of another physical assault, he told them that if they couldn't stop Flynn attempting to walk out of the camp he would be shot. Tamaki also suggested Flynn should be tied up with rope. The officers refused to comply saying he should be transferred to a proper hospital.

Most of us in camp were aware of what was going on. My own recollection was of Flynn doing the most outlandish things, such as entering areas into which we were not allowed and, what was more, he took no part in the daily work of the camp. If it was, as some people suggested, a big bluff on his part then it was either the act of a madman or a calculated risk. I am in no way capable of passing judgement. After a while the Japanese didn't touch him and he did later disappear, perhaps to hospital somewhere.

Lieutenant Tamaki asked for a medical report to be made out but it had to exclude details of how Flynn received his injuries. The wording of Captain Schneider's report was:

> *Insane prisoner, No 1105 Corporal J.Flynn, 2 Squad, has for the past five days been suffering from a mental illness which has close resemblance to a manic depressive psychosis. He is not aware of his present surroundings and he has alternating periods of depressed and violent activity. He believes people are plotting against him. He has tried to wander away from camp and it has become necessary to maintain a twenty four hour guard over him to keep him from doing so. Because of the inadequate facilities for treatment in this case at this camp, because of the undesirability of having him escape, and because he might remain in this condition for many weeks, or even months, it is requested that this man be moved to a camp where facilities to treat this type of case are available.*

Corporal Flynn's case arose because a Japanese sergeant suddenly changed his mind and ordered the work party to collect fifteen bundles of grass before lunch, instead of the original order for four bundles. Flynn was in that working party.

Not long after the episode with Flynn a prisoner, L/Bdr J. Bentley, went down with pneumonia. When the doctors asked for proper drugs to treat him they were told; "Dig up ten worms, wash them, cut in half, boil, and administer the soup to the patient." (Official Account). Bentley died the following day, not having had the benefit of the worm soup.

There were surprisingly few deaths in the Jungle Camp. Surprising because of the almost complete lack of drugs for treatment, the lack of a hospital and the extra rigours of daily life. A simple explanation is that if the war had lasted much longer the death roll would have been catastrophic.

We who were now in Kukutsu were considered to be the fittest of the survivors of Kinkaseki, though few of us in the Jungle Camp were of the original 523 who made up the mining camp in November 1942. We were, however, considered to have a little fat left to live on. During the first few months, though there were sick men, and some of them very sick indeed, we were not considered to have yet reached the end of our tether. Another two, or three months at the most, would have seen the end of us all. That is an unequivocal statement.

I came within a hair's breadth of not surviving. It was about a week before news of the end of the war broke upon us. After the months down the mine, with almost no rest, followed by hard labour in the Jungle Camp on very much reduced rations, increased work and increased brutality, I finally became more ill than I had ever been. My weight was down to around the six stone mark, and my morale was just about at zero.

I didn't discuss my state of mind with anyone, but I knew there was something happening to me, something I had managed to steer clear of all through my time in Kinkaseki. Something was happening to me that I had managed to defeat in the past. The will to die, and to see an end to all my suffering, was stronger than the will to live. I was down, and I was out as well.

Everything, my emotions and experiences, all had been on a knif-edge as a prisoner of the Japanese: the hunger and deprivations that led to the loss of weight; the physical and mental pain, reaching at times unbearable proportions; and the ever-increasing exhaustion that says everything has gone beyond the point of endurance. I eventually folded under the strain.

Under normal conditions it is possible to share the problem, to talk the matter out, but in these circumstances there is a reluctance to do so. Everyone else is suffering in the same way, and whilst the other man's problems may seem less than your own, they may also be as much as he can stand. Therefore, adding yours to his doesn't really help.

Physical pain is ever present in the extreme, mainly because of the lack of proper medical treatment. Pain is visible on everyone's face and in the bearing of their bodies.

And fear, that too is ever present to the nth degree. In normal life fear comes very rarely. A sudden noise in the night, the too close sound of a car on a busy highway, these are momentary fears. Under our circumstances fear was there all the time, not necessarily a physical fear, though that was present to a greater or lesser degree. But also a fear of the future, or even if there was going to be a future. I was aware that death was something people of all ages faced at some time in their life; but to a youth of twenty-two or three years it was a very worrying thing to have to consider. Even more so when one was aware that the whole question of the continuation of one's very life was in the hands of a people who, through their very actions, had shown themselves to be unstable and unpredictable.

The heat was extreme, the cold was extreme, and the reserves of the body were non-existant. Then comes the final straw. The time comes when it is easier to die than to go on living, and now, after three and a half years of continuous, hour after hour of pressure, I too had reached the limit.

As I lay there in my sick and demoralised state I tried to think of a way out of my troubles, a quick finish. When one of the American medical orderlies came to see me I tried to enlist his help. Sergeant Brodsky would have none of it. He talked to me like a sensible medical orderly would and the wisdom of staying alive was pointed out to me. It had to be somewhere near the end of the war, and having struggled through everything up to now it would be such a waste to give in, and so on.

The crisis passed. I was too weak to do anything about my predicament myself and I had at least begun to think right once more. Within a matter of hours my mental reserves revived, even if my body didn't, and once more I refused to succumb. I was determined to get through that day at least.

Before I rose from my sick bed I had another hurdle to climb. I was now suffering from the dreaded beri-beri. My face was all puffed up when I awoke the following morning. When I stood up the liquid in my body obeyed the laws of gravity and filtered down to my lower extremities, so that walking became more and more difficult. Whatever happened I had to stay away from any possible beatings there might be in the offing. They could be fatal. Beri-beri is caused by the lack of certain essential vitamins, in particular vitamin B1, available apparently in unpolished rice, but not in the polished version which had been our staple diet for three and a half years. However, we had been given what purported to be the polishings from the rice in the early days in Kinkaseki. This could only be described as eating sawdust, but we ate it. The sickness is a killer and was responsible for the death of many prisoners, though I was told that the dry form, which caused the skin to go shiny and scaly, with pains similar to those of rheumatism, was even more deadly.

Having recovered the determination to overcome my patch of black despair I began to rally and, though far from being well, I did feel a great deal better mentally. A day or so after my return to work we were compelled to take a rest, due to the very heavy rains, and it was during this period that a most extraordinary thing happened.

We were taking advantage of the enforced holiday and were lying about in the hut. Water was seeping through the walls and in one place there was a torrent actually flowing through the billet. Tamaki came into the hut and stood there for quite some time just looking at us. We were quite sure he had come to select for workers for one of his diabolical jobs and were all somewhat wary, having known Tamaki San for a long time. Suddenly and without any preamble, he announced, "Since you cannot go to work, I will tell you a story."

He then continued, for all the world like some practiced teller of tales at a medieval court.

"Many years ago in a small village in Japan there was a young boy who went down to the lake each day to fish. One day, while he was sitting on the bank of the lake, a young woman came up out of the lake and spoke to him.

" 'Would you like to visit my Underwaterpalace?' " The three words were run into one each time he used them.

" 'But it is not possible for me to go under the water, replied the boy, 'I will not be able to live, and my parents will wonder where I am.'

"Very quickly the Princess, for she was in fact a Princess of the Underwaterpalace, replied: 'If you come with me now you will be quite safe.'

"So the young boy went with her," explained our story teller, "and he explored the marvellous Underwaterpalace with her.

"Soon the young boy said he wanted to return to his parents, as they would be worried about him. So the Princess took him to the shores of the lake, and off he went back to his village.

"When he arrived he was not able to recognise any of the streets and he was unable to find his house. He saw an old man, with a long white beard, sitting on a seat, so he went to him and asked him if he knew his mother and his father.

"The old man said there was nobody with that name living in the village now. There was a family whose son, so the legend said, was drowned in the lake, but that was about three hundred years ago."

Tamaki smiled. "So this boy realised he had been away for a very long time. Not, as he thought, for just one day, but for three hundred years. Perhaps when you get home you will not know anyone.

"You will think you have been prisoners for three years. But when you get home it will be three hundred years."

Whilst it may have been a classical story, and a major part of old Japanese folklore*, to a hut full of weary, starving men, sitting in pools of water, with an unending downpour threatening to wash away the very building which was providing the only shelter available, it was a Japanese officer who had just gone off his rocker. On the other hand, it did seem to be just that – three hundred years since we had seen or spoken to a civilised person.

It was the next day, whilst I was working with the Garden Party, that Tamaki gave me a beating. I had been constructing some steps and he didn't seem to like what he saw, commenting on my handiwork in a rather derogatory way. My reply, considering Tamaki's command of English, was not quite as diplomatic as it might have been.

He beat me over the head with his stick and sent me off to get some water from the stream nearby. The containers were rather clumsy wooden buckets slung on each end of a bamboo pole and carried across the shoulders by means of a yoke. Negotiating the slippery path from the river bank I slipped, the buckets crashed to the ground and the bottom fell out of one of them. Unfortunately Tamaki saw what happened and I think he hit me with everything in sight. I suspected

---

* It would seem fairly reasonable to assume that Tamaki's story was based on the legend of "The Fisher-Boy Urashima". This in turn is based on the ballad of Urashima Taro, the Japanese Rip Van Winkle A.D.760. In the ballad the "Underwaterpalace" is called the Sea-God's Palace.

afterwards that he had remembered me from the episode on the first day of coming to Kukutsu and the retribution I had expected then was handed out in retrospect.

There was to be one more notable meeting with Tamaki before we finally parted company.

CHAPTER TWENTY

As cold water is to a thirsty soul,
So is good news from a far country.

—————————————— Proverbs.——————————————

It was Jack Brazier who first brought us the news of the end of the war, though at the time we were unaware of the importance of what he had been told. Over the years we had heard many such items of news, from "The Yanks are coming" in 1942, to the actual news item presented to us in August 1945.

The day had started like any other day, the usual parades and allocation of prisoners to working parties. I was with the Cultivation Party, and early that morning I dragged myself to the work area. The good thing about this morning was that I was planting new runners of the sweet potato, which was considered light work.

Jack, who was in a worse condition than I, was leading a buffalo and cart around the area under cultivation distributing tools. Whilst he was in a remote area he was approached by one of the local Formosans who spoke to him. As far as Jack could gather the words were:

"*Senso sunde. Takusan boom boom.*" Jack returned to us and told us what had happened. It wasn't particularly difficult to see what the man was getting at. *Senso* meant war; *sunde* was finish. The word *takusan*, in mine terminology meant big, plenty. *Boom, boom* was easy in almost any language. Speculation was rife, but we had also learnt to be very cautious when it came to anything which might give us false hope of freedom.

At lunch time our rest period seemed to go on for ever, serving to add to our hopes. A group of guards were sitting a little way up the hillside from us and, as we looked at them, we had a feeling that there was a little more animation than usual among them, though it could just have been imagination. One member of our group, whose knowledge of the Japanese language was a little better than our own, was sent off to get closer to them in the hopes he might overhear more, but the attempt didn't bring any further news.

The order eventually came to return to work, but it lacked the screaming we had come to expect. Our hopes rose a little higher still. Then came the crowning act. By mid-afternoon we were told to pick up our tools and returned to camp. Here, the day's events were received with the normal scepticism, although the fact that we had returned from work rather early meant there was cause for hope.

The following day, August 17, we were back at work as usual, but it was a perfunctory kind of work. We were told there was to be no cultivation, instead we were to weed the areas we had already planted.

Squatting on our haunches between the planted rows we pretended to pull out non-existent weeds. Stories were going around like wildfire and there was a distinct change in the atmosphere. Once again we finished work quite early in the afternoon. No official confirmation, or denial, came from the Japanese, though they must have been aware of the feelings in the camp, and even of brief snatches of our conversation.

The following morning Major Crossley was summoned by the Commandant, Captain Immamura. The Major was told that on 14 August peace negotiations had started, and that although the war was not yet over an Armistice had been agreed. He was also told that all working parties were to cease, except for the Town Party, who would be required to bring supplies from Shinten.

As soon as the morning roll call was over Major Crossley visited all the prisoner squads and told us:

"At 6.20 this morning the Commander informed me that negotiations between our two countries for peace had commenced. As yet the war is not exactly over, but peace reigns, it is hoped we will soon be completely free. The Commander has pointed out that we are definitely, as yet, still under their orders and regulations as before, and I hope none of you will do anything stupid or senseless."

The cheers that went up could have been heard in Tokyo, and there were tears too, but this time they were tears of absolute joy. It was true – I had survived. When we settled down there were a hundred things we wanted to say to each other, though it was noticeable that there was still an air of constraint, and it was even voiced that the whole thing was another diabolical trick on the part of the Japanese. From what we had seen and experienced in the past years anything was possible. After all, we were living in complete isolation in the hills. It was not a recognized prisoner of war camp and the Japs were the only ones with any firearms. So whilst there was joy, we certainly weren't going to do anything stupid.

It was interesting to note, with hindsight, that no one thought to ask who had won.

Major Crossley had a further meeting with Captain Immamura later in the day when the following question and answer session was held:

Q. "What is the position regarding more food?"

A. "The Commander will do his best."

Q."What is happening about hospital patients, especially the prisoners with beri-beri? Can we have food such as bean paste and eggs?"

A. "Permission for these will come from headquarters."

Q. "Can we have a bullock to kill for meat?"

A. "There is no meat."

Q. "Can we have Red Cross from town?"

A. "Yes, today."

Q "Can any sweets which are in the canteen be issued to prisoners?"

A. "Yes."

Q. "Cigarettes?"

A. "There are no spares."

Q. "Matches?"

A. "Burners will be issued."

Q. "Can we have the boots which were sent by the Red Cross?"

A. "Yes, today."

Q. "May an officer and a working party go out in order to tidy up the graves?"

A. "Yes, after lunch today."

Q. "May we hold a church service and sing *God Save The King*?"

A. "Yes to the first, no to the second."

Q. "May we hold a concert and a roll call later in the day?"

A. "Yes to both."

Q."What is the position regarding rules and regulations in the camp?"

A."They remain the same. There will be extremely severe punishment for stealing."

As a result of the approach by Major Crossley each prisoner was given 200 grams of crystalized sugar. This was obviously part of what was left from one of the many loads we had carried from Shinten. In the past it had, of course, been issued only to the guards, except for the small amount stolen with our niggling spoons.

During the afternoon Lieutenant R.W. Hellyer and four men visited the crude cemetery and tidied the graves. There was also a Thanksgiving Service for all denominations. It was a very emotional occasion. My thoughts were for the friends and comrades who had failed to survive Singapore, Kinkaseki and Kukutsu. Even worse, as I looked around, the thought entered my head that many of us were still in a bad way and there was still a long way to go before we could be considered to be out of the wood, literally and metaphorically.

There were at least twenty-five men who were incapable of walking out of the Jungle Camp to the nearest point which could be considered as civilisation, the village Shinten. The Medical Officer informed Sanitary Sid about the situation, but apparently the answer he got was: "The Medical Officer must do his best to make them well."

Attempts to get more food, such as eggs and meat, fell on deaf ears. Sanitary Sid's final words were that now that the camp hospital had been given a large supply of medicine and drugs, these should suffice. The items to which he referred were Red Cross supplies which the Japanese had been holding back for years, on the grounds that they didn't know how long the war was going to last. During the next week three more men died from beri-beri.

That night there were further harsh words. We were having a sing-song in one of the huts when the Japanese interpreter stormed in and demanded to know why we were singing. He called for Major Crossley who stuck to his guns and defended our high-spirited breach of the camp regulations. The singing went on until late into the night.

Slowly life began to improve. On 20 August a bullock was killed, and for the first time in years we tasted fresh meat. It was only a stew, but the meat was there. Shortly afterwards each man was given thirty cigarettes and some of the items which had been confiscated in the past.

Regretfully Lance Corporal R.R. Milne died from beri-beri.

The state of health of most men was still such as to give rise to a great deal of concern. Major Crossley, therefore, made a formal protest to Immamura when he demanded men for a Town Party, pointing out that it would be difficult, if not impossible, to find sixty men strong enough to carry loads from Shinten. The doctors supported him, and the Medical Officer stated that at least thirty men would have to be carried out of the camp on stretchers. The Commandant insisted we were still prisoners of war but changed his tune a little, saying that the loads would be as light as possible. It was, he said, for our own good, because the supplies would be our own food. A letter of protest was sent to the

182

Commandant regarding the work we were still being asked to do, and it was further requested that the letter be placed on file as a protest.

On 23 August Corporal Milne was buried, and on the same day we were told we would be leaving the Jungle Camp the next day at 7.30 am. For me 24 August 1945 was the day when I finally considered I was free from the grip of the Japanese. Another day that burns brightly in my memory.

There was a further touch of mirth as we stood there that morning, our last few minutes in Kukutsu, the dreaded Jungle Camp. We prepared to hold our final *tenko* – the last roll-call before we walked out of the camp and we decided to show just how free we were by numbering-off in English. Four or five times we tried, but each time something went wrong in the middle, and we felt quite ridiculous. Finally we reverted to Japanese, the language we had been using innumerable times every day for the past three and a half years, and we did it first time without a hitch. Even the guards saw the funny side of it and stood there laughing.

The stretcher cases left the camp first accompanied by their bearers, medical staff and a few spare men. The remainder of us left immediately after the roll call, and what a sweet day it was. I remembered my first walk along the track from Shinten when Jack and I carried two hundred and fifty pounds of blankets, and I particularly recalled the spot where we fell down for the last time. My bones were even wearier, but how much lighter was my heart. On the way down we passed the stretcher party who were also in very good spirits.

In Shinten there were a number of trucks waiting to transport us to our new, and final camp, on Formosa. Taihoku, the capital of Formosa at that time, was a journey of about about three quarters of an hour from Shinten, and on the way there we ran into the inevitable rain. Since we were riding in the back of an open truck, and we had no intention of getting wet, we pulled out a tarpaulin to provide ourselves with some cover. The lone Japanese guard in the truck with us also wanted shelter but we quickly asserted our new-found freedom and told him to stay outside and get wet.

The camp in Taihoku, where we were to await evacuation from Formosa, was the disused Matsuyama factory on the outskirts of the town, a two storey building constructed mainly of timber. It was enclosed in a barbed wire compound, intended perhaps to keep others out rather than for the purpose of keeping us in. The facilities were very rudimentary but much better than the camp we had just left at Kukutsu. We slept on the floor with just a blanket underneath us and one over, but it was certain nobody was going to complain about the spartan arrangements.

The sick party arrived at the camp about an hour after we did, and for them the journey had been more trying. Gunner T. Biggin died the same day from beri-beri, while on the following day Signalman E. Clack died, also from beri-beri. In my own case the beri-beri had stabilised and I began to hold great hopes for recovery. I realised that every day I remained on my feet now was a bonus. Over the next few days my illness began to show real signs of abating, though I succumbed to a dose of the squits, and while that was unpleasant in itself it seemed to be of some further help in reducing the effects of the beri-beri.

Requests were made for a funeral with full military honours for the men who had died recently, and for the British Padre, the Reverend T. Pugh, who was in another camp not too far away. The only concession granted, even at this late stage, was for a trumpeter to sound the Last Post at the funerals.

There was another meeting between Major Crossley and Immamura when once more the Japanese insisted we were still prisoners of war and that we should continue to salute them. As far as I was concerned, and in spite of whatever they might say or do, I had saluted my last member of the Japanese race, Commandant, private or Emperor.

On our way back from the funeral service for Gunner Biggin and Signalman Clack we met large gatherings of the local population who cheered us all the way back to camp. I hoped it was an indication of how they felt about the Japanese and not just a case of backing the winner after it was past the post. It certainly seemed to make our escort of Japanese guards more than a little uneasy and they didn't relax until they were back in camp.

Some fraternizing followed in the next few days. Not, I hasten to add, with the few Japanese military who were still with us, but with the civilians outside the camp area. They were prepared to barter eggs for blankets, and before long there was a considerable trade going on. We boiled the eggs in a large communal bowl, each man segregating his own purchases by putting them in a sock while cooking; after all, your eggs might just be bigger than his. The quality of the rice we were now getting was quite appalling, the worst we had had for some time. The excuse from the Japanese was that it had been in store for a long time.

A parade of the few remaining guards was held, many of the worst having folded their tents and stolen away in the night, as it were. We didn't see them going, they just weren't there one morning. The Commander in Chief of the Prisoner of War Camps in Formosa addressed the parade, though what was said was not revealed to us.

However, it was finally conceded that we were no longer prisoners of war. The guards were to remain in camp but only, as they put it, "to protect us" and to ensure that supplies of food were brought in. A couple of days later we were to get all the food and clothing we wanted. But this also brought tragedy.

The camp was advised that there would soon be a drop of food and other supplies by Allied planes and on 28 of August they appeared, literally out of the blue. In common with most men, I was resting, or perhaps we were chattering among ourselves, when suddenly we heard the sound of approaching aircraft. We rushed to the windows of the room on the upper floor. The whole scene was again one of those memorable sights and sounds that will never be forgotten. I remember the name of the man, Pat Dobbie, who was standing next to me and taking in the events of the next half hour or so.

We leant out of the window and there, at what would be considered as zero feet, the American B29s were heading directly for us from the right of the building. We cheered and waved for all we were worth as they passed over. A few minutes later they were again heading our way, having made a full circle. This time the leading airplane opened its bomb doors and out fell a number of bundles with parachutes trailing behind.

The technicalities of dropping supplies were lost on me, and I was only too pleased to see that we were about to receive much needed food. As the planes passed over us once more the bundles continued to plummet towards the ground. Then disaster struck, as some of the supplies dropped directly into the building just a few feet to our right, others crashed into the compound, while more fell outside the perimeter of the camp.

We rushed out only to discover that the planes were making another run towards the camp. We had to decide which side of the compound the loads were going to hit and we all charged to one side. It seemed to go on for hours, but in fact it was all over in a matter of minutes.

The bundles turned out to be huge oil drums packed with food and clothing. Two of them had landed on the building and gone down into the ground floor. Five men were injured, three of them dying later of their injuries, and a further sixteen men with injuries of varying severity. There was tragedy outside also – two civilians had been killed.

With others I rushed to help free the injured men from the damaged part of the building. One of them, a personal friend of mine, we carried out using a door torn from the damaged building to get him to a place of safety. As we did so he complained that his cigarette was burning his fingers. None of us told him his arm had been torn off.

185

The three men who died were Private B. Beardsworth, Gunner J. Howe and Private B. Leggett. One of the ironies was the fact that one of the drums which dropped on the building was full of nothing more than cartons of chewing gum.

The Official Account of the incident says no more than the fact that "A full account of the accident has been given to M.I.9." Obviously the loads were dropped from too low a height and there was insufficient time for the parachutes to open properly.

The remainder of the drums were collected from outside the camp, and in them were vital supplies of all kinds including tinned meats, fruit, chocolate and cigarettes. There was also a large quantity of American military uniforms, underclothing, socks and boots. Within a very short time we were kitted out with clean sanitized clothing, the first for four years. The food was distributed and, as we returned to normal, each man had a veritable grocery shop piled up by his bed space. The multi-coloured material from the parachutes was also used as covering for our beds. As the air filled with tobacco smoke from the many brands of American cigarettes the room took on the appearance of a scene from Arabian nights. It was a pity the whole day had to be marred by an act of incompetence which cost the lives of our friends.

On 30 August the B29s returned again and this time we were ready for them, having placed markers far outside the camp. Once more however, the parachutes failed to delay the speed of the drop, and one canister landed in the local jail, killing two more civilians.

During our time as prisoners we were obliged to hold our feelings in check, though the desire to strike out was very strong – to hurt them as we had been hurt, to crush them as they had tried to crush us. Even after we knew the war had finished we were still having to restrain ourselves at every turn. Our orders were to do nothing foolish. How then were we supposed to react when Captain Immamura made what was to be his final speech to us. A speech in which he disclaimed any personal responsibility for what had taken place during his time as Commandant of the camp at Kinkaseki?

It was 3 September and the Japanese were formally handing over command to our own officers. A parade had been arranged to link up with the time and date of the formal signing of the surrender of the nation of Japan. In his remarks Immamura said in all seriousness:

"You will be aware of the good treatment you have received at our hands. When things were not so good you will realise that it was not my doing, but because I had received orders from my superiors." He went on, "Because of the very fair treatment you have had I am sure you will

186

go back to Britain and be good ambassadors for Japan." We simply jeered him.

A day or so later I was driving a buffalo and cart around the camp to collect rubbish and as I drew near to the main gate a large American car approached. On the front of the vehicle were a number of flags, British, American and Chinese, and as it came to a halt a tall figure dressed in American army uniform stepped out.

"Is this a prisoner of war camp, buddy?" was his first question. When I said it was he asked me to take him to the senior officer of the camp. During the walk from the gate I asked if he had come to take us home and he said that was so, though it would take a couple of weeks to arrange. The news was welcome because we were soon to be going home, but disappointing because it was going to be such a long wait before anything happened.

I passed him over to Major Crossley and then turned my attention to the other person. He, apparently, was a military photographer, but dressed as he was, in gaiters and a Baden-Powell style hat, he looked to me more like a dough boy of the first world war. He asked if I would show him round. As I escorted him, he asked various questions and each time I pointed out a feature of the camp, like the row of busted toilets the B29s had demolished, he photographed them. He even took photographs of the stand-pipe sticking out of the ground because I said it was the bath-house. He photographed the quarters where we were living, including the badly damaged part of the main building. In fact, he photographed just about everything there was in the camp. But for me the best part was when he put the big question:

"Tell me, are there any war criminals around here?"

I was rather mystified by the question. "What's a war criminal?" I asked, "I can't really say that I understand."

"Well, has anybody been doin' you dirt?"

When I replied in the affirmative his eyes lit up. I followed up my remark with the fact that the whole Japanese army were guilty of that.

"Where are they? I'll photograph them," he said, at the same time looking around, as though they were all coming in for a group photograph.

He was carefully explaining what was meant by a war criminal when my old friend Tamaki came into view. It was a gift from heaven. I raised my hand with the palm down, opening and closing my fist in the approved Japanese fashion, and at the same time called out to him.

"*Hayaku kite kudasai, Tamaki San.*" – Come quickly Mr. Tamaki.

Tamaki hurried over, preening himself for what he thought was going to be an interview. I explained that the American wished to take his photograph, whereupon he preened himself even more. It was not until he had been photographed from every angle that I said: "He asked if there were any war criminals in the camp, so I have given him your name."

He was struck dumb for a few minutes, but his knowledge on the subject of war criminals was obviously much greater than my own.

"I am not a war criminal," he protested, "I am not a war criminal."

He was quite beside himself as he turned on his heels and left hurriedly. I must admit I couldn't help laughing. I had had very few opportunities for laughter at the expense of Tamaki San in the last few years.

‐╢EPILOGUE TWO╟‐

All cruelty springs from weakness.
Seneca 4BC – AD65.

It would be part of a life wasted if the one thousand three hundred days I had been a prisoner of the Japanese had not taught me something. Not only about the people who had held us captive and wielded the big stick for so long, but also about my fellow men. Adversity affects people in different ways, and it may well have been that some of the men who had died during captivity could have suffered an earlier demise without the Japanese guards to help them on their way – a sickness, a car accident, an accident at work, who knows?

On the other hand it is equally true that with reasonable treatment they could now be old men like me, remembering the lessons of the past. But whenever they died, and however they died, one thing of which I was quite certain, they did nothing in this life to warrant the pre-death treatment they were given. Their suffering in Kinkaseki was cut short and if there was a blessing in dying that was it.

Whatever I may have read in the past, or may read in the future, I do not expect to really understand the thinking, not only of the underlings who committed the various barbaric acts on prisoners, but of the men responsible for issuing the orders in the first place.

Surviving directives of the Prisoner Information Bureau leave no doubt in the mind of any student of the period, that it was the policy, from Emperor Hirohito down through to the Privy Council, that the extermination of prisoners was intended. Documentary evidence to this effect is extant, that prisoners should never be allowed to return to their homeland. One writer seeks to exonerate the Emperor from all blame in this matter, even to the point of attributing to him "unforeseen qualities of leadership in his readiness to divest himself of his supposed divinity and to accept his much diminished role as a symbol of the state."

How can this be? As the absolute head of the state he must have been aware that wherever the Japanese forces went; massacre, murder, torture, rape and many other atrocities were committed on a wholesale

189

scale, and in his name. There cannot be any doubt but what the cult of "Emperor worship" was one of the first causes of the bestial atrocities of the war in the Far East. The average indoctrinated soldier of Japan who was committing such atrocities against both civilians and prisoners of war was acting on behalf of the God-Emperor Hirohito – not in the dark corners of towns and villages through which they passed, or isolated acts by the occasional renegade soldier, but in the mass and under the instruction of his officers, and at times with their participation.

If it were otherwise, why then did he condone the nationalistic rousing of his troops by allowing the publishing on the eighth of every month in all the newspapers, and the reading in military establishments, including prisoner of war camps, the declaration of war against Britain and the U.S.A. to which he had affixed his name, as Emperor and head of the army?

After the war the International Military Tribunal in Tokyo reported: "During a period of several months the Tribunal heard evidence from witnesses who testified in detail to atrocities committed in all theatres of war on a scale so vast, yet following so common a pattern, that only one conclusion is possible. The atrocities were either secretly ordered, or wilfully permitted by the Japanese Government."

I therefore repeat, that to hold a trial of highly placed war criminals and to exclude the Emperor from that trial was almost as criminal as the acts themselves.

I was not privy to the conversations which took place between General MacArthur and the Emperor, or the power politics which existed after the cessation of hostilities. Certainly there was a great deal of discussion between the Allies regarding the position the Emperor was going to play in his country after the war. It was finally left to the U.S.A. to exploit his position in whatever way they thought best, consequently he remained as Emperor, but with his godly status removed.

Jukichi Inouye, in his *Introduction to Chushingura* in 1910, wrote, on the question of a *Samurai* in battle, " . . . shame to themselves not to die when their Lord was hard pressed . . . their own shame was the shame upon their parents, their family, their house and their whole clan, and with this idea deeply impressed upon their minds, the *Samurai*, no matter what rank, held their lives as light as a feather when compared with the weight they attached to the maintenance of a spotless name."

Was not the Emperor in the position of a *Samurai* of the highest class, or does the brainwashing into dying apply only to the lower orders?

When the Japanese Foreign Minister Shigemitsu reported to the palace after the signing ceremony on 2 September 1945, he asked Emperor Hirohito, "Would it have been possible for us, if we had won, to embrace the vanquished with such magnanimity?"

Hirohito's reply was, "Naturally, it would have been different."

I suspect that I, along with a few thousand others, know exactly how different it would have been. Japan's answer would have mirrored her history of the exploitation of the weak by the strong, of bloodshed, famine and disease.

The treatment of prisoners of war by the Japanese cannot be excused by use of the disgrace a Japanese soldier is supposed to feel at being captured. If this were the case there would have been thousands more dead Japanese soldiers after the war, for there were many who were taken prisoner, and returned to their homeland. It is the West who have fostered the act of suicide among the modern Japanese to atone for some real or imagined disgrace, the Japanese themselves are only too happy to keep the myth alive.

One thing I did learn about my enemies whilst in Kinkaseki was of the enormous, almost unbelievable conceit they have in themselves, a conceit more noticeable among the higher ranks, born perhaps of their appalling ignorance of the Western world.

I have heard people talk of their ability to forgive the Japanese for what we all now know to have been the most appalling treatment to both military and civilians, women and children as well as the sick and the helpless.

One account of an ex-prisoner who took up a post in Japan after the war wrote the following, "Many of my fellow prisoners found it was easiest to get along with our captors by treating them as youngsters, for clearly their sudden enthusiasms and wild tempers – often accompanied by fisticuffs, followed by apparent bursts of repentance, when they would buy their victims a cup of coffee, not so much from any sense of having done wrong but merely in order to satisfy a rather pathetic craving to be liked." He goes on to say that he gave the name "problem children" to his youthful guards. And later, after a visit to peacetime Japan he suggests that "Thanks to a more enlightened spirit," which he found in Japan (1945/46) he wrote, "problem children need careful handling, unstinted patience, and unremitting forgiveness." Charles A. Fisher was a prisoner on the Railway and was on General Percival's staff at the outbreak of war.

I have thought many times about the question of forgiveness since returning home but must admit to not making a serious attempt at it. I have only to reach into my most vivid memories to know that I have never had any trouble in pushing all thoughts of forgiveness out of my heart.

I have only to remember the statistics about the relationship between prisoners of war in Germany with their captors those of us who were prisoners in Japan. Discounting the holocaust and what happened to the Jews in Germany, the Japanese camps were infinitely more deadly. If one compares statistics relating to the British, American, Australian, Canadians and New Zealand troops, 4% of prisoners in Germany died; in Japanese hands the percentage was 28.65%. That does not include the Chinese military and the civilians of East Asia.

On the question of the dropping of the bombs on Hiroshima and Nagasaki, a debate I have had to cope with many times, my answer has been, and always will be, that at the time it was just another weapon. Most people who argue that they should not have been dropped do so from the benefit of hindsight.

I believe, as does Leo Rawlings in his book *And the Dawn Came Up Like Thunder*, that "The act has to be seen not in the light of the present, but kept in a proper context". And Laurens van der Post, in his *Night of the New Moon*, says, "Above all, for me, selfish as it may sound, there was the certain knowledge that if the bomb had not been dropped . . . Field Marshal Terauchi would have fought on and hundreds of thousands of prisoners in his power would have been killed. Even if we had not been deliberately massacred, we were near our physical end through lack of food. The war had only to drag on a few months longer for most of us to have perished. But quite apart from death through starvation which threatened us there was, most important for me, this question of deliberate massacre."

Again, I quote from the writings of Charles A. Fisher: "It wasn't until the next day that we learned that what had ended the war and so almost certainly saved our lives was the dropping of the atomic bomb on Hiroshima.

" Some of us wondered whether we were worth it."

Yes, I was then, and am now, of the same mind – it was the dropping of those two bombs that saved my life. A personal view maybe, but seen in the context of all that I and my friends had gone through, and were still going through, they felt as I did. But now I was free.

And though there are scars on my body which have healed, though I can count all my limbs as present and correct; though my health has been such that I have had no serious worries since I came home, there remain scars I can't show. I was twenty years old when I was taken prisoner, and I spent my twenty-first birthday working in the copper mine in Kinkaseki. I have left in the depths of that mine nearly four irrecoverable years of my youth that I would rather have spent in some other way. I do not forget, or forgive.

I have also pondered many times on other aspects of finding oneself in such extenuating circumstances and needing some sort of help other than temporal. I often felt slightly envious of those who seemed to have the crutch of religion on which to lean in times of great stress. Unfortunately I was unable to receive any comfort in that direction since when I made any attempts it seemed to me I always chose the wrong individual and I finished up feeling I had been let down. One example out of many was the Padre, Father Kennedy, a man who was meant to serve our theological needs in Kinkaseki. My first taste of his ministrations was during a spell in the camp hospital when, because my rendering of The Lord's Prayer was not identical to his, he suggested that perhaps it would be better if, during evening prayers, I didn't say the prayer at all. His other crime in my eyes was his refusal to officiate at any funeral unless the man was a Catholic, or that he converted to the Catholic faith before he died. On this last matter Major Crossley did in fact report Father Kennedy on his return to the U.K. Father Kennedy had many shortcomings in his ministrations during his time in Kinkaseki, which fortunately lasted only for a short period.

Generally speaking, religious comfort was in very short supply, though a lay person I knew quite well used to say a short prayer to the assembled company each night, finishing always with the same prayer of "God grant us speedy delivery from present circumstances." With that viewpoint I concurred.

193

PART THREE

Retribution

CHAPTER
TWENTY ONE

With freedom's soil beneath our feet.
And freedom's banner streaming o'er us.

———————— Joseph Rodman Drake ————————

Private A Kerr died in hospital on 4 September, the last fatality from our camp in Formosa. The following day a Colonel of the American Marines called rather unexpectedly at Taihoku to tell us we were to get everything ready as quickly as possible. We were going home. Apparently the representative who called at the camp a few days before considered our condition was such that we should be moved into safe hands as soon as possible. So, later that day, we walked out of camp wearing our brand new American uniforms, loaded with as much food and cigarettes as we could carry.

There wasn't a single Japanese in sight. The guards were obviously exercising a little discretion and stayed out of sight. My last memories of the camp at Taihoku were of the civilians to whom permission had been given to take whatever food and clothing we left behind. They were loaded up and away before the last of us were outside the gate.

A short walk from the camp brought us to a railway station where there seemed to be a very large number of civilians standing around silently watching our approach. There were a few Japanese troops in evidence also and still bearing arms, having taken up a position between the crowd and ourselves, though they were not the guards from the camp.

We boarded the train, but before it pulled away from the platform a young civilian – he looked no more than sixteen – scrambled into our carriage. He found himself a seat, quite indifferent to the fact that he was sitting in a crowd of what was, ostensibly, American military personel. Suddenly, without any warning, an officer of the Kempei Tai, the Japanese military police, approached the young man, shouted something at him, took him by his collar and threw him off the train. The police officer then turned towards us and bowed and grinned, indicating that we should approve of his action. One of our men, Private

Timlin, walked up behind the Japanese, tapped him on the shoulder and as he turned brought him a perfect right cross to the jaw, felling him to the ground. Others then bundled him off the train. There was great applause for our first physical act of vengeance.

We had been bottling everything up for so long it was natural to get a great kick out of such a small incident. As we continued our journey the train was halted for a short while at another station and through the windows, without blinds on this journey, we could see a large crowd of civilians on the platform. To the front of the crowd, and facing our carriage, were three or four armed guards, whether Japanese or Formosan I have no idea, but they appeared to be exercising some control in relation to the crowd.

Someone in our carriage threw a bar of chocolate onto the platform, just short of one of the guards. There was a slight surge from the crowd but the line held. Then someone threw a packet of cigarettes and a further bar of chocolate came from another carriage. It may well have been one of the soldiers who gave in to temptation, or perhaps the pressure from behind was too much. Whatever it was, within a few seconds the whole platform became one massive rugger scrum, with the soldiers underneath. Childish, perhaps, but to men like us it was highly hilarious.

The journey ended when the train pulled in at the quayside in Kiirun. It was an ordinary Formosan type of day, overcast and threatening rain, but inside we were glowing with anticipation. An American cruiser was lying alongside and we formed a ragged line moving towards the gangway guarded by two armed crew members. As we filed aboard they presented arms, I looked directly at the one on the right as I passed and watched the tears rolling down his face. He was not a young man but I imagine he hadn't seen anything like us before, still like skeletons but with a look of sheer joy on our faces.

The last memory I have of the island was going on deck to join a group of friends at the stern as the cruiser began to slip away from the quayside. From there we urinated towards the island, a gesture I had been promising myself for a long, long time. We stood and watched as distance and darkness began to make the land more and more indistinct.

The organisation on board was very good, though perhaps not quite *au fait* with the needs of a few hundred ex-Japanese prisoners of war. Within a short time of boarding we were served an excellent dinner, even if one of the ingredients was a helping of boiled rice. Every man passed it over so that within a few minutes it was removed from sight.

As we sailed out of Kiirun harbour after dinner I stood on deck in a sheltered corner talking to a couple of crew members. The sea was quite rough and the cruiser was developing quite a pitching, rolling motion. The leeward side of the deck soon became lined with men who had eaten well but not too wisely and their dinner was vanishing overboard. Soon we were out in the open sea, the night pitch black and a gale blowing up. There were too many sunken ships in the harbour so we were being ferried to a larger ship. It didn't occur to me to ask how we were supposed to get from the cruiser to the final transport, whatever it was, but when it happened it was a wonder no one was lost overboard. It was close on midnight when the forward motion of the cruiser stopped. Over the side went a number of rope landing nets, then about thirty of us at a time had to scramble down into a motorized craft bobbing up and down on the turbulent sea below.

I don't think the American authorities were aware of the physical weakness of many of the men. In some cases it was nothing more than an overwhelming desire to get home that took them in the pitch darkness of the night to climb safely down the net and into the waiting boats bobbing about on the surface of the equally dark sea.

Each small boat, then left the side of the cruiser and started out across the dark rolling sea. Soon the mass of an aircraft carrier loomed up. I have never seen anything that appeared so huge and daunting. From one of its decks searchlights scoured the sea, picking out both our boat and a gangway platform at sea level. As a wave carried the small boat towards the platform, one at a time we had to make a leap or catch hold of a rail and haul ourselves onto it. There was only a second or so for each man to make up his mind, it was his turn to make the death-defying leap, and there were several who had literally to be thrown onto the platform. A most hair-raising experience.

After scampering up the exposed gangway there were a number of crew members waiting for us and they began at once to process us, quickly and efficiently. Everything we were carrying had to be removed and thrown overboard. Personal items, such as photographs, letters and military documents, were placed in an envelope and taken away to be put through a de-lousing process. Not until we were completely nude of clothing and possessions were we moved into a nearby area where all body hair was shaved off. We were then sent into a shower room for a good scrub down, followed by an all-over de-lousing spray. Not until we had passed through this process were we allowed to advance more than a few yards into the main body of the carrier where we were issued with a complete outfit of American navy uniforms. I had never had such a speedy transfer from the army to the navy before, complete with the little round white hat.

We were on the *U.S.S. Santee*, an aircraft carrier with a distinguished fighting record in the Pacific as part of Task Force 58, including action in places like the Battle of Midway. The *Santee* was to be our home for the next few days as it ploughed its way through the China Sea towards the Phillipines. Other ex-prisoners from Taihoku went through the same routine but on another equally famous carrier, *U.S.S. Block Island.*

The aircraft carrier U.S.S. Santee.

How remarkable it was, after all the deprivation and brutality – the almost complete isolation of the past few years – to be met by extreme kindness, care and plenty. We were almost overwhelmed by them.

Dressed in new navy uniforms and looking like so many skinny Popeyes, we were taken on individually conducted tours of the carrier. Such solicitude was shown towards us that, coupled with the excitement of being free, we simply broke into tears. It was the first of many emotional moments during the next few months.

How we lapped up the luxuries of food, comfort and personal freedom! We were settled on the hanger deck containing nothing more war-like than rows of camp beds or cots, whilst on the work-benches down each side were plates piled high with food of all types and large stainless steel urns of coffee. We were told to help ourselves to whatever we wanted throughout the night, and it was only tiredness and the desire to sleep that eventually stopped me eating. During the night I awoke to go to the toilets and as soon as I raised my head an American

200

sailor was at my side with a flashlight to escort me to the "heads" with great concern for my welfare.

Breakfast next morning turned out to be another feast. A tray divided into compartments was filled with cereal, eggs, bacon, and hot rolls with butter. It was an orgy, impossible to stay away from, and I managed three trips, each with the same complete breakfast.

An hour or so later, back on the hanger deck, a voice boomed out over the ship's tannoy system: "Now hear this, now hear this." It was the ship's Medical Officer. His message was to welcome us aboard and explain that no matter how long we stayed on the carrier, and no matter how much food we ate, even we would be unable to consume all the food they had. It was not his wish to convey the impression that he didn't want us to eat; there was no question of introducing food rationing. But he asked us, for our own good, to go easy. That morning the stomach pump had to be used on two men, one of whom admitted to having had twelve breakfasts.

During the day we were allowed to wander round the carrier and talk with the crew. It was during a conversation among four or five of us that we were joined by one crew who explained that he wrote small articles for a newspaper back home and "could he ask us a few questions?" His first question was: what did we think about "the bomb". We didn't know what he was talking about and asked him which particular bomb he was referring to. Even when he explained about Hiroshima and Nagasaki we still failed to come up to his expectations and he seemed to be somewhat disbelieving. The enormity remained unknown to us for many months to come, though I remembered what Jack Brazier had said about his conversation with the local in the Jungle Camp – "*Takusan boom boom*". Like many of my friends I failed to connect "the bomb" with the end of the war and our own personal survival.

He still hadn't finished and his next question also floored us. After learning what we had been doing for the past few years, and yes, there were a number of women working in the mine in Kinkaseki – they were among the civilian workers – he asked: "So you were alright for sex then?"

Disbelief was almost stretched to breaking point when we reminded him that we were about half our normal weight, dying of malnutrition, beri-beri, dysentery and a dozen other killing diseases. Furthermore, given the choice between the finest woman in the world and a steak, then sex was a non-starter. His comment was expressive: "Boy, you sure got something saved up!" I would have loved to have seen his article to the folks back home.

Amid such solicitude it was quite surprising that very few people really did understand what our life had been like for the past three and a half years. Indeed, the truth about the camps took some time to penetrate into popular understanding, but as far as the crew of the *Santee* were concerned all that mattered were their efforts to begin to restore us to fit and healthy men again.

Whilst in Kinkaseki I had filled some of my spare time in a quite illegal hobby, illegal because I had aquired a piece of steel and had fashioned it into a small chisel. Had this been found it could have been construed as a weapon and I would have been in real trouble. Regularly sharpened by one of the Chinese workers down the mine I used it to produce a number of carvings, mostly of the various military cap badges in the camp. I used pieces of Japanese oak I found in the mine and, after completing the carvings, I polished them with boot polish from the Red Cross parcel. One of these carvings is the cap badge of the Argyle and Sutherland Highlanders, which I still have. It has my own personal forecast for freedom carved on the reverse – PoW 1942 to 1945. I suppose it was 1944 when I carved it and I was called a pessimist by one of the other prisoners at the time. Another was the badge of my own unit, The Royal Signals, with the names of the section to which I belonged carved on the reverse. This one was very precious to me, but so was the hospitality of the Americans on board the *Santee*, in particular Marvin Burns of Texas,. whom I got to know quite well. As a token of my appreciation of their hospitality I presented him with the carving. I would like to think he still has it. I still have the silver dollar I received in exchange.

Carving of the Argyle and Sutherland badge done by Arthur.

It was with some sadness that, eventually, we had to disembark from the *Santee*, in Manila harbour in the Phillipines. I remain more than grateful for the hospitality of men like Albert Jordan, Bob Voeller, Wayne Ponder, Charles Brockman and, of course, Marvin Burns.

Once ashore we were handed over to the Fifth Replacement Depot on the Madrigal Estate, about twenty-three kilometres south of Manila. Several hundred Japanese who had been taken prisoner during the war in the Phillipines were working around the camp, always grinning and being most polite and courteous whenever they passed anywhere near us. Most of us were able to ignore them but Timlin, the man who had struck the Kempei Tai on board the train at Taihoku, was quite unable to restrain his feelings. A Scot from Hamilton in Lanarkshire, he was not the sort of man to be in such a situation without leaving his mark on it. He was involved in several incidents, such as pushing one Japanese prisoner into a urinal pit, then giving another the weight of his fist when he was passing through one of the toilet tents where Timlin was sat cogitating. His anger also got the better of him as he was sitting one day watching a group of Japanese prisoners passing the open tent on their way to work one morning. They were giving their usual bow accompanied by the words "*O-hayo gozaimasu*" – "Good morning" – as they passed. Timlin could restrain himself no longer. "I'll give them *o-hayo*," he said. Each prisoner was carrying a long-handled spade over his shoulder and Timlin grabbed one of these from the last in line and hit him smartly over the head with it. Once more he was in front of the American Commander.

We had various medical inspections whilst we were in Manila. Our navy uniform was also taken from us and once more we were issued with American army uniform. Given the opportunity of returning to the U.K. via America or straight home, I opted without hesitation for the latter. By force of circumstances it turned out to be one of the slowest of sea journeys on what was probably one of the oldest and filthiest troopships that could be found, the *Empress of Australia*, formerly the *Empress of Japan*, so I was given to understand. We called in at Singapore after leaving Manila to pick up a number of civilian ex-internees. They were mainly women and children also returning to the U.K. The ridiculous administrative decisions made by the people in charge on the *Empress* are encapsulated in the order that was made after the first few days of leaving Singapore. We were kept strictly separated, civilian females on the port side of the ship and the military on the starboard. In other words we were to be excluded from any temptation. I thought back to our American friends expression on board the *Santee*, "Boy you sure got something saved up." Our answer to such a ridiculous order was to cross over to the port side en masse whereupon the order was rescinded. Compared to our recent voyage on the *Santee* the trip was appalling and the best that could be said was that we did, eventually, get to Liverpool.

Arthur Titherington and Fred Upton on the way home. The photograph was taken six weeks after they were released. Arthur's weight had gone from 6st to 13st 10ozs in those six weeks.

CHAPTER
TWENTY TWO

Be England what she will
with all her faults, she is my country still.

————————— Charles Churchill. 1731-1764. —————————

Seeing the coastline of England after many years absence was quite unforgettable – the patchwork of fields leading up to the hills beyond. Perhaps the first thing I noticed, even in October, was how green and sweet the land appeared. Even the dark line of smoke hanging over the city of Liverpool as we neared the quayside was familiar and engaging.

It was the end of October 1945, with the weather rather typical – a little drizzle as the clouds ranged in across the land. The *Empress of Australia* had taken an interminable time drifting through the Indian Ocean, the Red Sea, Suez, the Mediterranean and the final haul through the Atlantic and on towards Liverpool. There were times when we didn't think she was going to make it, beset as she was with mechanical problems.

We spent hours lying off Liverpool riding out a storm which prevented us from docking, and the landlubbers among us had to carry on suffering. I was almost prepared to try and walk on the water in order to reach land.

The cargo of ex-prisoners of war were now almost unrecognisable from the sick, gaunt scarecrows who had emerged from the isolated interior of Formosa two months before. We were fat and moon-faced from eating too much and lack of exercise. I was well over thirteen stone, more than twice my weight of eight weeks ago. The only clue a stranger could have had that there had been some harrowing experiences in our background was in our general nervousness and the occasional hysterical behaviour. It took only a mild joke to produce fits of laughter. On the journey home we had watched films on board ship, and even with some second rate comedies I had been doubled over in pain with laughter. Under normal circumstances they would hardly have raised a smile. From a few details in our conversation it was also obvious that we hadn't been part of the world for some time. We were unable, for instance, to join in the words of Lily Marlene when an entertainer sang it for us in an ENSA show in Suez.

But as the days passed we were slowly returning to the common stock of the civilized world, picking up the pieces we had missed out on. We were also returning to normal manhood. A buxom ENSA singer entertaining us with a sexy version of a song which contained a repeated line "What would you say if you had a little ghost like me?" recalled what the American had said aboard the *Santee*, and was emphasised by the reply from a wag in the audience as the line was sung, "Get up them stairs!"

Whilst in Suez we had been issued with British army uniform, the fourth uniform in about six weeks. There was also the issue of a couple of pieces of medal ribbon, the Pacific Star, for which the qualifications were, at the time, somewhat obscure. Simply to have been in hospital allowed us to wear the medal. At least that was what the man said, "But what if I have been in hospital with V.D., Sarge?"

"Don't matter, son," was the reply. "Got to have your ribbon."

Every soldier who comes home from a war knows the feeling when he first puts his feet on his own land again. As we disembarked there was a crowd shouting and cheering and everyone was looking for a familiar face. We boarded an army truck on the dock side, not being required to go through customs, so my kitbag full of cigarettes wasn't charged duty, a thought which only surfaced a few minutes before we walked off the ship. As we drove through the city it was dark and wet. There was, however, no sweeter sight than the crowds walking the glistening pavements and the lights shining from the shops, and still the sporadic cheers as we passed a crowd of people standing on a street corner. It was enough to make your heart burst.

For my part I knew my family was all right, as I had spoken to them by telephone and had cabled them not to try and meet me. Any tears to be shed would be shed in my own home.

At the reception camp in Magul, just outside Liverpool, we were asked if we wanted to go to bed and be processed in the morning, or go on through the night for as long as it took. Without question, we voted at once for a speedy process through what was left of the night.

The following morning another ex-prisoner and I boarded a train bound for Birmingham. We de-trained with all our luggage at New Street station and I suggested we should share a taxi, but before we could even decide which way to go we were approached by two very helpful and obviously well informed Red Cross ladies. How they knew or even guessed we were ex-prisoners I have no idea, but they insisted they had transport arranged for us. Picking up my full complement of kit I followed on after them. My friend had left one kitbag on the platform with the intention of returning for it, but within the minute or two that he was absent it had gone. Stolen! So much for the spoils of war.

As we neared my home the driver asked,"What was the address?" I repeated it for him and he said,"That must be the one with the flags outside."

I really had hoped to arrive home in a more unobtrusive way, but there was the banner "Welcome Home" and the front of the house covered in bunting. As soon as the car stopped I was out and into the house, so overwhelmed I didn't even bother to get my kit out of the car. Fortunately someone else did.

BUCKINGHAM PALACE

The Queen and I bid you a very warm welcome home.

Through all the great trials and sufferings which you have undergone at the hands of the Japanese, you and your comrades have been constantly in our thoughts. We know from the accounts we have already received how heavy those sufferings have been. We know also that these have been endured by you with the highest courage.

We mourn with you the deaths of so many of your gallant comrades.

With all our hearts, we hope that your return from captivity will bring you and your families a full measure of happiness, which you may long enjoy together.

George R.I.

September 1945.

A Message from the King.

CHAPTER
TWENTY THREE

I dare eat or drink, or breathe or live
I dare meet Surrey in a wilderness
And spat upon him, while I say he lies,
And lies, and lies.

———————————— Shakespeare. ————————————

It was more than thirty years after leaving Formosa, now known as Taiwan, that I had the chance to find out exactly what happened to some of the guards and the people responsible for treating me as they did during my time as a prisoner. The time to spare to carry out any research which would provide me with the answers to many questions had been denied to me after my return home, though I had promised myself that one day I would find the answers. My memories were as clear as yesterday as I leafed through the files on the war crimes trials in the quiet room of the Public Records Office in Kew. Sometimes there was complete satisfaction, sometimes anger.

The International Military Tribunal for the Far East had set up courts to try various political and military leaders as War Criminals. But the court papers, including verdicts, were stamped with a thirty year embargo and then locked away as soon as the trials were finished. The reasoning behind such a move never did become clear to me. I couldn't help feeling I had a right to know.

Few were actually reported in the British newspapers. Those that were tended to be the showcase trials dealing with major war criminals like Hideki Tojo, the Japanese Prime Minister of the period. Over 900 individuals were summoned before the courts held under British auspices and it was therefore impossible that each one should merit column inches. Consequently I had no way of knowing what had happened to our particular tormentors via press reports.

I never doubted, and still don't, that the trials were necessary, but I was wrong to think that the long arm of the military law would make each and every one accountable. They didn't, and many slipped through the net.

The trials were held under the Military Authority of the occupying powers following a Royal Warrant and Army Order made in 1945. War Crimes were defined as a "violation of the laws and usages of war" which were in turn enshrined in the Geneva Convention, and the Military Courts were authorised to pass sentences which included death.

From the start there was a major difficulty in bringing all possible war criminals to court. Apart from the leading officers of the camp at Kinkaseki, people like Immamura and Tamaki, many of them were only known to us by a nickname and these would obviously not have shown up on official records like Japanese army rolls or Nippon Mining Company employee lists. What is more, some of the guards and Runabouts, as we had already noticed, disappeared as soon as the war was over. What made the job of tracking them down rather difficult, including the *hanchoes* in the mine, was a definite closing of the ranks, a kind of sullen silence among those who were caught. Nearly all protested their innocence. A few turned Kings Evidence, but on the whole the availability of information from the Japanese and the Formosan side was less than perfect.

Even when it came to getting evidence from surviving ex-prisoners the operation was sketchy and rather half-hearted. Only three former Kinkaseki men appeared as witnesses at the trials: Major J.F. Crossley, Lieutenant J.T.N Cross and Sgt. J.O. Edwards. Neither of the officers had ever worked in the mine, and Edwards had worked mainly on only one level. He could not therefore have been cognisant of every *hanchoe* or every major incident, like the death of Gunner Cullop, except by hearsay.

Written evidence, or affidavits, were obtained from a limited number of other men, not all of whom had been in Kinkaseki from its beginning in November 1942, and some of them never went to the Jungle Camp. Their evidence in affidavit form was valuable in filling in the broad picture, but was limited because they could not be cross-examined. In the trial of Sergeant Tashiro – "Sanitary Sid" – for example, the Judge Advocate pointed out that if witness box evidence had been produced, specifically on the issue of medical supplies and treatment, the sentence would have been much harsher.

I can only assume that the military authorities who were responsible for organising the trials found it too expensive, or too formidable an operation, to gather together more of the ex-prisoners to attend the trials. At least, I hope the reason for the rather sketchy trials was an acceptable one and not just a matter of *laissez-faire*. Certainly, I find the excuse of a lack of finance a difficult one to swallow. On the other hand, our senior Medical Officer, Major Ben Wheeler, refused to have anything to do with the trials, except in affidavit evidence, and I have no way of knowing what happened to Captain Seed, our first Medical Officer.

Suspects were rounded up in a rather piecemeal fashion. There was no clean sweep, and they were tried together in batches. Senior officers appeared in the dock together, as did some of the *hanchoes*. This made sense in some ways because it allowed the court to focus in on particular crimes and criminals, but in other ways it seemed to have been very limiting. All in all, when going through the transcripts, there is an overwhelming impression that the trials performed the function of a rough and ready justice for a number of sample cases. Even an ex-prisoner might have to admit that, on the evidence presented at some of the trials, the verdicts were not always unquestionable.

Only one man who had any direct bearing on our lives and conditions in Formosa was actually given the death sentence: Major Taichi Uete, Commandant of all prisoner of war camps on the island from April to September 1945. He was hanged at Stanley prison in Hong Kong on 6 April 1948. I have no personal recollection of seeing him, but it appears that he did visit both Kinkaseki and the Jungle Camp.

Under examination he put forward the familiar defence of accusing those who were his seniors. "If there were any faults in any of these camps", he told the court, "the Commander in Chief of the Taiwan Army and the War Minister are to blame."

In a statement Major Uete said he forbade beatings, but suggested that they might have happened against his instructions because, among other things, "some of the prisoners of war were idle."

Colonel Hideo Sazawa

Uete, like many of the defendants, petitioned against his sentence. In his case it probably had some force because the two previous island Commandants, Colonel Nakano and Colonel Sazawa, had received not death but jail sentences of twenty and fifteen years. Nevertheless, during his short tenure of office, only a matter of six months, forty-five prisoners died, the majority of them from a lack of sufficient medical supplies. I must say that it would seem to me that the treatment in the period before he came to be Commandant of PoWs in Formosa would have had considerable bearing on the deaths of the forty-five men who died, and I can't help thinking that

211

Nakano and Sazawa were just as guilty as Uete.

The defence, not so much of obeying orders, but of being powerless to do anything about the excruciating treatment and conditions in Kinkaseki also came out in the trial of Colonel Sazawa. The following is an extract from his cross-examination:

Question. "You knew that conditions of work in the Kinkaseki mines was very, very irksome?"

Answer. "Yes I did."

Q. "And that in fact the Kinkaseki camp was the worst camp in Formosa?"

A. "Yes, it was."

Q. "And you had the welfare of the prisoners of war at heart since you have told the court that you believed in the *Bushido* Spirit?"

A. "Yes."

Q. "Why did you do nothing whatever with regards to the work which the prisoners were doing at Kinkaseki then?"

A. "It isn't that I did nothing. I did all I could in my power."

Q. "You have told the court nothing about the actual alleviation of any hardship which the prisoners experienced by working in the copper mine."

A. "It was beyond my power."

Q. "What do you mean beyond my power. What was beyond your power?"

A. "It was improper from the standpoint of humanitarianism, but my power was limited. I did not do anything."

Our own Camp Commandant, Captain Yaychachi Immamura, appeared under various charges, some relating to other camps in Taiwan where he was stationed before coming to Kinkaseki. Immamura was also in charge of the Jungle Camp at Kukutsu. He was sentenced to fifteen years in jail.

One of the charges specifically mentioned was that of sending sick prisoners to work down the mine. But he denied it and added "as far as I can remember". Because so many of the deaths in Kinkaseki were a result of

Captain Yaychachi Immamura

212

the vicious circle of starvation, work and disease, it is fitting to quote from Immamura's own statement about the procedure he adopted towards sick men and work:

"The Prisoner of War Headquarters gave orders that all men who were unfit, or too ill to work were to be withdrawn and their places taken by fit men from their (other) camps. Serious cases of illness were always reported to me immediately while minor illnesses were noted in the daily sick report.

"During my term of office over forty prisoners of war died from various illnesses, such as beri-beri, dysentery, pneumonia and intestinal troubles.

"As I was rather perturbed by this heavy death rate, which started about ten months after I reached Kinkaseki, I had specialists sent to the mine from the Japanese Military Hospital at Kiirun. These men made careful stool tests and found most of the men suffering from intestinal troubles were gravely infected by dysentery germs which had established a firm hold making it very difficult to effect a cure in most cases.

"In view of the fact that the work was very strenuous I decided to increase the number of holidays for prisoners by dividing them into two groups. One group would have a rest after four days work, the other after five days."

The last part of this statement certainly conflicts with my personal experience, but then, I had almost lost count of the days. And after all, Immamura was trying to make out that he had the prisoners welfare at heart. In another instance he asserts that the prisoners were given the same rations as the Japanese soldiers. He even suggests at one point that he thought the rations were insufficient because of the arduousness of the work and ordered the rations to be increased.

"When I arrived at Kinkaseki," his statement went on, "I found that the conditions were not very good, the prisoners were accommodated in buildings which had previously been used for coolie labour. Furthermore, it was reported to me that the mine officials treated the prisoners working in the mine harshly and that some prisoners were beaten. I informed the mine officials that this had to stop."

There was, in fact, supporting evidence that Immamura, on one occasion, and one only, cautioned two senior *hanchoes*, The Eagle and Frying Pan, about the beatings. The weight of information about the number of times he did nothing to prevent the violence, or was actually present to witness it not in the mine but in the camp, far outweighs this single instance of using his authority to good purpose.

The stunning part of Immamura's evidence was the mention of the Extreme Disposition, the tunnel which had been dug from the mine and led into the camp. Though it was used as a means of getting to work more quickly, I certainly never had any suspicion that its alternative use was as a possible mass grave.

Immamura's explanation and the reason for the move to the Jungle Camp, where he remained in charge of about 350 prisoners, was that "the site was better protected from air raids." He admitted having been present on some of the Town Party marches to bring supplies from Shinten, and of being a witness to some of the beatings.

"The prisoners had a tendency to go too slowly", he said, "I myself hit one or two with a bamboo stick."

In a question and answer session in court Immamura elaborated a little on this supposed single instance of personal violence: " . . . about my beating at Kukutsu. This I do not deny completely. However, if I be permitted to tell the circumstances of the time I wish to tell it."

Q. "Tell it briefly to the court."

A. "It was about 20 July. I took about a hundred prisoners of war to Shinten to transport goods. On the way coming back a batch of four or five were sitting on baggages and taking a rest, though it was not time for a rest, so I shouted "Go on, go on!" But they might not have understood these words and they would not go on, so I struck, aiming at the baggage. But the cane, which was aimed at the baggage, may have touched the buttocks of two or three, but I did not intend to give them physical suffering by striking them. But it is still bleeding."

One of the real villains of course was Lieutenant Tamaki, the man who told us the story of the "Underwaterpalace". Only samples of his brutality were produced to give damming evidence. But one which brought out the full terror of camp life was quite fully documented: the case of Corporal Flynn, the prisoner who went out of his mind after severe beating in the Jungle Camp.

The actual beating was carried out by one of the Formosan Runabouts, Korai Fuku – known to us as the Nasty Carpenter. Fuku actually managed to evade arrest after the war. Acting under the orders of Sergeant Mitoshi Nakajima, Flynn was knocked unconscious during a Garden Working Party. After lunch on the same day Major Crossley intervened to mark Flynn down as being too sick to go back to work.

Major Crossley recounted: "The following morning Tamaki sent for myself and Captain Schneider, the doctor, and without even saying anything he (Tamaki) knocked us both to the ground. He then commenced jumping up and down on the stomach of the doctor and took

214

him by the throat as if he were trying to strangle him. He then told us that there was nothing wrong with Flynn and that we were doing all this for propaganda purposes."

Major Crossley added, in a general description of Tamaki's personality, that though he spoke good English he "seemed to have an inbred [sic] hate of British and American personnel." Other evidence accused him of using prisoners for jujitsu practice. This was not something I had ever seen Tamaki doing.

Tamaki himself, while denying he had committed any war crimes submitted an unusual defence for some of the beatings. "I know that conditions in general for prisoners of war became worse during the last three to four months of the war," he explained. "Beatings increased, work became harder and the food less. My explanation of this is that Taiwan was being heavily bombed, the Japanese could see that the end of the war was near and that we were going to be defeated. In consequence we all became excited."Lieutenant Tamaki was sentenced to fifteen years in jail.

Another of the senior members of the guard staff who received one of the more severe sentences was Sgt Major Tatsuo Furuo. He was described as "the number one brute of this camp (Jungle)." Who took "a fiendish delight in beating a man until he was unconscious." He would select about six men for special attention and during the course of the day continue to beat, kick and shout at them until they were almost insane.

Sgt Major Tatsuo Furuo

Sergeant Major Furuo received ten years in jail.

Two prisoners at Kukutsu were singled out for special treatment after being accused of stealing sugar. One was Gunner Daly who was beaten up by Lieutenant Nobuo Suzuki. Daly ended up with a broken jaw which had to be set back into place with wire.

Suzuki was tried in a batch with Furuo, Nakajima and a Lieutenant Iwawo Tahara. During the case of Daly several of them suggested the reason for the considerable damage to Daly's jaw was that "It was easily dislocated." Suzuki also admitted tying up several prisoners for three days and nights, as he said "for stealing food."

The other prisoner involved in the charge of stealing sugar was an American, he was a medical orderly who only came to us at the Jungle Camp. The Commandant ordered him to be bound up with ropes and stood outside the guardroom. He was left there for seven days, in the open with the sun and tropical rains beating down on him, he was not allowed to sit and given only one small rice ball and some water at mealtimes.

Lieutenant Nobuo Suzuki

One of the interesting threads running through the evidence concerning men who were in second rank command in Kinkaseki and Kukutsu was the deliberate attempt to pass the buck either up to the first rank of Immamura and Tamaki, or down to the ordinary guards like Corporal Kuribayashi – known to us as So-So. In one incident Lieutenant Tahara claimed he was out of the room while Daly was being questioned, the inference being that Kuribayashi, who was involved in the interrogation, was responsible for the blood on the floor at the end of the interview.

Tahara also stated that Captain Immamura had ordered there should be no idling and that maximum work had to be extracted from each prisoner. He went on to say that Lieutenant Tamaki was to blame for the deteriorating conditions in the Jungle Camp.

Furuo, the number one brute, admitted slapping prisoners, but added, "I always tried to treat prisoners of war with kindness, and on the occasions I was in charge I bought things for them and gave them things to eat and drink." This was probably as outrageous a lie as it was possible to formulate. He further claimed that he had been punished by his own senior officers for being so kind to prisoners against orders. His description of how one prisoner, Signalman T.E. Roberts, ended up with severe injuries was also very curious.

"I went up to him with the intention of tapping him on the shoulder," explained Furuo. The prisoners were working with hoes on the Cultivation Party and the Sergeant Major thought somebody might get injured because they were standing too close to each other.

216

"Unfortunately the blow struck his neck with more force than I realised with the result he fell to the ground. I believe he fainted from shock."

One of Furuo's other victims, Signalman W. Barratt, was apparently caught stealing carbide whilst in Kinkaseki camp. The Sergeant Major hit him with his sword, kicked him, then poured water over the carbide which was in the waistband of his shorts. Furuo's version was, "I just scolded him and sent him away." Carbide was the fuel we used in our mining lamps, and it generates a great deal of heat, as well gas, when it comes into contact with water. Barratt had severe burns around his waist because of the treatment.

Suzuki and Tahara were jailed for seven years and Nakajima for three years.

Sgt. Mitoshi Nakajima

Gunner Daly's interrogation over the incident with the diary he was keeping in the Autumn of 1943 had involved the Japanese guard known to us as the Christian. Three years later this man appeared, giving evidence for the prosecution, one of the few who turned King's Evidence, in all probability to save himself from being put on trial. What he had to say was all given in an affidavit and was a strange mixture of self-preservation and truth.

Among other things The Christian, real name Yoshida, described the first Commandant at Kinkaseki, Lieutenant Wakiyama as "severe, unnatural and unjust" in his treatment of prisoners: "He did all in his power to make the lives of prisoners of war uncomfortable. I personally witnessed many beatings he himself committed and he became a kind of example for all those under him in the camp. I could not understand how a man could be so bad for nothing."

Yoshida continues, "Some of the worst beatings were given by two Japanese guards, Sergeant Namura and Corporal Kumakata during February of 1943. On one occasion Sergeant Namura sent for me and asked what my nationality was. I replied, 'Japanese, of course.' 'Why do you ask?' He replied I was too friendly and sympathetic towards the prisoners and the prisoners should be beaten and kicked, not sympathised with. On one occasion these two men were responsible for a very severe beating of Major G M Stewart, an Allied officer prisoner. He was kicked round the parade ground for one hour; most of the kicks were delivered in the crotch.

"At Kinkaseki many prisoners were sent down the mine who were not fit for work. The company asked Wakiyama for more men, so he sent the sick men down.

"On several occasions I have seen the bodies of prisoners being badly beaten, their bodies were very badly bruised.

"On one occasion I acted as interpreter when a foreman complained to the Nippon duty officer about the beatings in the mine. They showed their bodies to the officer who could see all the bruises and marks made by the *hanchoe*'s hammers. When these beatings were reported to the Nippon Mining Officer they were reported to him by Lieutenant Oita, but nothing was done about them. There was no doubt whatsoever that this treatment by the mine *hanchoes* was fully condoned by the Nippon army officers, especially Wakiyama.

"I do not consider Wakiyama was fit or competent to command the camp. I consider that the PoW camp and orderlies did everything in their power to stop the Red Cross representatives visiting Number One Camp because they did not wish the Red Cross people to see the conditions in this camp.

"Once a Mr Atsumi of the International Red Cross did visit Number Six Camp, and I personally asked him if he would look into the conditions at Number One Camp [Kinkaseki]. But he told me to shut up. I left Kinkaseki in October 1943 and was sent to Number Six Camp."

Corporal Mizuo Ueno

There was no way of corroborating whether The Christian actually made any formal protests to his superiors. If he did, they were never, as he admits, acted upon. His evidence also mentions three other Japanese guards: Sergeant Tashiro and Corporals Ueno and Kuribayashi, the so-called medical squad.

Each of these men had a nickname. Tashiro was the dreaded "Sanitary Sid", while Kuribayashi was "So-So", and Corporal Ueno was "Lancho".

These three men appeared together, charged jointly with "Inhumane treatment of British and Allied prisoners of war in their custody, thereby causing physical suffering and contributing to the deaths of many of them." Like everyone else brought to trial, they pleaded not guilty.

The Christian had this to say about them: "Sergeant Tashiro, the Medical Sergeant of the camp, was very savage and brutal and was not a fit man." I assume here that he was not referring to the state of his health, but his fitness to hold the position of medical sergeant. "Twice I spoke to him about the beatings of the prisoners and he became very abusive and threatened to beat me. He used a fencing stick – *kendo* – for most of his beatings which he administered regularly. Tashiro was also very much responsible for sending very sick men to work in the mines. The other two orderlies, Ueno and Kuribayashi, were more or less under his orders."

Left: Sgt. Taranosuke Tashiro
Right: Shigeru Kuribayashi

The nub of this particular part of the trial, however, was not so much the beatings. After all, virtually every guard, runabout and *hanchoe* was culpable, to a greater or lesser degree, of physical violence. It was really a question of where the responsibility lay for sending half dead men to work, and also who was in charge of the medical supplies and who was responsible for the deaths.

There were also men who became permanently disabled because of injuries in the mine.

"Day after day I saw men who were unable to walk by themselves dragged to and from the mine by their friends and frequently beaten up by the guards," said Major Wheeler in his affidavit.

219

"The first Red Cross medical supplies did not arrive until midway into 1944. Up to then no hospital equipment was provided to treat the sick. The sick lay on boards and were provided with four blankets apiece, and no provision was made for washing the blankets or providing extra ones. Sometimes we had well over a hundred sick men in hospital, with one and sometimes two medical officers, and four or five medical orderlies, two of whom were trained, and the Camp Commandant repeatedly refused further assistance.

"Throughout my stay in Kinkaseki," concludes Major Wheeler, "the Japanese would only allow a certain number of men to be off sick, regardless of the number of sick there were. This meant constantly sorting the sick and trying to keep the worst in camp. This did not give any of the sick a chance to recover. In addition, at variable intervals, the Japanese medical orderlies would hold a parade and send a large percentage of the sick to work despite any protest or suggestions on the part of the PoW medical officers."

The regime of cruelty and deprivation had started long before Major Wheeler arrived at Kinkaseki, from the very first landing at Kiirun in fact. Every prisoner who survived would remember the long march from Zeiho station and into the mountains. One Japanese officer was charged specifically with the suffering on that enforced march, Lieutenant Tsumoru Ashida. He pleaded not guilty and was actually acquitted because of the lack of evidence against him. Ashida claimed there were buses and trucks provided to ferry the sick who fell by the wayside, an assertion which certainly conflicted with eye-witness accounts. Unfortunately none of the sick were actually in court to give evidence.

Lieutenant Yoshijiro Oita was charged with causing suffering to the prisoners in the early days of Kinkaseki and was sentenced to eighteen months imprisonment. He was charged specifically with hitting prisoners with a golf club and a sheathed sword, and on one occasion of driving men with beri-beri out of hospital and submitting them to violence lasting about two hours. This was another incident which involved Sanitary Sid and was sparked off by the fact that fifteen sick men had failed to have their photographs taken for identification purposes.

Oita, who denied everything, said in evidence, "As to the regulations concerning the treatment of prisoners of war, I always had the following in my mind: to treat prisoners kindly. Because they were far away from their homes and I expected that they had many worries. Therefore I tried my best to do away with these worries."

The other major trial involved managers and employees of the Nippon Mining Company, and included several of the *hanchoes*. The story revealed from the court papers is no different from all the other trials involving war criminals from Kinkaseki: all pleaded not guilty, denied personal responsibility, played down the violence, and in several cases, were ready to put the blame on others in order to put themselves in a better light. There were also quite a few absences. Many of the mine *hanchoes* whose names, or nicknames, came up in evidence during the course of the trial, such as Goldie, Patchy, Blinker, Sammy, Monkey, Smiler, The Savage, Sporting Pink, Scruffy, Bobaday, and a few others were simply not caught.

Left: Seiichi Takeuchi
Right: Kozo Utsonomiya

This, of course, was attributable to the fact that some of them were not Japanese but, like the Runabouts, were Formosan, so it was quite easy for them to disappear to almost any part of the island until the hue and cry had died down. One who was missed – a fact I was sorry about – was Pan Face, a great friend of Frying Pan, real name Rin Kei. These two Formosan *hanchoes* were virtually in sole command of the first floor in the mine, the floor on which I spent almost the whole of my time when working. The collective beatings and crimes against humanity committed by both these men were enormous.

The manner of rounding up the suspects was rather haphazard, as was highlighted at the trials. One of the *hanchoes* in the dock, Nagi Takegoro, known to us as The Ghost, claimed they had caught the wrong man. He suggested that there were in fact two Ghosts, the real villain was the other one. Nagi was picked out of a crowd of about 2,000 men with their families who were about to board a ship bound for Japan in 1946. A massive identification parade was held, obviously at the last moment, on the dock-side. Edwards was required to scan every one. Not only did he pick out Nagi, but two other men also: Takeichi, nicknamed Nelson and Utsonomiya, known as Charlie Chaplin. One assumes that others had either left the island or were missed by Edwards. It was an unfair responsibility to put on the shoulders of one man when one considers the number of men capable of recognising the guards and *hanchoes* very well indeed, but were not called upon.

Toda Mitsgi, the mine Manager, and Nakamura Katsumi, Chief of the mining department, headed the list of mine employees. Then came Yonemura, a liaison officer between the camp and the mine, who was acquitted. The remainder who were tried at this time were all *hanchoes*, charged with contributing to the deaths of prisoners of war and to causing physical suffering to others. The documentation in this part of the trial was considerable Affidavits were obtained from eleven different ex-prisoners who had worked in the mine, also from Major Wheeler and three *hanchoes* who had turned King's Evidence.

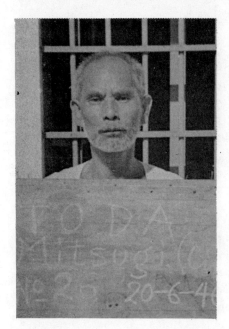

Left: Toda Mitsgi
Right: Katsumi Nakamura

Sergeant Edwards was called upon to give evidence regarding the number of accidents in the mine.

Question. "Were there ever any accidents in the mine?"

Answer. "Yes, there was never a week went by without a serious accident. Serious accidents occurred roughly every week."

Q. "Can you tell me some of these incidents?"

A. "The first man killed was Gunner Millership. He was killed by a fall down a chute. Next one killed was Gunner Sweeney, he was killed by a fall of the roof. The third one was Sergeant Bullinger, he was drilling near a chute and the floor just caved in and then the wall caved in. We couldn't get his body out until we cleared the chute."

Edwards then enumerated other accidents, though he became confused about some of them, mixing up Gunner Len Cullop's death through a mine blast with another man who was crushed by a roof fall.

By contrast, when it came to evidence offered under examination by the *hanchoes*, one of them Suenobu (Blackie), categorically stated that during his two years in the mine "there were no deaths or wounds among the prisoners of war." He put this down to the excellent supervision by his superiors, co-operation from the prisoners and "that God was always with us."

On the question of lamps in the mine, and their efficiency, Sergeant Edwards explained, "First of all every prisoner of war carried a carbide lamp. This lamp had no reflector, just a naked light.

During 1944 there was a lamp shortage and we were issued instead with a small candle lamp. The only place these lamps would work was outside the mine, it would not work when we got it in."

Q. "Which lamp are you referring to?"

A. "I am referring to the oil lamp."

Q. "Why didn't it work?"

A. "It was just a wick. It was just a bowl of oil with a little wick stuck in there [Diagram shown to the court]. The point was that just the slightest draught blew it out, and the air was so bad in the morning that it would not burn. A carbide lamp would burn a stronger jet."

Q. "What was the scale of lamp issues at this time?"

A. "Roughly two men in six had carbide lamps and four men had oil lamps in that period. Working it out, if six men were detailed for the hole and four were working upstairs cutting the ore out they would have one carbide lamp and one oil lamp, and one oil lamp below."

Q. "How many beatings took place down the mine?"

A. "Beatings started in 1943 and they became a daily occurrence on those top three floors. The men were first all lined up and asked about their quota of work and how many bogeys they had filled. If they had not completed their quota for the day they were beaten. They laid it on as hard as they could, they were hard blows. I have seen *hanchoes* using two hands. I have seen men beaten unconscious, not on one occasion, but many times."

When it came to the turn of the *hanchoes* who were in court they tried to make out that what had been said by Sergeant Edwards was exaggerated.

The mine at Kinkaseki had, in fact, been the fourth largest producer of copper ore under Japanese control and was already operating with coolie and civilian prisoner labour before we arrived. The management of the mine was supposed to be quite separate from the military. Captain Immamura and other camp staff had, in theory, no authority over them. Prisoners of war were formally handed over by the guards to the civilian *hanchoes*. In practice, though, the mine administration was inseparable from the camp, the principle being that here was more slave labour provided by the military. The mine management was forced to accept us, unskilled as we were in mine workings and conditions, and was also ordered to meet production quotas imposed by the military.

Toda, the mine manager, who was jailed for one year, said, in his petition to the court: "I never wanted to employ prisoners of war, but they were forced on me by the military authorities. I had no option but to co-operate with the military, for if I had done otherwise I would have been regarded as being unloyal to the Emperor."

Nakamura, Chief of the Mining Department, said in his defence, that while he was in charge, from June 1944 to February 1945, the accident rate decreased considerably. He produced statistics in order to back up his reasoning but the serious flaw was that, even allowing for his statistics, comprehensive safety measures like timber shoring were always very far from being adequate. During Nakamura's period in office deaths still occurred, including that of Len Cullop, victim of a faulty fuse. The report of this incident, which formed part of the evidence in the trial, was given by Edwards and was not entirely correct.

There was a suggestion that a *hanchoe*, known to us only as Long Tom, was to blame for the death of Len Cullop. Len and I were working together for quite some time under Long Tom as drillers, and not once during all the time we were together did I see, or hear, of Long Tom striking anyone. As for being responsible for Len's death, that was ridiculous. All Long Tom did was to draw the explosives from the store.

If it was a bad fuse which caused a premature explosion and killed Len, it could just have easily been among the fuses I was given. If anything, the real fault lay with the authorities of the mine for ordering inexperienced prisoners to handle explosives.

Nakamura was jailed for five years.

The examination of the six *hanchoes* which formed the bulk of the trial would, even to an objctive reader, provide an essay in human frailty. Lie followed upon lie. Each one tried to paint himself as a victim of the prosecution's exaggeration. They even resorted to blaming each other in the dock for the cruelties. And, most incredible of all, the argument was produced that beatings were actually good for the prisoners.

This last one came from Teruo Zushi, The Eagle, a senior *hanchoe* who was said, with complete justification, to be the worst of the worst among the *hanchoes*. He said he could only recall three beatings. And he went on to explain, "I hit them on the back with my hammer shaft. I wanted to increase the daily production for the good of the prisoners, because if production was good as shown on the daily report they were to get better rations." The logic of this kind of defence, however, had its own inbuilt shortcomings; if we only needed beating three times, then for most of the time we must have been pretty good workers.

One of the main witnesses for the prosecution was a For-mosan mine *hanchoe* whom we referred to as Scotch Jock. His real name was Cho Sho Ki. He produced a long state-ment in which he named some of the worst culprits.

"My name is Cho Sho Ki, thirty-four years old, born in Giran, Formosa, I am married, I have five children, I live with my family in Giran.

"I worked in the Kinkaseki Copper mine from 1935 to 1945. I was a squad worker Supervisor during the time the prisoners of war were working in the mine, starting in the Fall of 1942 and ending

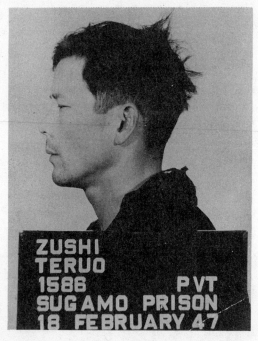

Teruo Zushi

225

in the Spring of 1945 when the mine was closed. I worked on the third level, seventh hole. Working with me over the prisoners of war were Cho Kon Toku [Frying Pan], Rin Kei (Pan Face], Ktoku Boku [unknown], Zushi[The Eagle], Miya [unknown], Nagi [unknown], and one civilian Mancy [Long Tom].

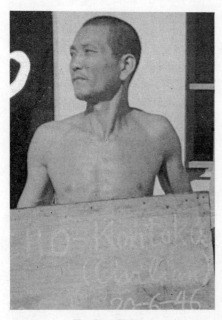

Cho Kon Toku

"I saw various crimes committed by the first six I have named, they were Mine Worker Supervisors who mistreated prisoners of war under them. I will tell in detail everything I saw and only what I saw.

"Cho Kon Toku, a squad supervisor beat prisoners of war so often his beatings were an almost every day occurrence. He beat them with the mine hammers, the head not the handles, and with his fists and open hands, he also kicked them. His blows came on the head, the body and legs and arms of the prisoners.

"Rin Kei, another supervisor, beat prisoners also with the hammer in the same way as Cho Kon Toku but he was not quite so bad.

"Ko Toku Boku, another squad supervisor, was about the same as Rin Kei, they both beat prisoners of war with the hammers and they were not good supervisors. I just mean they were not quite so bad as Cho Kon Toku.

"Zushi, a Group Supervisor who directed the squad supervisors, was the worst man in the area of the mine, worse even than Cho Kon Toku. He personally ordered the One Bar Squad Directors to beat prisoners. He beat them himself with his fists and with hammers. He is responsible for the striking of prisoners.

"Miya, the top Supervisor on the level, did not mistreat prisoners himself. He ordered them to produce about three times as much copper as it was possible for one man to produce and if they did not produce what he asked he would order them to be beaten, but the beatings were done by somebody else.

"Nagi, another Group Supervisor, was responsible for daily beatings and the men in the level were lined up and systematically beaten if they

226

did not produce as much as was expected. One day I saw him beat one man twenty strokes with a hammer after the man had already been beaten by the One Bar Supervisor. He frequently beat men with hammers.

"I swear that everything I have said is the truth and that I have revealed nothing but the truth and concealed nothing but the truth. [sic] Signed Cho Sho Ki."

The Eagle's (Zushi) reply to these allegations not only contained the self-defence of trying to be helpful to the prisoners, but also the following addendum: "I did not beat with any intention of torturing or hurting the prisoners. I do not recall ever causing any bodily injury.

"I never saw any blood shed."

On the other hand, Nelson, who was in the dock with him, blamed The Eagle for most of the beatings. He said he personally was scared of him.

"He was a violent-tempered man. He was a heavy drinker and was extremely brutal. During his frequent rages he acted like a wild beast," added Nelson, who went on to explain that at the end of the working day, when prisoners were paraded, Zushi selected those he thought had not done enough work. They were made to hold onto a pipe which ran along the wall and were systematically beaten with hands, feet and hammer shaft.

Teruo Zushi received ten years imprisonment.

Nelson himself received one of the lighter sentences, two years imprisonment. One of the occasions he recalled when he had to beat a prisoner – and he only admitted to two – was in one of the holes where a man was supposed to be drilling. He says that each time he appeared the prisoner explained his idleness by pointing to a faulty drilling machine. He went on to say that this might work once or twice, but obviously this man tried it too often, claiming he did not know the difference between the store for good machines and the store for faulty ones.

Cho Kon Toku, one of the worst villains, also denied everything, making a plea in mitigation however that, "Whilst working at Kinkaseki mine I always acted on the order of my spirit."

In his statement Frying Pan used the customary defence of "acting on orders". The following is an extract of what he had to say:

"The incidents in which I involved myself, or saw others involved, regarding prisoners of war took place as follows. The first occasion took place in January 1943. Our overseers gave us orders to punish PoWs who did not do the required amount of work. Under my supervision were twelve men working in groups of four.

"Each group was expected to produce sixteen bogeys of ore, or four bogeys per man. Four of these men, all members of our group, failed to complete their task.

"By the use of pidgeon English and pidgeon Japanese they were able to explain to me that they had been delayed in their work by fixing a broken shaft, they also had to carry their ore further then the other eight men. I accepted their excuse because I could see it was reasonable but Kugiyama [?] would not and ordered me to punish them. I slapped them all across the face with my open hand. Kugiyama said that was not enough and he himself slapped them several times.

"The second occasion was also in January 1943 and was of a very similar nature, the PoWs were not the same men but another group of four who were ordered to be punished by Kugiyama. I slapped them. During this period of 1943 I saw Kugiyama mistreat PoWs on several occasions by slapping them, on one occasion I saw him use a hammer shaft to beat one of the PoWs. Except for the two instances mentioned I did not involve myself again during this period."

Frying Pan (Cho Kon Toku) received seven years imprisonment.

Affidavit after affidavit mentioned The Eagle, Frying Pan and The Ghost (Takegoro Nagi) as the worst of a bad bunch.

The Ghost also admitted to only two incidents of violence, one to punish a prisoner for hiding and the other after a worker had dropped a drill bit down a ladder, "a thoughtless and dangerous act," he explained. He was also involved in a roof fall death, but said he was not responsible since his superiors should have tested the roof properly, and although he carried a hammer "he was not sufficiently trained, or experienced, to test the safety of the roof." This from a senior, two bar *hanchoe*.

The Ghost, like The Eagle, received ten years imprisonment.

Evidence against Blackie was not as fierce, and part of his defence was to tell the court that there were no injuries or deaths down the mine. The reason for this he said "was that God was always with us." He tried always to ensure that the prisoners worked "pleasantly and willingly."

Blackie (Fumio Suenobu) got three years imprisonment.

Charlie Chaplain (Kozo Utsonomiya) in one part of his defence expected the court to accept a statement that after beating a prisoner for being idle "he later said he was sorry and we became good friends." His statement went on to say, "About the month of June 1944 I remember striking a prisoner of war". They always seemed to be able to remember what month it was. "The incident took place as I was convalescing and while walking through one of the main tunnels I saw two PoWs sitting beside a derailed empty bogey. These bogeys are heavy but can be put on the rails by three men. I said I would help them, but one said he would go and fetch an iron pipe to use as a lever. I told him this was not necessary and that we could do it ourselves. He made faces at me and shouted loudly.

"He went off to get the pipe, returning about half an hour later. I remonstrated with him and by signs gave him to understand I was angry about the affair and his attitude. He shouted at me again and made faces. I became angry and excited and I struck him across the face with my open hand. We then put the bogey on the rails and went our way."

As a postscript it is worth mentioning that two other ex-*hanchoes* also provided evidence in this trial against mine officials and supervisors. Sannomiya and Kameda claimed to have written letters to senior officers in the camp, including Captain Immamura, complaining about the number of sick prisoners who were being sent to work. "I have seen prisoners carried out unconscious," said Sannomiya. "They did not produce much ore anyway."

The protests, if written and delivered, were ignored.

Left: Sgt. Arashi Chiba, "The Beast".
Right: Lieut. Kozi Tamaki.

CHAPTER
TWENTY FOUR

As far as I am aware there are only three men who were prisoners in Kinkaseki who have ever returned to the camp after the war – Major Crossley, Lieutenant Cross and Sergeant Edwards – who went back in connection with the preparations for the War Crimes Trials. Over 1,000 men had passed through Kinkaseki and Kukutsu during 1942-1945 and a large proportion of them had died, some during their time in the camp and others in camps to which they had been transferred. Of course some had died after their return home. Among the survivors there had always been talk of the possibility of returning one day – this used to come up regularly at the Annual Reunions.

However, I did discover that one other person had retraced our footsteps – the daughter of Major Ben Wheeler, a Canadian and one of our medical officers in Kinkaseki. Ben had apparently kept some notes he made while he was a prisoner. After he died his notes remained with the family, and years later his daughter, Anne, was so moved by the contents of the notes that she went to the camp with a film unit to record what she considered to be the story of Kinkaseki.

I knew nothing about any of this at the time, and my own reason for wanting to return to what had been the most unhappy time of my life was to find out if I could lay any of the ghosts that had been bothering me for years. For me the experience would be most critical because nearly four decades later I still knew those years as a prisoner had shaped my life. But to explain why I felt compelled to make the journey it is necessary to understand the legacy of the experience; the same feelings that were shared by others who, if not physically scarred were, like me, concealing deep mental wounds.

There was very little understanding in the U.K. of what life had really been like in the camps under the control of the Japanese. The popular conception of a PoW camp had largely been focussed through

231

the newspapers and broadcasting on camps in Germany, though in comparison they were as different as chalk and cheese, both in the way they were run and in their construction.

Stirring tales of breakouts from Colditz, or from others by the use of a wooden horse, brave though they were, bore no resemblance to PoW camps in the Far East under the Japanese. It was true that the gruesome details of the concentration camps in Germany gave the public an insight into the depths of barbarism reached by the Nazi regime, but it took some time for Britain to realise that many of its own servicemen had been subjected to inhuman treatment also. An announcement was made to The House of Commons in January 1944 by Anthony Eden that, "The British Government are reasonably satisfied that conditions generally in this area [Formosa] are tolerable, although, as the Secretary for War has said on more than one occasion, the scale on which food is provided is not adequate for long periods to maintain the health of the prisoners in Japanese hands." A somewhat understated and misinformed statement, though it might have served to allay the fears of the families of those taken prisoner.

I suspect that in the begining there was a degree of embarassment about the war in Malaya and Singapore, as the British Government had hardly covered itself with glory in the planning, or the execution, of that phase of the war. I don't suppose for one moment the British public were told the real reason why Singapore fell at the time it happened, therefore we were just the troops who had capitulated and been put out of action for over three years, having failed to hold a fortress. It was better for all concerned if we could be the forgotten army for the time being.

Having come home to roost, as it were, we were also bringing some of the government's ghosts home with us. In retrospect it is easy to say that some attempt at rehabilitation should have been made. What form it should have taken I do not pretend to know, but at the time there was little understanding of how deep the wounds had been in ex-prisoners.

On the outside, apart from those who were crippled and wounded, we were back to our normal weight, and had healthy complexions. We were fit enough to work and to get on with normal life. Though on the inside it was completely different, the hurt and the hate continued to boil away, fuelled by every instance of public ignorance and mis-understanding.

In my own case there were the nightmares which began soon after I got home and carried on for years. The scars also affected my personal and social life. I recall my first grandson inadvertently hitting me across the face in play and the sudden, almost overwhelming desire to retaliate in the hardest way I could. I had to leave the room very quickly.

Outside my home my reputation was that of a man with a very short fuse. I didn't stand too much provocation, and I don't think this was all just inherent temperament. On no account would it have been advisable to come into personal contact with a Japanese person, certainly not in the early years after the war. Later I would learn to live, against my will, with the unexpected sound of the Japanese language coming from behind me while walking down the street or in a store.

When the Queen received the Emperor of Japan on a State visit I felt so angry I had to force myself to stay away from the capital on that day.

My inability to forget, fed by anger, resentment and the nightmares, led me to the paradoxical pursuit of wanting to find out everything I could about the Japanese and the war in the Far East. Was I trying to understand, or just feeding an obsession? There is no doubt that at first it was simply therapeutic, setting down as much as I could in notes about my experiences in the camps. Memories would come flooding out, demanding to be put into words. It was not simply a matter of going to the re-unions where old memories would be revived, but where, with each succeeding year, it became depressing to find that there were fewer and fewer of us around. I stopped going, because those were the wrong sort of memories. We were pledged not to forget, to "keep going the spirit that kept us going." But what record of the camps at Kinkaseki and Kukutsu would survive us?

There is a reasonably wide selection of literature available on many of the camps in the Far East, a large number concentrated on the notorious Burma railway. And yet, surprisingly, nothing on Formosa's Number One Camp at Kinkaseki. As I ploughed through book after book the omission took on a serious note, and more resentment crept in. It wasn't just the fact of being forgotten. It was also the picture which was being painted through the medium of popular films, though I must admit to not being able to see any of them in their entirety. Then there were so many myths in the popular imagination about the Japanese themselves which, after having studied them at close quarters I was not prepared to accept. I certainly didn't believe that they were going to fight to the death with the name of the Emperor on their lips.

In the last weeks in Formosa it was surprising how many of the guards slipped off into the undergrowth, undoubtedly frightened out of their skins at possible retribution. With the advantage of my own experience it was very clear, even miles away from the battleground in Kinkaseki, that the ordinary Japanese soldier was frightened, bullied and humiliated by his superior officers. We were at the end of a vicious line, just like thousands of Chinese, Manchurians, Koreans and the people of Malaya.

To me it seemed that their culture veered between two extremes: the Buddhist peacefulness of a garden full of lotus and cherry blossoms, and the growling, sword flashing *Samurai*. But the average Japanese however belonged neither to one or the other.

Prime Minister Tojo had on several well documented occasions exhorted Camp Commandants to "Supervise your charges rigidly and permit no idleness", also "Let them eat as long as they work." Under such conditions if the sick would not be permitted to eat, they would die. This was the way it was at Kinkaseki and later in the Jungle Camp, but to discover it was the policy of a nation, emanating from the very top and then filtering down through a chain of command to our miserable encampment in the hills of Formosa, obviously gave me a greater perspective of where we fitted in, where our sufferings began and ended.

It was not just a sadistic Japanese N.C.O. or mine *hanchoe* we were up against, but a system, a command, leading all the way back to Emperor Hirohito himself.

In the method of waging war against defenceless people, and I do not only refer to men who have fought honourably and been defeated, but also to the thousands of civilians who lived or died through the chill wind of Japanese expansionism, there was infinitely more blood than blossom.

My readings confirmed and then expanded my opinion. Above all I wanted to try to find out why the Japanese had done all these things. I could not believe that my own countrymen, from the head of state downwards, could have acted collectively in such a way. The Japanese seemed to be so different, they didn't seem to have any sense of their own individuality, or independence of mind.

Above everything else I was drawn back to the experience itself, whether it had any meaning. I had learned that one of the basic philosophies about life for me was to take things one day at a time, and this still held true. As I awoke each morning I considered that compared to some I had at least been given a time bonus. Ten, twenty, thirty, forty years!

What was the recipe for survival in a grim captivity? Had I stumbled on it in Kinkaseki, and was it worth it? Was survival no more than taking one day, one moment, at a time? Was it necessary to be angry and fighting underneath? To resist with all the defiant strength you can muster, to be patient and live in hope? When do you snap, and what causes it? My refusal not to forget was eventually bringing me more and more to the stage where I felt my own experience was incomplete without actually going back to the island that was now called Taiwan, and to tread it again in the flesh. There was an undoubted challenge because Kinkaseki still represented the worst that I had known in life. My fear of the place was not just an imaginary fear. Nightmares are real, and the sweat in which I was bathed when I woke up was also real. All our past is real, not just the good things which most people like to remember, but the bad too.

I had heard that it was possible to exorcise the evil in a person who is supposed to be possessed. Maybe there was a sense in which I too was possessed and felt it necessary to confront the evil spirits of the past locked inside me. Exorcism is dangerous I had been told, and if that was what I was up to in resolving to go back I certainly was aware there were dreadful dangers involved. What if I broke down under the strain? What if the experience of seeing those places again proved too much for me? My wife was coming with me, so there would be at least one sane person present. Even so, a feeling more than simple butterflies in the stomach began to take hold of me as the days of my return to Kinkaseki drew nearer.

CHAPTER
TWENTY FIVE

The Return

Finding a map of Taiwan was one of my first problems. The Bodleian Library in Oxford have a number of maps which were produced by the American Military about 1945, but for reference only. The larger map-selling shops in London failed to produce one single copy.

A further stumbling block was that even though the island exports its goods to this country by the thousand, there is no Embassy as such in the U.K. The nearest thing to it is a Tourist Bureau, and in order to get the necessary visa one has to obtain a letter from the offices in London and then exchange the letter for a visa on arrival in Taiwan.

On making enquiries in London they expressed great surprise at the reason I gave for my wish to return to Taiwan. Fortunately I was helped in a most unexpected way. Whilst trying to explain matters to the person on duty, and having almost reached the exasperated stage, a young man, on my side of the counter, came forward and in very good English asked if he could help. His name was Chen Ning Ming, but he suggested I should call him Steve. He was on holiday in the U.K. and was due to return to Taiwan very soon. Though he also appeared to find the reason for my visit rather strange he went on to say that if, and when, I ever got to Taiwan I was to call him and he would provide whatever help he could. He lived just outside Taipei which was to be my own destination.

As the day of departure drew ever nearer I had the occasional impulse to call the whole thing off, a strange attitude when I consider how many years I had been planning it. My wife wasn't really going to get a great deal of joy out of the trip, because where I was heading was not generally considered to be on the tourist trail. But, once started, the whole adventure began to gather its own momentum. My feeling of tension lasted the whole of the journey. As I tried to relax in the comfort of a modern airliner I was brought food and drink which I didn't really want. Mercifully most of the time on the final leg of the flight, from Hong Kong to Taiwan, was taken up by the requirement to complete various landing and entry forms.

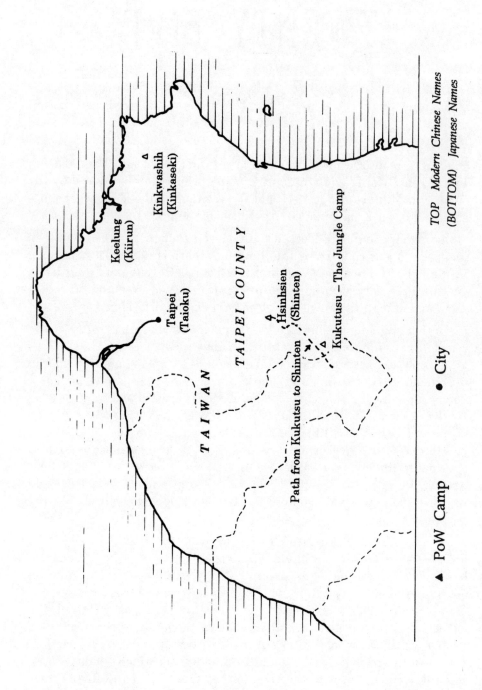

Keelung
(Kiirun)

Kinkwashih
(Kinkaseki)

Taipei
(Taioku)

TAIWAN

TAIPEI COUNTY

Hsinhsien
(Shinten)

Path from Kukutsu to Shinten

Kukutusu – The Jungle Camp

▲ PoW Camp   ● City

TOP Modern Chinese Names
(BOTTOM) Japanese Names

We came out of the clouds and I looked out of the window in an attempt to recognise the island. The plane taxied to a halt, the doors opened and I stepped out onto the airport concourse. I was on Taiwanese soil again, even if it was only the hard surface of an airport.

That first night in the Taipei Hilton was a bad one but the crisis point came and went and I eventually subdued the desire to quit.

More than anything else I felt the challenge of coping with, and overcoming, fear. There was no doubt I considered my survival as a PoW as an achievement, something gained against all the odds. I was proud at having come through all the deprivations and degradations and maybe I felt, in a small way, that people like me were a little bit special. But it had been bought at the price of nightmare and fear. What was more, the fears were the kind that one had to keep to oneself; they could not be shared, because there really was no one who could understand.

When I awoke the doubts were gone. There were things to do, some of them proving almost impossible, certainly infinitely harder than I anticipated.

The room boy came to the room and introduced himself as Peter. He was in fact a forty year old Formosan whose job was to attend to our needs. So the first thing I did was to get him to provide some tea and answers to a few questions. Incredibly, I discovered that he was virtually ignorant of the fact that there were Allied prisoner of war camps on the island less than forty years ago. His father had told him very little of the war and beyond what I would call just a child's knowledge he had no conception of what went on. I wondered if this was simply a lack of curiosity, or a racial reticence?

Naturally, I shuddered at the thought that out here my past, and that of a few hundred tortured souls, seemed to have receded without a trace. Peter said he would ask his father about some of the matters of which we had spoken. In the meantime I thought the best thing I could do was to rally some of my contacts and try to get things moving. Peter telephoned Steve on my behalf and told him I was now in Taiwan and was in need of help. He said would be over at once and he was as good as his word for in less than thirty minutes he was in my hotel room and we were chattering away like old friends.

Steve's own knowledge of the events of the past was even less than that of Peter, who was at least twice his age, but I pressed on with my questions. Where was Kinkaseki in relation to Taipei? Was it very far away? What did Steve know of the war years in Taiwan? Had he been told anything at school? All my questions drew blanks. He knew nothing, not even the location of the place I knew as Kinkaseki. But like Peter he would make enquiries of his father.

It was, in fact, an Englishman in Taiwan who came up with the first piece of practical help. I telephoned a businessman, Brian Gazely, whose name had been given to me by friends back home, and the same day he was able to furnish me with a detailed map of the island.

Apart from Brian's help the first two days in Taipei were frustrating. I was unable to get answers to what, seemed to me, simple questions. Indeed I began to think I was never going to get out of the city. The main stumbling block was the actual location of Kinkaseki, and how I could get there. No one seemed able to understand what I was looking for, or for that matter why I should want to go there. It was not until the map arrived at the hotel that some light began to shine on my problem, and with no small degree of annoyance I realised I should have seen the answer earlier. Since Formosa had become Taiwan it was obvious that the place names would no longer be Japanese but Chinese. Taipei, where I was staying, had formerly been Taihoku.

With that realisation I now began to ask different questions. What was the name now of the place I knew as Kinkaseki? Another look at the map, which was in Chinese, provided the answer. The place that had epitomes the lowest point of my life had received a name change and was now Kin Kwa Shih. Though I am unable to be certain of the precise translation into Roman characters I now seemed to be moving in the right direction. However, it was evident this was not going to be a well-charted visit like the tourist trips to the supposed Bridge on the River Kwai, a prescribed track for returning prisoners of war and other tourists to follow.

My first sight of Taiwan (Formosa) in November 1942 had been when I was arriving at the island on board the *England Maru* at the docks of Kiirun. Now I was heading for the same city, with the new name of Keelung, on a cold, very grey and wet morning in February 1983. If the sun had been shining I would have felt cheated, since I wanted it just the way it was. It was the same weather I remembered from my previous visit, only now I was sitting in a pleasantly warm car with Steve as my guide, translator and chauffeur with a friend of his, Gary, as an extra companion, and my wife Iris.

Keelung is about twenty-four miles from Taipei and the road is a good dual-carriageway. We made good speed to the city but on entering the port area nothing stirred in my memory; there were no positive landmarks and the place was quite unrecognisable. I walked around the harbour but still nothing stirred, though there was no doubt that geographically this was the place where we had disembarked in 1942 from The *England Maru*. I decided to take a few photographs of the area, an act which almost landed me in an incident because official permission was required to take photographs.

The next town I was looking for was Zeiho and our route took us up among the mountains, the road disintegrating at times into nothing more than a track. We took a few wrong turns and it was necessary for Gary to ask for directions. I was no help because my previous journey from Kiirun (Keelung) to Zeiho had been by train with the blinds drawn, so the landscape meant nothing to me. In any case I couldn't see how I was going to be much help if, like many other places, the name had been changed.

When we eventually arrived and I was pleased to see that nothing had changed. The station at which we had detrained was still there, as was the square where we had lined up before the march to Kinkaseki.

If Zeiho had had unpleasant associations in 1942 this time it was to leave a distinctly different memory, a blend of the quaint and the surprising. While I was photographing the station I ran out of film, discovering that in my haste to leave the hotel I had neglected to put any spares in my camera case; a lapse of memory that led me to a totally unexpected findin this out-of-the-way place in the mountains – a professional photographer and his studio. My curiosity was soon satisfied. I was invited to see the studio, and it became clear how the ancient and the modern were working together: a vintage camera studio stand and a mahogany and brass camera of the 1920s stood in the centre of the floor. Alongside these items of Victoriana was a modern Hassleblad, but both of served him as the tools of his trade. The man himself, like others in the town, was most helpful and insisted I use his studio to take a photograph of Steve and Gary.

The route from Zeiho was now somewhat different from my first experience. We wend along a metalled road out of the town which, whilst it went in the same general direction towards Kinkaseki, followed a line along the side of the hill rather than the track down in the valley. As we drove slowly along the higher road I could, however, see to our left the track along which we had stumbled in 1942.

About seven miles outside Zeiho we came to a junction of the roads and I was assured that the signpost to the left did say Kin Kwa Shih.

I decided to get out of the car and walk the road into Kinkaseki rather like a pilgrim. Iris and our two companions carried on in the car along the main road while I walked through the back streets. The village was built on the side of the mountain and had no particular associations for me, except for the school playground, the site of the parade in the cold rain on the 14th November 1942.

As I wandered nearer the centre of the village I began to feel I was indeed on the right road, and then I knew that as I turned the corner up

241

ahead I was going to see the school. It was still raining and the conditions were just right for my memory to transport me backwards in time.

Hurrying along I saw nothing, except a straggling line of prisoners making their way along the road. Then suddenly there was the school. It was exactly as I remembered it, though there may have been one or two slight alterations. I walked into the playground and stood there whilst the words of the Japanese Camp Commandant seemed to hang in the air. Tears came into my eyes – not tears of self pity, but tears of joy that I was able to return and stand once more in this spot. My tears were also for the men who, in death, were unable to stand here.

Steve and Gary went into the school in order to make some enquiries and it was while I was still in my reverie that a young man on a motor cycle, with a young woman on the pillion seat drove up, interrupting my thoughts to ask if he could help me. Not for the first time I explained who I was and why I was there. Of course he wasn't old enough to remember but he also was on a pilgrimage, so he told me. He was showing his girl friend where he had attended school before he went on to Taipei University. This was a coincidence which could not be ignored; two totally different experiences, two different sets of emotions and two different pasts meeting in the same location for a completely different reason.

By now a few villagers, young and old, had gathered outside the school gates talking with Gary in an animated way. I kept interrupting to ask what they were saying. The older people remembered the camp, just a few metres down the road. It was known, one of the women said, as High Nose Village. The reason for this Gary explained was because of the foreigners who had been kept there – Westerners with their different shaped noses.

Another villager volunteered the information that a more sinister name for the camp was The Devil's Castle. For many years after the war local children had been forbidden to play within the camp area "because of the bad spirits which were living there". This made the point that "they" were aware, therefore, of the things that had happened in the camp. They also told a story, of which I had known nothing, of the village girls who had been raped by Japanese soldiers from the camp. Another account was of an execution which had taken place in an area nearby which was now the local football field. I explained I knew nothing of such matters that had happened outside the camp.

On our previous walk from the school to the camp the route had taken us across a bridge spanning a deep gorge, but now I went by a different route which the villagers pointed out to me. I had to climb a set of very steep steps cut into the bank, an area of which I had no previous knowledge. It brought me out to a vantage point which I could clearly see was the lower parade ground that formed the central part of the camp at Kinkaseki. I knew it, not just from the mountains with their memorable contours forming a back-cloth to the camp buildings on the hillside, but also from all the feelings stirring inside me.

Most of the original buildings had gone, blown away in a hurricane, I was told. A couple of replacement building had been erected and were inhabited by people from the village. The actual camp area appeared to be rather smaller than I remembered. I was able to trace the foundations of most of the buildings and it was not a difficult matter to visualise each one, from the bath house to the cookhouse and the guardroom. I walked around for a while quite unable to speak to anyone. The Commandant's office and, just below, the long building which comprised the hospital were still there, serving as homes for some of the villagers.

To the left of the lower square, where the two single storey wood and brick houses had been built, came a man with two young children. He was quick to understand why I was there and, when Gary and Steve had explained matters to him, he seemed to want to help. He told me his name was Hsieh Jie Chauag, we called him Mr Shey. He went on to explain that during our time in Kinkaseki he was a boy of twelve or thirteen years of age living in the village and he was aware of many of the things that happened to us during the years 1942 to 1945.

I explained to him the part I had played in the mine as a driller whereupon he told me that was also what he now did for a living. I expressed some surprise that the mine was still producing copper but he told me that this was not the case, it was no longer a copper mine, but a gold mine owned by the government. My mind raced back to the noise and the sweat of drilling holes for Long Tom. In my imagination I could once again feel the darkness closing in on me as I walked the mile or so underground. Whether we had been drilling for gold or copper, the end result would have been just the same. Through Gary I questioned Mr Shey about his work and how they carried out the drilling and the chunkle and basket work. Not surprisingly things hadn't changed a great deal. He went into a small shed by the side of his house and brought out a carbide lamp, exactly the same as the ones we carried. But these, at least, were no longer used down the mine – instead, they had electric lights fixed to their helmets. For old time's sake he gave me the carbide lamp. Lampo would have been proud of me – I was on parade and I had remembered to bring my lamp.

Mr Shey then offered to take me to the mine. Our route took us up the identical set of steps out of the camp that I had climbed all those years ago, through the depression in the hillside and on to an area which provided me with a long-remembered view overlooking my nightmare of almost forty years ago. The steps up which we had dragged our tortured bodies were gone now and the area was completely overgrown, though still easily recognisable. The route down to the mine-head was now by means of a wooden platform running on a funicular type of rail.

Several other men had joined us by this time, more mine employees. They were told by my two interpreters who I was and why I was there, information which resulted in a flood of memories about what they were doing in the village as children when we were prisoners, though I obviously couldn't follow much of it. Not only because of the language problem, but because by now I was being transported to a place I swore I never wanted to see again. My mind was bursting with memories and my heart with tears through these self-inflicted wounds.

When we reached the mine-head and I stepped off the wooden platform I wanted to scream. The effort of holding back the emotion I was feeling was almost overwhelming. Even the approach of an armed policeman questioning my friends as to why I was there failed to arouse me as I walked towards the mine entrance. Apparently I was in an area I was not supposed to enter. However, the situation was explained to the guard who then came over and shook my hand. The area was even more broken down than it had been when I last saw it, and oddly enough, it was once again a great deal smaller than I had remembered. One of the old miners, to whom things had been explained, must have sensed how I was feeling. He came over and gave me a warm handshake. Another talked of how his father had worked in the mine and used to tell him about the prisoners, going on to say that his father had also told him that they used to try to smuggle food into the mine for us, "Very much against the orders of the Japanese." Another miner pointed out the spot where the Japanese shrine used to be. I stood there and remembered Len Cullop's death, and how our prayers, for him and others, had been quite ineffective. I also remembered our many requests for "a tin of bully and a packet of fags", said in the most meaningful way we could muster as we bent forward to make our compulsory obeisance. The entrance to the mine was before me, I was unable to go any further, and the tears came to me eyes once more.

I acquired a permanent record of the place, posing for a photograph outside the mine entrance and flanked by some of the miners. Again, as at Zeiho, there was some doubt about the legitimacy of taking photographs, and the armed mine guard who had joined us was a little angry that he had not been consulted about my visit, though again, before I left, he once more shook hands with me and explained through Gary how sorry he was for what had happened to myself and my friends. After a further short conversation with the other miners, I climbed onto the wooden platform to be taken back to the top of the mountain. Each of the miners, and the policeman, made a great show of their friendship and good wishes as I left. The weather was still cold and very wet as I gently rode up the hillside. On my return drive to Taipei sat still and quiet, disturbed only by my own thoughts and memories.

I had one more place to visit, and more ghosts to exorcise – in the village of Shinten. When we first collected supplies for the Jungle Camp it appeared to me to be a hamlet of rather squalid houses and nothing more. In 1983 I was amazed that this could have been the village I thought I remembered so well as just a single row of dilapidated shops and houses, where Jack Brazier and I had begun our never-to-be-forgotten journey to Kukutsu with a stretcher loaded with blankets.

Hsintien, as it is now known, is a large urban area, almost a suburb of Taipei. It is a town of large shops and office blocks, with a large bustling population. I almost despaired, being quite sure this was not the place I wanted, though both Steve and Gary assured me it was. I asked to be taken to the railway station, knowing that from there, if we were in the right place, I could orientate myself. However, after a couple of false starts and various enquiries had been made we learnt that the station had been closed down.

I then thought of the river – they couldn't have closed that down -and after more directions, and more walking around in the rain, I finally found what I was looking for – the suspension bridge that spanned the wide muddy river. True, it wasn't the same bridge. A rather more sub- stantial one had been built, though it was still a suspension bridge, and in the same place as I remembered. Making my way towards it I stood with my back to the river, walked forward a few yards and turned right.

There, in front of me was my village street, exactly as it had been in my mind all those years. In spite of the pouring rain I walked slowly along the road, which now had a hard surface, though everything else was the same. As I walked I could feel the weight of the stretcher on my arms and once again I wondered if I had done a very wise thing in coming here. The pain was very strong indeed.

I needed confirmation of what I already knew and it could only come from someone of my own age, or older. As I walked towards the end of the street I saw a shopkeeper in one of the small shops who looked as though he was about the right age. Retracing my steps I brought my two interpreters back to the shop to question the old man. His name was Yong Chi Gey and for the next hour or so memories, his as well as mine, came flooding back.

"Yes," he said, "we used to watch the prisoners coming into the street from out of the hills on the other side of the bridge to collect stores from a warehouse across the street," pointing out the building to me. "Now it is a government printing works", he explained, "and perhaps you ought not to let them see you photographing it." Once again my camera seemed liable to get me into trouble.

The area around the Jungle Camp at Kukutsu, he went on to explain, was now being used for some form of industry.

"Yes," Mr Yong kept repeating, "we used to watch you. We knew you were British prisoners, and that you were being treated badly." He went on to say that he and his neighbours could see we were starving, which was the reason why they put out the trays of food when they saw us coming, so that we might take some as we passed by. They were afraid to give us the food, as the Japanese would have punished them.

All through my captivity in Formosa I believed the island was totally hostile, not just the climate and the environment, not just the Japanese and Formosan guards, but the native population as well. There were few points of contact with them but those we did know were the people in a position of authority. There were also the odd few down down the mine, men like Stropper Joe and Shanghai Lil, but these were Chinese, brought in, like us, for the purpose of labour to improve the war situation for the Japanese. Our eyes had told us that the most we could expect from the local people was indifference.

On the few occasions when we were out of the camp, such as the initial march from Kiirun, and later the Town Working Parties in Shinten, when the impassive faces we saw betrayed no hint of what I was now learning, their anti-Japanese feelings. When the war was over and they began to appear at the fence of the camp in Taihoku they were, for the most part, just a bunch of civilians who wanted to trade for what we were offering. They, like us, were very relieved that the war had ended. But to us, throughout the years of our captivity, the Formosans belonged to the same basic race as our enemies, the Japanese. We had the feeling that all around us was a large sea of hostility, and the only help we were going to get was from each other.

It was many years after the war, however, that I realised I was going to have to revise some of the assumptions I had made. They were largely a Chinese people who, in 1895, had been subjugated when the island, in the infancy of the Japanese drive towards expansion, had been ceded to them after the first Sino-Japanese war of 1885. They were a subject race and not as I, and every other prisoner had imagined, an active ally of the Japanese.

I had been one of the men who took their food when the opportunity presented itself. I had always thought I was stealing it, though I had to admit I could never understand why, when it was so obvious they had seen us, and didn't raise the alarm. Now I knew. Mr Yong's father, a man of ninety-four, stood nearby nodding his head in confirmation of everything his son was saying.

Mr Yong's business was that of a herbalist and before I left him and his family that afternoon he presented me with a small blue and white jar. He explained that the jar had been brought from China to Formosa by his father some seventy years before when he had first arrived to set up the business in the very shop in which we were now standing. The old man, carrying a hand warmer which in some way was built into a basket, expressed his feeling for me, said how sorry he had been to see us as prisoners of the Japanese, and hoped that all the men had returned home to their families.

It was not until that day that I realised the precise relationship of the local people with the Japanese, and that for some ninety years the local population had been fighting skirmishes with the Japanese. It would have been such a comfort to know that we had potential friends on the outside of the camp. What a pity the language barrier prevented us from knowing it.

I made one more visit to Kinkaseki two days later. It was raining hard as we turned off the coast road outside Keelung to head towards the mine by a different, shorter route. Very quickly we were up into the cloud line. The constant mist shrouded everything as we climbed the mountain road. At Kinkaseki Mr Shey invited us into his houe on the site of the camp. While Iris, Steve and Gary went in to talk and drink a cup of hot tea I wandered round outside on my own. A couple of hens were scratching about on the ground outside the buildings where the Commandant had had his office. The steps down which he had made so many theatrical entrances for the *presento* parades, and which had been the indirect cause of the death of many of my friends when used as punishment for failing to produce a work quota were gone now. In their place was a steep concrete drive which allowed the residents to have vehicular access to their premises. A mangy-looking dog barked to assert his territory, recalling the other dog that had dared invade the camp area so many years ago. Two single storey shed-like dwellings now stood on the site of the hospital building where Sanitary Sid would barge in with his stick ready to beat the hell out of somebody.

It was still raining hard as I wandered round, looking this time for the alternative entrance which had been excavated into the face of the mountain. I was unable to find it. Finally a neighbour of Mr Shey's told me that the old entrance was now blocked by the gable end of his house. The Extreme Disposition tunnel into which, according to instructions, we were to be shepherded and killed off, was now no more.

Then up the steps leading to the mine-head for the last time . . . It had all been so unnecessary, unforgiveable and unjust. So many good, ordinary men, wasted. And for what purpose?

The Japanese had attempted to subjugate the other races of the Far East. They were brutal and inhuman and I still hated them for all they represented. Of course, torture, suffering and slaughter has happened many times before, and it still goes on. It has been documented by one means or another almost since the beginning of time, and sooner or later we all learn about it, though some are fortunate enough not actually to experience it. But how easily it is forgotten, almost as if we could get used to it. Complacent almost. I have always considered I was fortunate to survive without any physical scarring, to get my extra forty years, to have come through, perhaps by sheer will-power, or maybe good fortune, by taking each day as it came. Yet without the hope that some day it would all be over I don't know that I could have gone on. Even with that vital hope a rock fall in the mine or the Extreme Disposition could have brought everything to an end.

The fear of the place was still there. I suppose it was partly that feeling I resented. Did I return to rid myself of that fear? Or was it simply to lay a few ghosts?

I took a last look at High Nose Village and The Devil's Castle. Maybe those names alone would preserve a fraction of the reality, get entangled in local legend and perhaps become some sort of Chinese myth, a memory, however dim.

Along with a few hundred other men *it* had been the biggest challenge of my lifetime, a challenge to come through with some sort of belief in myself, and not to have given in.

The last thing I did was to ask Mr Shey about the cemetery. He told me that some years after the war the bodies of those who had been buried in this awful place had been removed and taken elsewhere. May they rest in peace.

We would not forget them. We would carry on a little longer, blessed with the good fortune of having been to the gates of hell, and come back, to keep going the spirit that kept us going one day at a time.

The site of the "Extreme Disposition" behind the building on the right.

⊣┐ POSTSCRIPT ┌⊢

Death of An Emperor

Power without responsibility – the prerogative
of the harlot throughout the ages

Kipling.

Emperor Hirohito, the 124th in a line of Japanese Emperors, finally died on 7 January 1989 after a very long illness. One does not rejoice at the death of another human being, but in this case it would be beyond the bounds of reason to expect anyone with my particular enduring ordeal to feel a deep sorrow. This postscript represents my thoughts and findings on the passing of what I, and no doubt a few thousand others who shared that experience, consider to be the last of the major war criminals of World War Two. His escape from the judgement of his enemies was, without a doubt, because it was considered politically expedient, in particular by the Americans who felt Hirohito could be better used as a live Emperor than a dead war criminal. A point of view not universaly popular. Hirohito was allowed to go unpunished for his share in the war crimes of the military leaders of Japan extending over a period of at least twenty years.

After his death Emperor Hirohito became known, as is the custom in Japan, by the name given to the period of his reign, hence Emperor *Showa* (Enlightened Peace): a man with only one name, but never permitted to be so called by the citizen of Japan, or the press. He is always referred to by one of the many descriptions reserved for Japanese Emperors: *tenno* (Son of Heaven), *tenno heika* (Lord Son of Heaven), *tenshi* (Heavenly King), *kotei* (Sovereign Ruler of Nations), *denka* (Imperial Royal Highness), and in the west by the more romantic name *Mikado*.

The names given to him by us, his prisoners, under the control of his military forces, were equally flowery but not quite so flattering. One such appellation given to him by PoWs which suggested he was born out of wedlock was not so far wrong since his mother and father were not married until some days after the birth, this event being kept secret for a year before the announcement of the birth on 29 April 1901.

251

The culpability of the Emperor for the declaration of war against the allies, initiated by the attack on Pearl Harbour on 7 December 1941, has been discussed at great length since the surrender of Japan. The question has been asked many times, "Did Hirohito know of the intentions of his war chiefs"? A consensus of opinion, by both Japanese and Western writers, is that he was aware of the impending attack on Pearl Harbour and its ramifications. This puts him in a position of not only being aware, but taking an active part in the planning. So, was he a puppet? On the day Singapore fell, and the Japanese began to celebrate, was it just a coincidence that he was out for a ride on his white horse during the celebrations when he stopped to pose on the drawbridge of his palace for a celebratory photograph, was it also a coincidence that he was wearing full military uniform? It has been said in order to mitigate, or to excuse such a coincidence, that nearly all Japanese males at that time were wearing military clothing, and that it signified nothing. Nevertheless, the person, the clothing, the horse, the pose, the location and the timing indicated something more than coincidence.

There had been a shift in the emperor's relationship with the military after the Meiji Restoration in 1932. For this reason, if for no other, this made him much more responsible when Japan planned and executed her territorial excursions into an Asia which had, heretofore, been outside the normal borders of Japan. From then onwards the emperor had a responsibility for what happened, he could no longer be, as I have heard him referred to, "a master of inaction".

I find it difficult to accept that Emperor Hirohito was unaware of the trials and tribulations, not only of prisoners of war, but of the ill treatment, torture and murder of the civilian population in the countries which were to become part of the Japanese dream of a "Greater East Asia Co-prosperity Sphere". Emperor Hirohito, who was aware of the European way of life, having mixed with members of our Royal family before the war, had it in his power at least to allow the women and children who had been caught up in his war to be repatriated. This would have meant not only survival for many of them, but from a Japanese point of view would have been infinitely fewer mouths to feed and people to guard. He failed even in this humanitarian act.

When it became obvious that his illness was certain to be terminal the debates on his responsibility began. The Association of Historians in Japan issued a statement, backed by the Historical Society of Japan, to the effect that, "Hirohito was the person with supreme responsibility in militaristic Japan, the obvious responsibility of Emperor Hirohito for the war should not be dissolved with his death."

Sosuke Uno, the Foreign Minister, and a critic of the Emperor, was reported as saying after the death of the Emperor, that, "The historians could now claim it was Hirohito who tried to prolong the war before speaking up in order to play a part in ending it." In other sections of the government every effort was made to provide clean hands for Hirohito by trying to prove it was the Emperor who persuaded his Generals and the army that they should cease fighting. History records that the debate on the question of bringing the war to an end had been going on for some time. The military leaders and the government ministers who had been conducting the progress of the war failed to agree when they met in June 1945. They again failed to arrive at a conclusion in early August after the dropping of the first atomic bomb on 6 August. It was left to the emperor to resolve the situation on the third meeting which took place on 14 August 1945.

When the question is asked, "If Hirohito could stop the war in 1945 why then did he not go the whole hog and prevent it in the first place?" The Japanese Foreign Minister's answer was: "Established constitutional practice (was such) that the Emperor performed the affairs of state with the advice and assistance of his ministers and he would not think of rejecting recommendations made to him by his advisors."

Another school of thought in Japan states that in the debates on ending the war, where one faction wanted to carry on with the fight whilst another wished to sue for peace, the Prime Minister of the day, Kantaro Suzuki, failed to make his wishes in the matter clear and appealed to the Emperor to break the deadlock. Accordingly he came down on the side of peace. But not until a further atomic bomb had been dropped. This is not easy to equate with the side of the coin which espouses the edict that "None of the Emperor's subjects would dream of disobeying their Emperor."

One writer, Shumon Miura, says, "The atrocities committed during the war were carried out in the Emperor's name – yet it was we ourselves, our fathers, our husbands and our brothers who committed them, the emperor's responsibility cannot be separated from his people's responsibility."

Hirohito took his people into the dark valley. His responsibility is undeniable. One Japanese remarked to a critic of the Japanese actions during the war when he remonstrated with him, "The trouble is that you refuse to forget what happened in the war against Japan." Whereupon the critic replied, "Yes, and you have failed to remember."

My personal past convinces me that experience is life's great teacher. And there is no way one can forget the lesson which came out of the experience of being a prisoner of the Japanese for three and a half years. It is all very well for the past President of the United States, Ronald Reagan, to say, on the ocassion of Hirohito's funeral, "His Majesty played a truly heroic role in bringing hostilities between our two peoples to an end."

Mr. Reagan was one of the people of an age to be available for war service to whom the principle "The further from the battle zone the easier it is to talk", having spent the war years "fighting the war on the film lots of Hollywood and sleeping in his own bed every night."

From the lips of the emperor we have the quote when asked by General MacArthur after the war, "If you felt so strongly against the war, why did you not step up to the microphone and pronounce an Imperial Rescript against it?" Hirohito's reply contained the words, "If I had taken such action in 1941 I should most certainly have had my throat cut." Had Emperor Hirohito taken such a step there are those who would have said, "His majesty played a truly heroic role in preventing hostilities between our two countries." But, since he used the expression "having his throat cut" was there a clue in this? Was it possible that the warmongers in The Cabinet were threatening to murder him?

┉ APPENDIX ONE ┉

List of Prisoners at Kinkaseki

Camp Number relates to the issue of numbers we were required to wear and to give to a guard or *hanchoe* on demand. Like our army number it served the same purpose as a name.

Numbers 1 to 523 represent the original members of Kinkaseki from November 1942 and were in alphabetical order. There was, for some reason or other, a deviation from this system as other men entered the camp. The military rank was the criteria used.

Where it is known the record shows that some men died in certain camps after they left Kinkaseki.

(T) represents the camp at Taihoku, Formosa.

(H) is the camp at Heito, Formosa.

(S) is Shirakowa, Formosa.

(K) is Kagi.

Arrivals from other camps came from Shirakowa, Heito, Kagi, Taihoku and Taichu.

The asterisks *** denote the men who remained in Kinkaseki after their arrival and went on to The Jungle Camp at Kukutsu near Shinten where they remained until the war finished.

A copy of the orignal address of each man is held by the author.

There are some names which are followed by a ? This is all that is shown in the Official Record after they left Kinkaseki.

Camp No.	Name	Rank	Address	Disposition
1	Adams. J.	Gnr.	Buxton	Left 20.8.43 Died (S)
2	Adamson. J.J.	Sgmn.	Brydekirk	Died 14.12.42
3	Agass. E.	L/Cpl.	Stevenage	Left 20.8.43 (T)

4	Albone.H.J.	Gnr	Beds.	Left 8.11.43 (T)
5	Allardyce.A.	L/Cpl.	Aberdeen	*** March 1945
6	Anderson.M.L.	Capt.	Not given	Left 20.8.43 Died
7	Anderson.W.G.	Sgt.	Lanark	Died 13.1.45.
8	Andrews.E.G.	Gnr.	Surrey	Died 26.3.43
9	Angus. G.	Bdr.	Thetford	Left 21.2.45
10	Appleton. J.A.	Gnr.	Harrogate	Left 21.2.45
11	Askew. H.	L/Bdr.	Not given	Left 13.11.43 (H)
12	Atkinson.D.F.H.	Sgt.	Halifax	Left 20.8.43 (T)
13	Aylward.P.B.	Bdr.	W.Norwood	*** March 1945
14	Badgett.J.L.	Capt.	Twickenham	Left 20.8.43 (S)
15	Baigent.G.	Gnr.	Midhurst	*** March 1945
16	Bailey.E.	Gnr.	Hull	*** March 1945
17	Baillie.T.W.	Gnr.	Douglas	Left 25.10.44 (S)
18	Baker.A.W.	L/Bdr.	London	Left 20.8.43 (T)
19	Baker.B.N.	Sgt.	Anerley	Left 13.11.43 (H)
20	Barber. G.	Sgmn.	Nottingham	Died 29.1.45
21	Barker.H.	Gnr.	Bulwell	Died 3.3.43
22	Barnes. E.	Gnr.	Not given	Left 20.8.43 (T)
23	Barnes.F,V.	Gnr.	Grimsby	Died 18.11.45
24	Barrett.H.G.	R.S.M.	Brighton	Left 13.11.43 (H)
25	Barrie.W.	Gnr.	Lesmahgow	Left 21.2.45 ?
26	Barritt. C.	Gnr.	Todmordon	Died 13.1.43
27	Bartelot.R.J.G.	Capt.	Timsbury	Left 20.8.43 (S)
28	Bartholomew.A.E.	Gnr.	Leeds	Left 20.8.43 Died
29	Batrick.W.	Gnr.	Not given	Left 8.11.43 (T)
30	Beaument.A.	Gnr.	Sheffield	Left 20.8.43 (T)
31	Beaumont.S.	Bdr.	Liverpool	Left 21.2.45 ?

32	Bell.D.T.	L/Sgt.	Glasgow	*** March 1945
33	Bell.H.N.	Gnr.	Hetton le Hole	Left 25.10.44 (S)
34	Bell.J.M.	Gnr.	Dublin	Left 20.2.45 ?
35	Benson.C.	Gnr	Winson Green	*** March 1945
36	Bentick.J.H.	Gnr.	Mildenhall	Left 21.2.45 ?
37	Bentley.J.	L/Bdr.	Elland	Died 24.6.45
38	Beszant.S.	Pte.	Market Rasen	Left 8.11.43
39	Bidwell.H.A.	Gnr.	Buttisham	Left 8.11.43 (T)
40	Biggins.S.	Gnr.	Hebden Bridge	Left 30.3.45 (T)
41	Bilham.L.	Gnr.	Not given	Left 8.11.43 (T)
42	Bingham.J.	Sgt.	Lanark	*** March 1945
43	Bird.J,C.	Gnr.	Hoddesdon	*** March 1945
44	Black.J.	L/Bdr.	Sanquhar	Died 11.3.43
45	Blair.D.	Gnr.	Stirlingshire	Left 22.3.45 (S)
46	Blair.W.B.	L/Bdr	Belhaven	Died 6.2.45
47	Blakely.J.	Gnr.	Glasgow	*** March 1945
48	Blezzett.R.	Gnr.	Peterbrough	*** March 1945
49	Boughey.J.G.	Cpl.	Wishaw	Died 21.2.43
50	Bowers.A.R.	Gnr.	London	Left (S)
51	Brain.K.H.G.	Gnr.	Clapham	Died 28.12.42
52	Brandon.W.J.	Gnr	Glasgow	*** March 1945
53	Brazier.J.L.	L/Cpl.	Moseley	*** March 1945
54	Brennan.J.	Bdr.	Not given	Left 13.11.43 (H)
55	Brentnall.R.	Gnr.	Not given	Left 20.8.43 (T)
56	Brewster.W.	Bdr.	Durham	Left 22.3.45 (S)
57	Briggs.L.G.	Gnr.	Walthamstow	Left 20.8.43' (S)
58	Brodie.J.	L/Sgt.	Glasgow	*** March 1945
59	Brooke.E.	Sgmn.	Glossop	Left 25.10.43 Died

60	Brooks.W.S.	B.S.M.	Not given	Left 13.11.43 (?)
61	Brookes.K.G.	Gnr	Not given	Left 20.8.43 (T)
62	Brown.G.H.	Gnr.	Carluke	Died 6.4.43
63	Brown H.	Gnr.	Havant	*** March 1945
64	Brown J.	L/Sgt.	Lanark	*** March 1945
65	Brown W.M.G.	Lieut.	Newbury	Left 31.2.45
66	Bruce D.	L/Bdr.	Not given	Left 3.11.43
67	Bruce E.	Gnr.	Not given	Left 8.11.43
68	Brunton	Bdr.	Farnborough	Leeft 20.8.43
69	Buchanan R.	Gnr.	Not given	Left ? Died.
70	Buckham J.	Gnr.	Hamilton	*** March 1945
71	Buckton T.E.	Gnr.	Middlesbrough	Left 21.2.45 (?)
72	Buntin J.	Pte.	Motherwell	Left 22.3.4 (S)
73	Burgess J.	Gnr.	Not given	Left 8.11.43 (T)
74	Burnhill.W.	Gnr.	Cleckheaton	Left 8.11.43 (T)
75	Burns.H.	Gnr	Edinburgh	Died 8.2.45
76	Buttifant.F.I.	Sgmn	Norwich	Left 30.3.45 (T)
77	Calder.W.	Gnr.	Edinburgh	Left 13.11.43 (H)
78	Caldow.J.	Gnr.	Wishaw	*** March 1945
79	Callaghan.D.	Gnr.	Durham	*** March 1945
80	Callan.R.	Gnr.	Not given	Left 20.8.43 (S)
81	Calland.D.	L/Bdr.	Lancaster	Died 5.2.43
82	Cameron.R.N.	Gnr.	Rosewell	Left 25.10.44 (S)
83	Cameron.W.G.	Gnr.	Battersea	Left 21.2.45 (?)
84	Cameron.W.J.R.	Gnr.	Gifford	Left 22.3.45 (?)
85	Campbell.A.	Gnr	Glasgow	*** March 1945
86	Campbell.G.	Gnr.	Hurlford	*** March 1945
87	Campbell.W.	Gnr.	Glasgow	*** March 1945

88	Campion.F.	Sgmn.	Leominster	Left 20.8.43 (S)
89	Cant.B.	Gnr	Fullbeck Heath	Left 20.8.43 (S)
90	Carey.R.E.	L/Bdr	Whitehaven	Left 20.8.43 (T)
91	Carlyle.I.	L/Bdr.	Brydekirk	*** March 1945
92	Carmichael.A.	Gnr.	Glasgow	Left 21.2.45 (?)
93	Carr.A.	L/Bdr.	Not given	Lfet 13.11.43 (H)
94	Carroll.E.A.	Gnr.	Glasgow	Left 22.3.45 (S)
95	Carol.J.	Gnr.	Not given	Left 13.11.43 (H)
96	Carruthers.W.	Gnr.	Lanark	*** March 1945
97	Carson.B.	L/Bdr.	Coatbridge	*** March 1945
98	Cartwright.D.	Gnr.	Raskelf Yorks	*** March 1945
99	Chadwick.A.	Pte.	Littleborough	Left 8.11.43 (T)
100	Channon.C.J.	Cpl.	Cardiff	Left 8.11.43 (T)
101	Chivers.W.H.	Gnr.	Aberdeen	Left 21.2.45 (?)
102	Christie.R.H.	L/Bdr.	Sunderland	Left 25.10.44 (S)
103	Clack.E.A.	Sgmn.	Sheffield	Left 20.8.43 (S)
104	Clark.W.S.B.	L/Bdr.	Glasgow	*** March 1945
105	Clingan.W.	Gnr.	Not given	Left 20.8.43 (T)
106	Coates.W.H.B.	Sgmn.	Leeds	Left 22.3.4 (S)
107	Collins.F.C.	Gnr.	Not given	Left 13.11.43 (H)
108	Coogan.A.	Gnr.	Not given	Left 13.11.43 (H)
109	Cooke.R.T.W.	BQMS	Watford	Left 13.11.43 (H)
110	Cooper.G.A.	L/Bdr.	Islington	Left 13.11.43 (H)
111	Cousin.J.	Sgt.	Coalsnaughton	*** March 1945
112	Cowan.J.	Gnr.	Eastriggs	Died 8.2.43
113	Cox.J.	Gnr.	Glasgow	Left 5.12.44 (T)
114	Cragg.M.J.	Gnr.	Burnley	Left 25.10.44 (S)
115	Craig.D.	L/Bdr.	Not given	Left 13.11.43 (H)

116	Craig.J.	Sgmn.	Dundee	*** March 1945
117	Cresswell.J.	L/Sgt.	Not given	Left 20.8.43 (S)
118	Cross.J.T.N.	Lieut,	Bromley	*** March 1945
119	Crossley.J.F.	Major.	Halifax	*** March 1945
120	Dalgliesh.G.	Gnr.	Lockerbie	Left 25.10.44 (T)
121	Daly.R.W.	Gnr.	Glasgow	*** March 1945
122	Davey.J.S.	L/Bdr.	Bagthorpe	Left 22.3.45 (H)
123	Davidson.T.	Gnr.	Not given	Left 13.11.43 (T)
124	Davies.A.	Gnr.	Porth	Left 20.8.43 (T)
125	Davies.D.	Gnr.	Swansea	*** March 1945
126	Davies.E.B.	Lieut.	Gillingham	Left 20.8.43 (S)
127	Davies.J.A.	L/Cpl.	London.	Left 21.2.45 (?)
128	Davis.E.G.	Sgt.	Walthamstow	Left 21.2.45 (?)
129	Davis.I.	Gnr.	Blaenllechav	Left 20.8.43 (T)
130	Davis.K.A.W.	Lieut.	New Barnett	*** March 1945
131	Davis.L.E.	Sgmn.	Sunbury	*** March 1945
132	Day F.	Gnr	Enfield.	Left 20.8.43 (T)
133	Dell .R.	L/Bdr.	Not given	Left 20.8.43 (T)
134	Denny.C.	Gnr.	Dartford	Left 8.11.43 (T)
135	Denton.R.O.	Gnr.	Newcastle-Tyne	Left 30.3.45 (T)
136	Devere.E.	Gnr.	Harbourne B'ham	*** March 1945
137	Dewar.W.	Gnr.	Glasgow	Left 30.8.43 (T)
138	Desnap.D.J.	Sgt.	Gretna	*** March 1945
139	Dickson.A.	Gnr.	Carluke	*** March 1945
140	DicksonW.J.	Gnr.	Not given	Left 8.11.4 (T)
141	Dixon J.M.	Pte.	Blythe	Left 8.11.43 (T)
142	Dobbie P.H.	Gnr.	Wishaw	*** March 1945
143	Docherty R.	Gnr.	Glasgow	Left 25.10.44 (S)

144	Dodds T.	Gnr.	Not given	Left 8.11.43 (T)
145	Donaldson L.A.	Sgt.	Tiverton	Left 25.10.44 (S)
146	Donnelly H.H.	Gnr.	Not given	Left 20.8.43 (T)
147	Donnelly T.	Bdr.	Not given	Left 13.11.43 (H)
148	Douglas J.W.	Gnr.	Guardbridge	Died 25.1.44
149	Douglas J.C.	L/Bdr.	Langholm	Left 22.3.45 (S)
150	Downie A.	Bdr.	Lanark	*** March 1945
151	Downie J.	L/Bdr.	Lanark	*** March 1945
152	Downs A.K.	Gnr.	Norfolk	Left 20.8.43 (T)
153	Dubock H.	BSM	Coventry	Left 21.2.45 (?)
154	Duncan A,	Gnr.	Not given	Left 20.8.43 (T)
155	Dunsmure W.	Bdr.	Newcastle	Left 13.11.43 (H)
156	Edgar P.F.	Gnr.	Maughline	*** March 1945
157	Edwards C.J.	Gnr.	Pontypridd	Left 21.2.45 (?)
158	Edwards G.	Gnr.	Wrexham	*** March 1945
159	Edwards J.O.	Sgt.	Cardiff	*** March 1945
160	Edwards S.A.	Gnr.	Gosport	*** March 1945
161	Ellerby G.	L/Bdr.	Bury	Died 18.12.42
162	Embury G.	L/Bdr.	Tunstall	Left 22.3.45 (S)
163	Fairbrother E.B.	Gnr.	Liverpool	Died 27.11.44
164	Farmer J.A.	L/Sgt.	Not given	Left 13.11.43 (H)
165	Farmer J.C.	L/Bdr.	Not given	Left 20.8.43 (T)
166	Fasson J.C.H.	Lt/Col	Jeddburgh	Left 20.8.43 (S)
167	Ferguson A.	Gnr.	Gateshead	Left 20.8.43 (S)
168	Ferguson D.J.	Gnr.	Glasgow	Left 21.2.45 (S)
169	Fergusson J.	Bdr.	Lanark	Left 21.2.45 (S)
170	Field A.	Pte.	Bath	Died 10.2.43
171	Fisher B.W.J.	L/Bdr.	Pontnewydd	*** March 1945

172	Fisher F.C.	Gnr.	Hull	Left 20.8.43 (S)
173	Fitzgerald J.A.	L/Bdr.	London	*** March 1945
174	Flanagan.W.J.	Gnr.	Birr, Eire.	*** March 1945
175	Fleming W.	Gnr.	Glasgow	Left 21.2.45 (?)
176	Fletcher W.	Gnr.	Not given	Left 20.8.43 (?)
177	Flux F.	Gnr.	Gosport	Left 8.11.43 (T)
178	Foot A.	Gnr.	Hayling	Left 8.11.43 (T)
179	Ford G.P.	Lieut.	Harrow	Left 20.8.43 (S)
180	Ford J.	L/Sgt.	Ilford	Left 21.2.45 (?)
181	Forrest W.W.	Gnr.	Edinburgh	*** March 1945
182	Foster F.	Gnr.	Fulham	Left 8.11.43 (T)
183	France B.A.	Lieut.	Newcastle-Tyne	Left 20.8.43 (S)
184	France J.E.R.	Capt.	Not given	*** March 1945
185	Fraser P.	Gnr.	Ballater	Left 20.8.43 (T)
186	Freeman S.	Sgt.	Swansea	Left 20.8.43 (T)
187	Freeman W.	Gnr.	Not given	Left 20.8.43 (T)
188	Frew S.	Gnr.	Not given	Left 20.8.43 (T)
189	Gale R.	Gnr.	Not given	Left 20.8.43 (T)
190	Guardhouse J.	Gnr.	Chichester	Left 20.8.43 (T)
191	Germany E.R.	Gnr.	Bracebridge	Left 22.3.45
192	Gibson W.McG.	Sgmn.	Kirkcudbrightshire	Left 22.3.45 (S)
193	Gilboy D.S.	Sgmn.	Halifax	Left 20.8.43 (T)
194	Giles A.L.	Gnr.	Halifax	Left 21.2.45
195	Gill F.	Sgmn.	Not given	Left 20.8.43 (T)
196	Glencross W.	Bdr.	Sanquhar	Left 21.2.43
197	Glendinning R.	Gnr.	Not given	Left 13.11.43 (H)
198	Goodman R.G.	L/Sgt.	Croxley Green	*** March 1945
199	Gordon T.	Gnr.	Not given	Left 20.8.43 (T)

200	Gore H.M.	L/Sgt.	Prescot	Died 22.12.42
201	Gotobed J.	Gnr.	Beverly Yorks.	Left 8.11.43 (T)
202	Gough B.	Bdr.	Hamilton	*** March 1945
203	Gowland C.	Gnr.	Middleburgh	*** March 1945
204	Graham J.	Gnr.	Annan	*** March 1945
205	Grant D.	Gnr.	Pitenween	Died 10.7.43
206	Green J.	Gnr.	Glasgow	*** March 1945
207	Griffiths J.F.	L/Cpl	Hucklecote	Died 16.11.42
208	Griffiths T.	Gnr.	Trelaw	Left 13.11.4 (H)
209	Grundy G	Bdr.	Sutton Coldfld.	Left 23.10.44 (K)
210	Gunn A.	Gnr.	Glasgow	Died 18.10.42
211	Gunn L.	Gnr.	Huddersfield	Left 21.2.45
212	Guscott S.	Gnr.	Exeter	*** March 1945
213	Guthrie J.	Gnr.	Not given	Left 20.8.43 (T)
214	Haines J.J.E.	Bdr.	Carshalton	Left 21.2.45 (S)
216	Hands J.A.	Gnr.	Not given	Left 13.11.43 (H)
217	Hanford D.	Sgmn.	Not given	Left 20.8.43 (S)
218	Hardy K.	Gnr.	Leeds	Left 8.11.43 (T)
219	Harley D.B.	Gnr.	Glasgow	Left 20.8.43 (T)
220	Harrington W.	Gnr.	Woodham Ferrers	Died 27.12.43
221	Harrison J.V.	Gnr.	Todmorden	Left 20.8.43 (S)
222	Harrison T.	L/Sgt.	Buxton	Left 21.2.45
223	Harrod D.E.	Gnr.	Manchester	Left21.2.45
224	Hart F.T.	L/Bdr.	Knutsford	Left 25.10.44 (K)
225	Harvey D.A.	Gnr.	Eastriggs	*** March 1945
226	Haslam F.	Sgmn	Bolton	Left 21.2.45
227	Hay W.L.	Gnr	Lanark	*** March 1945
228	Haynes G.W.	L/Sgt.	Not given	Left 20.8.43 (T)

229	Haynes H.	Gnr.	Hitchin	Left 22.3.45 (S)
230	Healy F.J.	Gnr.	Stoke on Trent	Left 22.3.45 (S)
231	Heaver L.A.	Sgt.	Lanark	Left 21.2.45
232	Hellyer R.W.	Lieut.	Bradford	*** March 1945
233	Henderson S.	L/Sgt.	Not given	Left 20.8.43 Died
234	Henderson S.	Gnr.	North Sheilds	Left 20.8.43 (T)
235	Hiddleston A.	Gnr.	Dumfriesshire	Left 25.10.44 (K)
236	Hiddleston D.M.	L/Bdr.	Not given	Left 20.8.43 (T)
237	Higgins R.F.	Gnr.	Not given	Left 20.8.43 (T)
238	Higham J.	Gnr.	Doncaster	Died 5.11.44
239	Hill H.	Lieut.	Not given	Left 20.8.43 (S)
240	Hill N.	Gnr.	Wednesbury	*** March 1945
241	Hinton G.N.	Lieut.	Ilmister	Left 20.8.43 (S)
242	Holdsworth F.	Gnr.	Halifax	Left 21.2.45
243	Holmes F.	Gnr.	Walthamstow	Died 13.10.43
244	Holt W.G.	Gnr.	London	*** March 1945
245	Hook G.	Gnr.	Nunhead	Died 29.3.43
246	Hooks D.J.	Bdr.	Glasgow	***March 1945
247	Hope-Johnstone P.	Capt.	Canisan, Surrey	Left 20.8.43
248	Hopkins G.L.	Gnr.	Leamington Spa	*** March 1945
249	Horton G.	Gnr.	Walsall	*** March 1945
250	Houston	Sigmn.	Selkirk	Left 8.11.43
251	Hudson H.A.	Lieut.	Bristol	Left 20.8.43
252	Hufton R.	Gnr.	East Kirby.	Left 20.8.43
253	Hughes B.	Gnr.	Wincanton	Left 20.8.43 (T)
254	Hugo J.W.	Lieut.	Lanark	Left 20.8.43 (S)
255	Hunt I.	Gnr.	Liversedge	*** March 1945
256	Hunter J.	Gnr.	Leeds	Left 30.3.45

257	Ingram H.	Gnr.	Not given	Left 20.8.43 (T)
258	Irving W.	L/Cpl.	Annan	Left 20.8.43 (T)
259	James K.	Gnr	Leeds	Left 20.8.43 (T)
260	Jennison T.	Gnr.	Leeds	Left 20.8.43 (T)
261	Jess H.S.	Gnr.	Lanark	Left 22.3.45 (S)
262	Johnson J.	L/Bdr.	Sunderland	Left 21.2.25 Died
263	Jones E.	Bdr.	Dundee	Left 20.8.43 (T)
264	Jordan J.	Pte.	Acton	Died 2.2.43
265	Joy L.R.	L/Bdr.	Catford	*** March 1945
266	Kane J.	Gnr.	Wishaw	*** March 1945
267	Kappelhoff J.	Sgmn.	Hounslow	Died 12.1.43
268	Keith J.	Gnr.	Edinburgh	Left 21.2.45
269	Kelso F.	Gnr.	Not given	Left 20.8.43 (T)
270	Kennedy M.	Gnr.	Not given	Left 8.11.43 (T)
271	Kennedy R.	Capt.	Carrickmines	Left 20.8.43 (S)
272	Kepple M.	Lieut.	Great Bookham	Left 20.8.43 (S)
273	Kerton R.H.M.	Gnr.	Bakewell	Left 20.8.43 (S)
274	Kilvinton N.	Gnr.	Not given	Left 20.8.43 (T)
275	King J.R.	Gnr.	Ilford	Left 25.10.44 (S)
276	Kingsland J.	Sgt.	Hurstpierpoint	*** March 1945
277	Kirk L.	Gnr.	Sheffield	Left 21.2.45
278	Kirby W.	Gnr.	Liversedge	Left 21.2.45
279	Kramer E.G.	Gnr.	London	Left 25.10.44 (S)
280	Lang W.R.	Gnr.	Poplar	*** March 1945
281	Langford T.E.	Gnr.	Mold	*** March 1945
282	Lapsley R.	Gnr.	Newcastle -Tyne	Left 20.8.43 (S)
283	Larkin F.	Gnr.	Edinburgh	*** March 1945
284	Lawson G.	Gnr.	Glasgow	Left 20.8.43 (T)

285	Lawton W.	Gnr.	Leeds	Left 8.11.43 (T)
286	Leaman G.	Gnr.	Torquay	Left 20.8.43 (T)
287	Leamer W.	L/Bdr.	Watford	Died 10.12.44
288	Ledwidge V.	Gnr.	Not given	Left 12.11.43 (H)
289	Lemm J.	Gnr.	Havant	Left 8.11.43 (T)
290	Levett.C.	L/Bdr.	Not given	Left 20.8.43 (T)
291	Lightowler D.	Gnr.	Bradford	Died 5.11.43
292	Limb.R.	Gnr.	Not given	Left 8.11.43 (T)
293	Lindley.F.S.	Gnr.	Langholm	Left 25.10.44 Died
294	Lindsey.J.N.R.	Gnr.	Sheffield	Left 20.8.43 (S)
295	Linvingstone.A.	Gnr.	Glasgow	Left 21.2.45
296	Lockhead.S.	Sgt.	Castle Douglas	*** March 1945
297	Lowing.F.S.	Gnr.	Leeds	Left 20.8.43 (T)
298	Lowther.C.S.	BSM	Dumfriesshire	Left 21.2.45
299	Lowther.M.	Gnr.	Beatock	Left 20.8.43 (T)
300	Lunness.L.	Sgt.	Bradford	Left 21.2.45
301	Macauslan.J.	RQMS	Not given	Left 13.11.43 (H)
302	Mackenzie.J.	Capt.	Edinburgh	Left 20.8.43 (S)
303	Mackie.R.	Gnr.	Glasgow	Left 31.5.45
304	Main.T.	Gnr.	Edinburgh	*** March 1945
305	Manley.H.	Gnr.	Hastings	Left 20.8.43 (T)
306	Markham.W.	Gnr.	Sidcup	Left 20.8.43 Died
307	Marriott.J.	Gnr.	Sheffield	Left 20.8.43 (T)
308	Marshall.J.M.	Gnr.	Bellshill	*** March 1945
309	Marshall.W.	Sgmn.	Not given	Left 20.8.43 (T)
310	Marson.J.	Gnr.	Not given	Left 8.11.43 (T)
311	Martin.A.W.	Gnr.	East Ham	Left 21.2.45
312	Martin.A.A.	Gnr.	Not given	Left 20.8.43 (T)

313	Martin.W.J.	Sgt.	Charlton	Left 21.2.45
314	Mather.J.	Bdr.	Edinburgh	Left 25.10.44 (K)
315	Mathewson.J.	Gnr.	Not given	Left 20.8.43 (T)
316	Mcadam.R.A.	Pte.	Liverpool	Left 30.3.45 (T)
317	Mcallister.J.	Gnr.	Glasgow	*** March 1945
318	Mcausland.J.M.	Sgt.	Edinburgh	Left 20.8.43 (S)
319	Mcallum.D.	Gnr.	Not given	Left 13.11.43 (H)
320	Mcallum.J.W.	Gnr.	Not given	Left 8.11.43 (T)
321	McCartney.J.	Gnr.	Glasgow	Left 13.11.43 (H)
322	McCredie.W.	Gnr.	Glasgow	Left 13.11.43 (T)
323	McCutcheon.J.	Gnr.	Lanark	Left 22.3.45 (S)
324	McDill.W.	L/Bdr.	Glencaple	Left 20.8.43 (T)
325	McKewan.J.	Gnr.	Wishaw	*** March 1945
326	McGhie.F.D.S.	Gnr.	Blackpool	Left 21.2.45
327	McGhie.R.G.	Gnr.	Blackpool	Left 21.2.45
328	McGill.A.	Gnr.	Londonderry	Left 21.2.45
329	McGuninness J.L.	Gnr.	Motherwell	Left 21.2.45
330	McIntosh.A.	Sgmn.	Inverurie	Left 20.8.43 (T)
331	McIntyre.T.	Gnr.	Glasgow	Left 13.11.43 (H)
332	McKay.H.	Gnr,	Not given	Left 20.8.43 (T)
333	Mckew.F.	Bdr.	Hamilton	Died 2.12.42
334	McKnight.J.B.	Lieut.	Lancaster	Left 20.8.43 (S)
335	McLean.A.	Gnr.	Not given	Left 20.8.43 (T)
336	McLean.I.G.	Lieut.	Newcastle-Tyne	Left 20.8.43 (S)
337	McLean.J.	Gnr.	Perth	Left 13.11.43 (H)
338	McLeod.J.A.	Gnr.	Inverurie	Left 25.10.44 (K)
339	McLoughlin.MG.	L/Cpl.	Trenherbert	*** March 1945
340	McPhail.A.	Sgt.	Wishaw	*** March 1945

341	Medlock.A.	Gnr.	Not given	Left 8.11.43 (T)
342	Melrose.R.G.	Gnr.	Dumfriesshire	Left 21.2.45
343	Merridan.A.T.	Gnr.	Wilsden	Left 21.2.45
344	Miles.R.T.	L/Sgt.	Rickmansworth	Left 6.12.44 (T)
345	Millership.H.	Gnr.	Nottingham	Died 1.2.45
346	Milne W.	Gnr.	Kinrosshire	March 1945
347	Mitchell C.B.	Sgt.	Dartford	*** March 1945
348	Mitchell H.	Bdr.	Not given	Left 20.8.43 (S)
349	Money.F.T.	Gnr.	Liverpool	Left 20.8.43 (T)
350	Moorhouse.F.	Gnr.	Huddersfield	*** March 1945
351	Moran.J.	Gnr.	Haydock	Died 7.4.43
352	Morley.W.J.	Gnr.	London	Left 22.3.45 (S)
353	Morris.E.J.	Sgmn.	Penclawdd	*** March 1945
354	Morrison D.O.	Gnr.	Linlithgow	Left 21.2.45 (S)
355	Motley R.A.H.	L/Bdr.	Lanark	Left 20.8.43 (S)
356	Mouland C.H.	L/Sgt.	Emsworth	Left 21.2.43
357	Muir.W.	Gnr.	Paisley	*** March 1945
358	Mulliner.E.	Sgmn.	Manchester	Left 20.8.43 (S)
359	Morgatroyd.J.	Sgt.	South Elmall	*** March 1945
360	Murphy.J.J.	Gnr.	St.Athen	*** March 1945
361	Myson.E.	Gnr.	Haselmere	Left 20.8.43 (S)
362	Napier. W.E.S.	Lt.Col.	Peebles	Left 20.8.43 (S)
363	Nash.R.S.	Gnr.	Clapton	Left 21.2.45
364	Norbury,F.	Bdr.	Lanark	*** March 1945
365	Notley.W.R.	Gnr.	Battersea	Left 21.2.45
366	Offord.F.	Pte.	Sheffield	Died 9.3.43
367	Ogden.J.A.	Gnr	Salford	*** March 1945
368	Olsen.S.	Gnr.	Hull	Left 8.11.43 (T)

369	Ostler.J.A.	Gnr.	Paddington	*** March 1945
370	Pannell.G.	Gnr.	Not given	Left 20.8.43 (T)
371	Parry.G.	Sgt.	Mold	Left 20.8.43 (T)
372	Parsons.S.F.	Gnr.	Birmingham	Left 21.2.45
373	Paterson.J.	Gnr.	Lansholm	*** March 1945
374	Paterson.W.J.	Bdr.	Lansholm	*** March 1945
375	Paterson.I.	L/Cpl.	Ross on Wye	Died 12.2.43
376	Peacock.T.W.	L/Sgt.	Bristol	*** March 1945
377	Pedley.I.C.	Major.	Carlisle	Left 20.8.43 (S)
378	Pelling.J.A.S.	Bdr.	Brighton	Left 25.10.44 (K)
379	Perman.G.	L/Bdr.	Not given	Left 20.8.4 (T)
380	Pestell.J.G.	Gnr.	Yarmouth	Died 22.2.43
381	Peters.C.V.	L/Sgt.	Bedhampton	*** March 1945
382	Pett.K.E.	Gnr.	Petersfield	*** March 1945
383	Phillips.J.	Bdr.	Portsmouth	Left 25.10.44 (K)
384	Pickles.S.	Gnr.	Burnley	Died 24.1.45
385	Plumridge.L.	Gnr.	Wembley	Left 21.2.43
386	Popple.C.	L/Bdr.	Wombwell	*** March 1945
387	Porteous.P.B.	Lieut.	Bridge on Weir	Left 20.8.43 (S)
388	Powell.J.	Gnr.	Willesden	Died 29.11.43
389	Pryke.A.G.	L.Bdr.	Emsworth	Left 25.10.44 (K)
390	Puckering.L.V.	Bdr.	Not given	Left 13.11.43 (H)
391	Rae.H.	Gnr.	Glasgow	Left 25.10.44 Died
392	Ramsay.S.	Gnr.	Forfar	Died 21.1.43
393	Rankin.C.	Sgmn.	Glasgow	*** March 1945
394	Rawlingson.W.H.	Gnr.	Knaresborough	Left 8.11.43 (T)
395	Reid.G.	Gnr.	Nor given	Left 20.8.43 (T)
396	Readman.W.	Gnr.	Thirsk	Left 8.11.43 (T)

397	Reeve.H.	Gnr.	Sidcup	Left 20.8.43 (T)
398	Roberts.A.	Sgmn.	Chester	Left 20.8.43 (S)
399	Roberts.E.W.	L/Bdr.	Rhyl	Left 30.3.45
400	Ronaldson.P.H.D.	Lieut.	East Lothian	Died 9.1.43
401	Rook.F.W.	Capt.	Dublin	Left 21.2.45
402	Ross.W.	Gnr.	Heckmondwike	Left 21.2.45
403	Rossiter.T.	Gnr.	Nottingham	Left 22.3.45 (S)
404	Rowney.W.T.	Gnr.	Manchester	*** March 1945
405	Ryder.T.	Gnr.	Derby	Left 20.8.43 (T)
406	Sams.R.J.	Gnr.	Not given	Left 20.8.43 (T)
407	Sanderson.G.B.	Major.	Edinburgh	Left 20.8.43 (S)
408	Sanderson.W.	Gnr.	Not given	Left 20.8.43 (T)
409	Sargent.A.G.	BSM	Brighton	Left 8.11.43 (T)
410	Savage.L.V.	Cpl.	Watford	Left 21.2.45
411	Scarsborough.E.	L/Sgt.	Blackpool	Left 21.2.45
412	Scott.G.	Gnr.	Not given	Left 8.11.43 (T)
413	Scott.J.	Gnr.	Motherwell	Left 22.3.4 (T)
414	Scott.J.	Gnr.	Annan	Left 25.10.44 (K)
415	Scott.W.	Gnr.	Annan	*** March 1945
416	Scullion.P.	RSM	Not given	Left 13.11.43 (H)
417	Sears.F.	Gnr.	St.Albans	Left 21.2.45
418	Seed.P.G.	Capt.	Manchester	Left 22.3.45 (S)
419	Sephton.R.	Sgt.	Southampton	Left 25.10.44 (K)
420	Sewell.E.R.A.	Capt.	Radlett	Left 22.8.43 (S)
421	Shaw.J.	Sgt.	Lanark	Died 16.12.42
422	Sheldrick.E.F.	Sgmn.	Maidenhead	Left 21.2.45
423	Shelvey.D.A.	BSM	Deal	Left 21.2.45
424	Shephard.R.A.	L/Sgt.	Northampton	*** March 1945

425	Shephard.E.	Gnr.	Wickford	*** March 1945
426	Shephard.E.	Gnr.	Rhondda	Left 20.8.43 (S)
427	Shields.W.	Gnr.	Wishaw	Left 21.2.45
428	Shipley.L.C.	Gnr.	Glasgow	Left 30.3.45
429	Sibley.N.A.H.	Bdr.	Not given	Left 13.11.43 (H)
430	Sim.J.D.	Gnr.	Not given	Left 20.8.43 (T)
431	Slater.W.	Gnr	Northampton	*** March 1945
432	Smith.A.	Gnr.	Not given	Left 8.11.43 (T)
433	Smith.D.D.	Lieut.	Not given	Left 21.2.45
434	Smith.C.H.W.	Sgmn.	New Barnet	Left 20.8.43 (S)
435	Smith.H.	Gnr.	Coalburn	Died 24.8.43
436	Smith.J.	L/Bdr.	Stockport	*** March 1945
437	Smith.J.M.M.	Gnr.	Alloa	*** March 1945
438	Sorrell.P.	Gnr.	Hoxton	Left 13.11.43 (H)
439	Southerton.H.H.	Gnr.	Small Heath	*** March 1945
440	Speed.H.	Bdr.	Not given	Left 20.8.43 (T)
441	Spooner.R.	Gnr.	Not given	Left 13.11.43 (H)
442	Spurrier. A. W.	Gnr.	Not given	Left 8.11.43 (T)
443	Stanhope.T.E.	Gnr.	Not given	Left 20.8.43 (S)
444	Stevenson.J.D.McK	Bdr.	Perth	*** March 1945
445	Stevenson.W.	Gnr.	Glasgow	Left 13.11.43 (H)
446	Stewart.G.M.	Major.	Glasgow	Left 20.8.43 (S)
447	Stewart.J.H.F.	Capt.	Lanark	Left 20.3.4 (S)
448	Stockford.R.	Gnr.	Not given	Left 20.8.43 (T)
449	Stone.S.D.J.	Gnr.	Not given	Left 8.11.43 (T)
450	Strong.C.C.	L/Bdr.	Durham	*** March 1945
451	Swan.G.E.	Gnr.	Leicester	Left 22.3.45 (S)
452	Swan.W.	Gnr.	Not given	Left 13.11.43 (H)

271

453	Sweeney.D.	Gnr.	Glasgow	Died 18.8.43
454	Sweeney.T.A.	Gnr.	Glasgow	Left 21.2.45
455	Tabeart.F.	Capt.	Littleport	Left 20.8.43 (S)
456	Tait.J.	Sgt.	Glasgow	Left 13.11.43 (H)
457	Taylor.J.	Gnr.	Bradford	Left 20.8.43 (T)
458	Taylor.L.V.	Gnr.	Palmers Green	Left 20.8.43 (T)
459	Telfer.J.M.	Sgmn.	Jedburgh	Left 21.2.45
460	Terry.E.	Gnr.	Carlton	Left 21.2.45
461	Thackaberry.G.	Gnr.	Glasgow	*** March 1945
462	Thomas.F.	Sgt.	Glasgow	Left 30.3.45
463	Thompson.R.	L/Bdr.	Not given	Left 20.8.43 (T)
464	Thompson.R.W.	Gnr.	Brighouse	Left 20.8.43 (T)
465	Thornton.J.E.	Gnr.	Pudsey	Left 25.10.44 (K)
466	Titherington.T.A.	Sgmn.	Birmingham	*** March 1945
467	Topping.K.G.	Gnr.	Whitley Bay	Left 20.8.43 (T)
468	Topping.J.	Gnr.	Manchester	Died 8.2.43
469	Tough.R.	L/Bdr.	Not given	Left 20.8.43 (T)
470	Townley.W.	Gnr.	Not given	Left 20.8.43 (T)
471	Travis.N.S.	L/Bdr.	Portsmouth	Left 22.3.45 (S)
472	Trimm.J.J.	Gnr.	Bury St Edmunds	Left 20.8.43 (T)
473	Tuck.S.H.	Gnr.	Middlesburgh	Left 25.10.44 (S)
474	Turner.J.	Gnr.	Halifax	Left 8.11.43 (T)
475	Turner.M.	Gnr.	Glasgow	Left 20.8.43 (T)
476	Turhill.G.W.T.	Gnr.	Liverpool	*** March 1945
477	Vacher.G.W.	Gnr.	Tottenham	Left 30.3.45
478	Vacher.W.M.	L/Bdr.	Hornsey	*** March 1945
479	Vanstone.R.H.	Gnr.	Not given	Left 8.11.43 (T)
480	Vere.A.	Gnr.	Langholm	Left 25.10.44 (S)

481	Viccars.J,V.	L/Bdr.	Rotherhithe	*** March 1945
482	Waldron.T.	Gnr.	Not given	Left 8.11.43 (T)
483	Walker.A.	Gnr.	Lanark	*** March 1945
484	Walker.W.	W/O1	Not given	Left 13.11.43 (H)
485	Wallace.T.	L/Bdr.	Annan	*** March 1945
486	Walsh.H.	Gnr.	Not given	Left 20.8.43 (T)
487	Ward.E.	Gnr.	Not given	Left 20.8.43 (T)
488	Ward.T.B.	Gnr.	Dundee	*** March 1945
489	Warner.J.	Gnr.	Not given	Left 20.8.43 (T)
490	Warnock.H.	Gnr.	Glasgow	Died 19.12.42
491	Warwick.R.D.	Sgt.	Annan	Left 21.2.45
492	Watson.A.	Gnr.	Glasgow	Left 20.8.43 (T)
493	Watson.B.	Gnr.	Rochdale	Left 13.11.43 (H)
494	Watson.J.L.	Sgt.	Torthorwald	Left 22.3.45 (S)
495	Watson.T.	Sgmn.	Dumfries	*** March 1945
496	Waugh.J.D.	Sgt.	Thornhill	Left 21.2.45
497	Wearing.G.W.	Gnr.	Lockerbie	*** March 1945
498	Wearing.T.S.	Gnr.	Birmingham	Died 14.12.42
499	Weedall.E.	Gnr.	Not given	Left 20.8.43 (T)
500	Weighill.F.	RQMS	Wirral	Died 18.12.43
501	Wheeler.A.F.	Sgt.	London.	Left 20.8.43 (T)
502	Whitbread.R.L.	Gnr.	Walthamstow	*** March 1945
503	White.C.F.	Gnr.	Penwaun	Died 25.1.45
504	White.C.J.	Gnr.	Gravesend	Left 8.11.43 (T)
505	White.G.	Gnr.	Not given	Left 8.11.43 (T)
506	White.J.C.	L/Bdr.	Bradford	Left 21.2.45
507	Whitehead.H.	Gnr	Rotherham	Left 31.2.45
508	Whitehead.J.	Gnr.	Not given	Left 20.8.43 (T)

509	Whitfield.G.H.	Pte.	Grimsby	*** March 1945
510	Williams.A.M.	Gnr.	Manchester	Died 24.10.43
511	Williams.D.	Gnr.	Liverpool	Left 20.8.43 (T)
512	Williams.E.	Gnr.	Dudley	Left 21.2.45 (T)
513	Williams.G.H.	Gnr.	Wishaw	*** March 1945
514	Williams.K.	Gnr.	Wrexham	Left 20.8.43 (T)
515	Williamson.W.B.	Gnr.	Sanquar	*** March 1945
516	Wilson.B.	Gnr.	Leeds	Left 20.8.43 (T)
517	Wilson.S.W.	Gnr.	Not given	Left 20.8.43 (T)
518	Wiseman.J.	Gnr.	Hampstead	Left 20.8.43 (T)
519	Wright.C.R.	L/Bdr.	West Wykham	Left 20.8.43 (T)
520	Wylie.T.	Gnr.	Loch Winnoch	*** March 1945
521	Wyllie.J.S.	BQMS	Not given	Left 8.11.43 (T)
522	Wyllie.T.C.	Bdr.	Girvan	*** March 1945
523	Pereira.F.P.	Pte.	Singapore	Left 22.3.45 (S)

All the above comprised the makeup of the first party to enter Kinkaseki in November 1942.

On 3 May 1943 thirty-one men arrived at Kinkaseki from No.3 Camp at Heito, Formosa.

524	Hunter.G.	L/Sgt.	Hindley, Wigan	Left 21.2.45
525	Bayliss.	L/Cpl.	Not given	Left 20.8.43 (T)
526	Corp J.	L/Cpl.	Vauxhall	*** March 1945
527	Davies T.J.	L/Cpl.	Penrhivceiber	*** March 1945
528	Emmett.J.H.	L/Cpl.	Glenlivet	*** March 1945
529	Bailey.A.	Pte	Westhoughton	Left 21.2.45
530	Baillie.	Pte.	Kincardine	Left 8.11.43. (T)
531	Baxter.B.	Pte.	Harlesdon	*** March 1945

532	Bird.H.	Pte.	Bradford	Left 8.11.43 (T)
533	Bolton.P.	Gnr	Wakefield	*** March 1945
534	Buckley.	Pte	Not given	Left 8.11.43 (T)
535	Coverdale.C.	Pte.	Manchester	*** March 1945
536	Dootson.J.	Tpr.	Wigan	Left 21.2.45
537	Grimley.L.	Pte.	Bermondsey	*** March 1945
538	Leggett.B.E.	Pte.	Norfolk	Died 29.8.45 Killed
539	Morgan.		Not given	Left 20.8.43 (T)
540	New.G.	Gnr.	Sunderland	Left 22.3.45 Died.
541	Parking.J.	Pte.	Eastwood. Notts	Left 21.2.45
542	Pounder.	Pte.	Not given	Left 8.11.43 (T)
543	Qhinn.D.	Pte.	Paisley	*** March 1945
544	Reynolds.R.	Pte.	Coventry	*** March 1945
545	Rigby.P.E.P.	Pte.	Kearsley	Died 13.8.43
546	Rowland.M.S.	Tpr.	Wigan	Left 6.12.44 (T)
547	Spurr.T.	Pte.	Carlton.	*** March 1945
548	Stafford.	Pte.	Not given	Left 8.11.43 (T)
549	Wilson.R.	L/Cpl.	Bolton	*** March 1945
550	Winstanley.J.A.	–	Wigan	Left 22.3.45 (S)
551	Turner.	–	Not given	Left 20.8.43 (T)
552	Wright.J.T.	Gnr.	Dunstable	Left 21.2.45
553	Yore.	Pte.	Not given	Left 8.11.43 (T)
554	Young.R.	Pte.	Perth	Left 21.2.45

On 12 June 1943, three more men arrived in camp from Heito, Formosa.

| 555 | Donnelly.D.H. | Cpl. | Kirkintilloch | *** March 1945 |

| 556 | Parker.T. | Pte. | India | Left 22.3.45 (S) |
| 557 | Thompson.J. | Pte. | Salford | *** March 1945 |

On 10 August 1943, a further 121 men arrived in Kinkseki from No.6 Camp Taioku, Formosa.

558	Archer.W.	Gnr.	West Hartlepool	Left 6.12.44 (T)
559	Ashley.H.	Sgmn.	Romford	Left 25.10.44 (K)
560	Ayscough.W.A.	Gnr.	Halifax	Left 21.2.45
561	Baker.J.	Sgmn.	London	Left 30.3.45 (T)
562	Barratt.W.	Sgmn.	Newcastle-Lyne	*** March 1945
563	Barrow.A.	Bdr.	Stoke on Trent	Died 26.1.44
564	Bean.L.W.	CSM	West Looe	Left 21.2.45
565	Beeby.E.A.	Gnr.	Bermondsey	Left 31.5.45
566	Benfield.G.	Sgmn.	Leicester	Left 6.12.44 (T)
567	Birtwistle.G.E.	Gnr.	Pennington	*** March 1945
568	Bishop.E.A.	L/Sgt.	Coventry	*** March 1945
569	Bishop.	RSM	Not given	Left 13.11.4 (H)
570	Blackham.H.C.	L/Sgt.	Selly Oak	Left 21.2.45
571	Bosi.I.	Sgmn.	Wolverhampton	*** March 1945
572	Bowkett.H.Y.	Cpl.	Abergavenny	*** March 1945
573	Bradley.H.M.	Gnr.	Preston	*** March 1945
574	Bramford.	L/Cpl.	Not given	Left 13.11.43 (H)
575	Brompton.D.F.	Sgmn.	West Bridgeford	Left 30.3.45
576	Browell.J.	Sgmn.	Durham	Left 30.3.45
577	Bruton.S.F.	CQMS	Durrington	Left 21.2.45
578	Carter.C.F.	Gnr.	Watford	*** March 1945

579	Campbell.G.	L/Cpl.	Belfast	Left 21.2.45
580	Catton.J.	Gnr.	Keighley	*** March 1945
581	Carson.J.	Bdr.	Not given	Left 13.11.43 (T)
582	Carter.A.J.	Sgmn.	Hounslow	Left 25.10.44 (K)
583	Cassidy.D.	Gnr.	Kilmarnock	Left 21.2.45
584	Clarke.E.A.	Gnr.	Farnbrough	*** March 1945
585	Collins.J.M.	Gnr.	Ealing	Left 6.12.44 (T)
586	Collingwood.W.	Gnr.	Newcastle-Tyne	Left 22.3.45 (S)
587	Cornthwaite.j.	Gnr.	Blaenavon	*** March 1945
588	Couper.J.P.D.	Sgmn	Edinburgh	*** March 1945
589	Cripps.R.E.	L/Bdr.	Chippenham	*** March 1945
590	Crocker.W.S.	Gnr.	Wolverhampton	*** March 1945
591	Curry.W.	Pte.	Irthlingboro	*** March 1945
592	Cutler.B.I.	Gnr.	Selly Oak	Left 21.2.45
593	Daley.C.	Gnr.	Warrington.	*** March 1945
594	D'arcy.G.R.	L/Bdr.	Liverpool	Left 22.3.45 (S)
595	Dare.	Gnr.	Not given	Left 13.11.43 (H)
596	Davies.L.J.	Gnr.	Reading	*** March 1945
597	Deegan.M.	CQMS	Chertsey	*** March 1945
598	Edwards.R.	Sgmn	Brighton	*** March 1945
599	Elliott.A.T.	L/Sgt.	Willsden Green	Left 25.10.44 (K)
600	Essay.N.I.T.	Sgmn	India	Left 21.2.45
601	Ewing.A.C.	Sgmn.	India	*** March 1945
602	Finn.W.H.H.	Gnr.	Wimbledon	Left 21.2.45
603	Foster.A.J.	Gnr.	Beckenham	*** March 1945
604	Gettie.J.	Gnr.	Glasgow	*** March 1945
605	Gibbons.J.	Sgmn.	Leeds	Left 25.10.44 (K)
606	Gill.J.M.	Gnr.	Glasgow	*** March 1945

607	Guest.W.	L/Bdr.	Exeter	*** March 1945
608	Harrison.G.W.	L/Bdr.	Bromley	*** March 1945
609	Hayde.W.E.	Sgmn.	India	Died 14.1.44
610	Haynes.W.F.	L/Bdr.	Forrest Gate	Left 22.3.45 (S)
611	Henderson.G.	Sgmn.	Liverpool	Left 25.10.44 (K)
612	Hill.W.L.	Gnr.	Barnsley	Left 21.2.45
613	Holmes.F.	L/Cpl.	Sheffield	*** March 1945
614	Holmes.	Gnr.	Not given	Left 13.11.43 (H)
615	Howe.J.T.	Gnr.	Barnsley	Died 29.8.45
616	Hunt.C.S.	Cpl.	Downham Market	Left 21.2.45
617	Irvine.J.S.	Gnr.	Liverpool	Left 21.2.45
618	James.J.W.	CQMS	Dublin	Left 30.3.45 (T)
619	Ker.T.McD.	Bdr.	Edinburgh	Left 6.12.44 (T)
620	Kingate.W.	Gnr.	Islington	Left 21.2.45
621	Marshall.J.C.	Gnr.	Bradford	Left 21.2.45
622	May.F.W.	Bdr.	Vauxhall	Left 21.2.45
623	May.R.	Gnr.	Egham	*** March 1945
624	McGill.R.	Gnr.	Lanark	Left 21.2.45
625	Miller,J,	Gnr.	Newcastle-Tyne	*** March 1945
626	Molyneaux.	Sgmn.	Not given	Left 3.11.43
627	Morgan.S.L.	Gnr.	Enfield	Left 6.12.44 Died
628	Moule.B.J.	L/Bdr.	London	*** March 1945
629	Muirhead.J.E.	Gnr.	Fife	Left 21.2.45
630	Newman.W.T.	Sgmn.	Romford	Left 21.2.45
631	Noble.W.A.	Bdr.	Rochford	Left 25.10.44 (K)
632	Oaff.L.S.	L/Bdr.	Newton Abbot	Left 25.10.44 (K)
633	O'Toole.T.F.	Sgt.	Dublin	Left 6.12.44 (T)
634	Painter.F.	Gnr.	Camphill, B'ham	*** March 1945

635	Perrett.F.J.	BQMS	Portsmouth	***	March 1945
636	Perry.C.	Gnr.	Evesham	Left 22.3.45 (S)	
637	Perrin.J.H.	L/Bdr.	Londonderry	***	March 1945
638	Pullinger.C.A.	Sgt.	India	Died 25.11.43	
639	Ratcliffe.D.W.	Gnr.	Scarbrough	***	March 1945
640	Reynolds.G.H.	Bdr.	Newport	Left 22.3.45 (S)	
641	Richards.M.F.	Gnr.	Llanelly	Left 21.2.45	
642	Ritchens.J.D.	Bdr.	Bath	Left 22.3.45 (S)	
643	Rivers.E.	Sgmn	Wembley	Left 25.10.44 (K)	
644	Roberts.J.	Gnr.	Balsall Heath	Left 30.3.45 (T)	
645	Robinson.T.F.J.	Gnr.	Essex	Left 25.10.44 (K)	
646	Rogers.W.J.	Sgt.	Eastleigh	Left 21.2.45	
647	Ross.R.W.	Gnr.	Newport	Left 21.2.45	
648	Rotherford.F.	L.Bdr.	Leeds	Left 21.2.45	
649	Russell.D.	L.Bdr.	Halesowen	Left 21.2.45	
650	Scargill.J.C.	Gnr.	Leeds	***	March 1945
651	Scott.L.G.	Cpl.	Battersea	Left 25.10.44 (K)	
652	Scriven.R.G.	Gnr.	Not given	Left 13.11.43 (H)	
653	Shorto.W.K.	Sgmn.	Warminster	Left 25.10.44 (K)	
654	Simpson.A.J.	Sgmn.	Brentwood	Left 30.3.45	
655	Slater.C.	Sgmn.	Matlock	Died 8.12.43	
656	Stone.J.	Gnr.	Gateshead	***	March 1945
657	Stratford.	Sgmn.	Not given	Left 13.11.43 (H)	
658	Telford.J.	Gnr.	Glasgow	Left 21.2.45	
659	Thomas.R.N.	BSM	Swansea	Left 22.3.45 (S)	
660	Tufrey.R.W.	L/Cpl.	Woodgreen	Left 21.2.45	
661	Walker.J.	Sgmn.	Walsall	***	March 1945
662	Wallace.R.	Sgmn.	Glasgow	Died 25.1.45	

663	Ward.R.V.	L/Bdr.	Rhuddlan	*** March 1945
664	Warwick.W.F.C.	Sgmn.	Broughton	Left 25.10.44 (K)
665	Watson.M.	Sgmn.	Ilkeston	*** March 1945
666	Webber.S.A.	Sgmn.	Stoke Newington	Left 30.3.45
667	Webster.G.W.	Sgmn.	Gravesend	*** March 1945
668	Wersby.L.	Gnr.	Malden	Left 25.10.44 (K)
669	West.H.	Sgmn.	Walworth	Died 13.11.45
670	Wheatley.T.	Gnr.	Belper	Left 25.10.44 (K)
671	Wheeler.B.M.	Major.	Canada	Left 22.3.4 (S)
672	Whyatt.J.C.	Gnr.	Bradford	*** March 1945
673	Willders.L.S.	L/Bdr.	Lincoln	*** March 1945
674	Wilson.M.W.	Gnr.	Middlesborough	Left 21.2.45
675	Wilson.W.	Gnr.	Sparkbrook	*** March 1945
676	Winder.R.	Sgmn.	Lancaster	*** March 1945
677	Woodburn.E.B.	Cpl.	Cumberland	*** March 1945
678	Yeats.	Sgmn.	Not given	Left 13.11.43 (H)

On 12 August 1943 a further 100 men arrived in Kinkaseki from No2 Camp Taichu, Formosa.

679	Birks.E.	CSM	Bolton	Left 21.2.45
680	Cameron.A.	Sgt.	Perth	Left 22.3.45 (S)
681	Duell.A.E.	L/Sgt.	Sunderland	Died 29.12.44
682	Lowndes.G.L.	Sgt.	Burslem	Left 22.3.45 (S
683	Parkes.J.	L/Sgt.	Derby	Left 23.10.44 (K)
684	Pearson.L.	Sgt.	Manchester	*** March 1945
685	Pickles.T.A.	L/Sgt.	Grange Town	Left 25.10.44 (K)

686	Slack.B.	L/Sgt.	Codnor	Left 22.3.45 (S)
687	Woodage.P.D.	Sgt.	Durrington	Left 21.2.45
688	Aspinall.J.	Cpl.	Bolton	Left 25.10.44 (K)
689	Barry.J.	Bdr.	Middlesborough	*** March 1945
690	Bell.G.H.G.	Bdr.	Horden Colliery	Left 25.10.44 (K)
691	Bemstead.F.W.	Cpl.	Dover	*** March 1945
692	Dorse.J.C.	Cpl.	Cleveden	Left 22.3.45 (S)
693	Locke.J.A.	Cpl.	Ashton U Lyne	*** March 1945
694	McFarlane.W.G.	Bdr.	Luton	*** March 1945
695	Simpson.J.B.	Cpl.	Portsoy	Left 30.3.45 (T)
696	Wilkinson.J.P.	Cpl.	Preston	*** March 1945
697	Durrant.E.	L/Cpl.	Hardwick. Cambs	*** March 1945
698	Gee.J.A.	L/Bdr.	Shepshed	Left 22.3.45 (S)
699	Hockley.D.G.	L/Cpl.	Ipswich	Left 25.10.44 (K)
700	King.G.	L/Cpl	Gateshead	*** March 1945
701	Kingston.C.	L/Cpl.	Cheshire	Left 21.2.45
702	McFarlane.A.	L/Cpl.	Glasgow	*** March 1945
703	McLernon.	L/Bdr	Gt. Yarmouth	*** March 1945
704	McLoughlin.S.	L/Cpl	Chatham	Left
705	Smith A.	L/Cpl.	Nottingham	Died 18.5.44
706	Street A.S.	L/Bdr.	London	Left 21.2.45
707	Turnbull P.	L/Bdr.	East Largo	Left 22.3.45
708	Whitall.A.	L/Cpl.	Cheadle Heath	Left 21.2.45
709	Adcock.R.	Gnr.	Acocks Green	Left 21.2.45
710	Aldred.D.	Pte.	Wigan	Left 25.10.44 (K)
711	Allen.F.J.	Tpr.	Croydon	Left 25.10.44 (K)
712	Auger.H.W.	Gnr.	Millwall	Left 21.2.45
713	Baker.F.W.	Gnr.	New Barnet	Left 6.12.44 (T)

714	Bamsey.A.E.J.	Pte.	Rainham	***	March 1945
715	Barnes.J.	Pte.	Bolton	***	March 1945
716	Beresford.	Pte.	Not given	Left 13.11.43 (H)
717	Bridges.W.A.	Pte.	Peterborough	***	March 1945
718	Burch.E.P.H.	Spr.	Norbury	Left 21.2.45
719	Byford.L.E.	Pte.	Southend	Died 21.9.44
720	Chambers.W.E.	Gnr.	Wakefield	Left 22.3.45 (S)
721	Clark.K.G.	Gnr.	West Croydon	Died 19.12.44
722	Coleman.P.	Gnr.	Sunderland	***	March 1945
723	Darby.B.D.	Spr.	Stourport	Left 22.3.45 (S)
724	Davison.G.	Fus.	Wrothbury	Died 4.3.45
725	Day.	Gnr.	Not given	Left 13.11.43 (H)
726	Denyer.H.R.	Pte.	London	Left 21.2.45
727	Dixon.J.P.	Spr.	Manchester	Left 21.2.45
728	Down.H.F.	Spr.	Barking	Left 21.2.45
729	Eardley.L.	Gnr.	Audley,Stoke	Left 30.3.45 (T)
730	East.E.J.	Gnr.	Dunstable	***	March 1945
731	Eldridge.W.H.	Gnr.	Winchester	***	March 1945
732	Fletcher.J.W.	Pte.	Nottingham	Left 22.3.45 (S)
733	Fowler.J.V.	Pte.	Lowestoft	Left 22.3.45 (S)
734	Greenwood.S.	Pte.	Wigan	***	March 1945
735	Grubb.C.	Pte.	Kirkaldy	Left 21.2.45
736	Harrison.L.R.	Gnr.	Hemel Hempstead	Left 25.10.44 (K)
737	Hart.L.J.	Gnr.	Bradford	Left 21.2.45
738	Higgins.A,	Gnr.	Sheffield	***	March 1945
739	Hill.D.	Gnr.	Salford	Died 3.4.44
740	Hill.J.R.	Spr.	Mold	***	March 1945
741	Hooper.R.J.	Spr.	Bristol	Left 21.2.45

742	Jackson.A.	Spr.	Liversedge	Left 22.3.45 (S)
743	Jones.L.B.	Gnr.	Scarbrough	*** March 1945
744	Kelly.R.	Gnr.	Dundee	*** March 1945
745	Kerr.A.R.	Pte.	North Chingford	Died 4.9.45
746	King.E.	Gnr.	Fulham	*** March 1945
747	Lawton.A.	Spr.	Doncaster	*** March 1945
748	Marshall.A.C.	Pte.	Waltham Cross	*** March 1945
749	McAlpine.G.	Spr.	Tenby	*** March 1945
750	McArthur.J.	Pte.	Peterhead	*** March 1945
751	Milleer.M.G.	Spr.	Bedlington	Left 21.2.45
752	Mohshi.A.O.	Gnr.	Cardiff	Died 8.12.43
753	Mulrainey.T.	Gnr.	Coatbridge	*** March 1945
754	Murray.J.	Gnr.	Glasgow	Left 21.2.45
755	Owens.W.	Spr.	Pinmore Girvan	*** March 1945
756	Parkes.L.R.	Spr.	Burton on Trent	*** March 1945
757	Payne.H.G.	Spr.	Baldock	Left 22.3.45 (S)
758	Peach.W.	Pte.	Hucknall	Left 30.3.45 (T)
759	Prescott.J.	Pte.	Wigan	*** March 1945
760	Preston.D.	Pte.	Rotherham	*** March 1945
761	Randall.E.J.	Spr.	Ilford	Left 22.3.45 (S)
762	Rawsthorne.J.	Tpr.	Preston	*** March 1945
763	Richardson.E.E.	L/Cpl.	Battersea	*** March 1945
764	Riley.L.	Pte.	Manchester	Left 30.3.45 (T)
765	Roe.C.F.	Pte.	Mitcham	Left 21.2.45
766	Rooney.M.A.	Spr.	Norwich	*** March 1945
767	See.A.H.	Pte.	Kilburn	Left 25.10.44 (K)
768	Sillett.F.G.	Spr.	Norwich	*** March 1945
769	Southgate.W.G.	Pte.	Ipswich	Died.18.3.45

770	Stevenson.R.	Pte.	Glasgow	*** March 1945
771	Strongie.J.	Pte.	Cheetham	*** March 1945
772	Togher.J.	Gnr.	Edinburgh	Left 21.2.45
773	Upton.R.E.	Spr.	Cheltenham	*** March 1945
774	Watson.G.	Spr.	Glasgow	Left 6.12.44 (T)
775	Watts.A.P.	Pte.	Brentwood	*** March 1945
776	Wood.J.	Spr.	Brierley Hill	Left 22.3.45 (S)
777	Woods.A.	Pte.	Woodbridge	Left 25.10.44 (K)
778	Young.J.	Pte.	Airdrie	Left 21.2.45

There was a further intake of 100 men to Kinkaseki from No.3 Camp at Heito on 2 September 1943.

779	Allen.R.	L/Cpl.	Peckham	*** March 1945
780	Atkins.J.A.	Gnr.	Tipton	Left 21.2.45
781	Bagnall.A.W.J.	Spr.	London	*** March 1945
782	Baker.H.	Gnr.	Not given	Left 8.11.43 (T)
783	Bannister.H.	L/Cpl.	Rainham	*** March 1945
784	Barlow.E.	Gnr.	Todmorden	Left 25.10.44 (K)
785	Bailey.T.W.	Pte.	Ipswich	Left 22.3.45 (S)
786	Beardsworth.B.	Pte.	Morecombe	Died 28.8.45
787	Bennett.H.	Pte.	Manchester	Died 10.11.45
788	Black.W.A.	Pte.	Seg Hill	Left 21.2.45
789	Blease.H.	Pte.	Congleton	Left 22.3.45 (S)
790	Blowers.J.W.	Pte.	Caister on Sea	*** March 1945
791	Bodell.W.	L/Cpl.	Frodsham	Left 25.10.44 (K)
792	Bortoft.J.	Pte.	Manchester	*** March 1945

793	Broome.N.J.	Cpl.	Oldham	*** March 1945
794	Brown.J.	Tpr.	Hackney Wick	Left 22.3.45 (S)
795	Butters.W.J.	Pte.	Norwich	*** March 1945
796	Carter.A.W.	Pte.	New Basford	Left 25.10.44 (K)
797	Carter.E.	Pte.	Nottingham	*** March 1945
798	Cheesebrough.F.	Gnr	Sunderland	Left 25.10.44 (K)
799	Cherry.H.G.	L/Sgt.	Lambeth	*** March 1945
800	Claridge.S.	Pte.	Luton	Died 8.2.44
801	Condon.W.	Sgt.	Manchester	Left 21.2.45
802	Cooper.H.	Pte.	Beeston	Left 25.10.44 (K)
803	Copping.R.	Pte.	Ledbury	*** March 1945
804	Corfield.D.	Tpr.	Bolton	Left 21.2.45
805	Cox.J.W.	Gnr.	Birmingham	Left 21.2.45
806	Daulby.W.	L/Cpl.	Manchester	Left 21.2.45
807	Dennison.C.	–	Not given	Left 13.11.43 (H)
808	Derbyshire.W.	Tpr.	Wigan	Left 21,2,45
809	Dougan.M.	Pte.	Lanarkshire	*** March 1945
810	Dunn.J.	Marine	Warrington	Died 22.6.44
811	Forbes.J.M.	Pte.	Cambusland	Left 21.2.45
812	Fossey.H.	Pte	Ampthill	*** March 1945
813	Gallagher.M.F.	L/Cpl.	Bolton	Left 25.20.44 (K)
814	Goldring.A.	Gnr.	Tottenham	Left 22.3.45 (S)
815	Griffiths.T.H.	Cpl.	Haverfordwest	Left 22.3.45 (S)
816	Hayles.H.W.	Cpl.	Alum Rock B'hm	Left 25.10.44 (K)
817	Hansard.G.W.	Pte.	Scunthorpe	*** March 1945
818	Harwick.J.E.	L/Cpl.	Southport	Left 30.3.45 (T)
819	Heathcote.W.R.	L/Cpl.	Oldham	Left 30.3.45 (T)
820	Hickman.E.	Gnr.	Bilston	*** March 1945

821	Hillditch.H.	Pte.	Crewe	Left 21.2.45
822	Hiscock.G.	L/Cpl.	Sidcup	Left 22.3.45 (S)
823	Hitchen.L.T.	Cpl.	Bolton	*** March 1945
824	Horsefall.G.	Gnr.	Huddersfield	Left 21.2.45
825	Housego.E.C.G.	Pte.	London	Left 25.10.45 (K)
826	Hughes.T.A.	L/Cpl.	Rainham	Left 21.10.44
827	Hume.A.	Pte.	Motherwell	*** March 1945
828	Hynes.J.	Pte.	Glasgow	Left 22.3.45 (S)
829	Fletcher.J.	Cpl.	Glasgow	*** March 1945
830	Ingram.J.	Pte.	Wolverhampton	*** March 1945
831	James.N.	Pte.	Cotham. Notts	Left 22.3.45 (S)
832	Jones.H.	Bdr.	New Brighton	Left 25.10.44 (K)
833	Kinniburgh.R.S.	Sgmn.	Glasgow	*** March 1945
834	Kirk.F.	Pte.	Loughborough	Left 22.3.45 (S)
835	Knight.C.R.	L/Cpl.	Not given	Left 8.11.43 (T)
836	Knight.R.	L/Cpl.	Bristol	*** March 1945
837	Lamb.J.B.	L/Bdr.	Glasgow	Died ?
838	Langridge.C.H.E	Gnr.	London	Left 21.2.45
839	Lawrence.R.H.	L/Cpl.	Cambridge	*** March 1945
840	Livingstone.S.	Pte.	Bognor Regis	*** March 1945
841	Loskey.	–	Not given	Left 8.11.43 (T)
842	Lovett.H.	L/Cpl.	Watford	Left 30.3.45 (T)
843	Luck.J.	Gnr.	Not given	Left 13.11.43 (H)
844	Martin.A.	L/Sgt.	Hull	Left 22.3.45 (S)
845	McGregor.J.	L/Cpl.	Aberdeenshire	Died 4.11.44
846	McShane.W.	Pte.	Aberdeen	Left 21.2.45
847	Millman.W.	L/Cpl.	Ilkley, Yorks	Left 21.2.45
848	Mills.G.	Pte.	London	Left 21.2.45

849	Milne.R.	L/Cpl.	Aberdeen	Died 22.8.45
850	Morris.G.W.	Pte.	Liverpool	Left 30.3.45 (T)
851	Nash.W.	L/Sgt.	Thornaby /Tees	Left 21.2.45
852	Oldham.N.	Gnr.	Spennymoor	*** March 1945
853	Oswin.	–	Not given	Left 13.11.43
854	Perkins.A.	Pte.	Ipswich	*** March 1945
855	Pollard.E.E.	Sgmn.	Thornaby /Tees	Left 25.10.44 (K)
856	Poole.A.J.	Pte	Not given	Left 13.11.43 (H)
857	Porter.E.	Pte.	Ashton U Lyne	Left 22.3.45 (S)
858	Presland.W.J.	Pte.	Hitchin	Left 21.2.45
859	Roast.G.E.	Gnr.	Rushden	*** March 1945
860	Robertson.W.A.	Pte.	Manchester	Left 21.2.45
861	Robinson.A.	Pte.	Burnley	*** March 1945
862	Seaton.A.J.	Spr.	Linton. Cambs	Left 30.3.45 (T)
863	Shearer.A.J.B.	Gnr.	West Hagley	*** March 1945
864	Singleton.W.	Gnr.	Preston	Died 22.6.44
865	Soutar.W.	Gnr	Arbroath	Left 22.3.4 (S)
866	Stalham.G.W.	Pte.	Chesterfield	Left 21.2.45
867	Street.T.	Pte.	Bolton	*** March 1945
868	Swindlehurst.J.	Sgmn.	Blackburn	Left 21.2.45
869	Taffs.F.	SA	Catford	Left 6.12.44 (T)
870	Tiffney.D.	Gnr.	Glasgow	Left 25.10.44 (K)
871	Tonne.A.F.	Pte.	Greatford	Left 21.2.45
872	Tracy.A.A.	Spr.	Glasgow	Died.13.1.45
873	Wallwork.A.	Pte.	Rossendale	Left 25.0.45 (K)
874	Waring.H.	Spr.	Bolton	Left 25.10.44 (K)
875	Wilson.H.	Gnr.	Blackburn	*** March 1945
876	Winsper.H.V.	Pte.	Oldbury	Left 22.3.45 (S)

877	Worthington.J.	Gnr.	Manchester	Left 21.2.45
878	Wragg.J.A.	Gnr.	Dunstable	Left 21.2.45

A further fifty men came to Kinkaseki on 8 November 1943 from No.6 Camp at Taihoku.

879	Armstrong.J.	Gnr.	Workington	*** March 1945
880	Avins.H.	Gnr.	Leicester	Left 21.2.45
881	Bird.C.H.C.	L/Bdr.	Dulwich	*** March 1945
882	Bradburn.R.	Sgmn.	Sutton, Surrey	Died 18.10.44
883	Bradley.F.	Sgmn.	Sheffield	Died 11.10.44
884	Brant.H.J.	L/Cpl.	Walsall	Left 21.2.45
885	Brewster.P.J.T.	L/Cpl.	Christchurch	*** March 1945
886	Burton J.	Cpl.	Tunstall	Died 10.1.45
887	Casey J.	Gnr.	Twickenham	Left 25.10.44
888	Clark R.C.	Gnr.	Llanelly	Left 25.10.44
889	Colton J.J.	Gnr.	Blackpool	*** March 1945
890	Croucher.A.E.	Sgmn.	Middlesbrough	Left 21.2.45
891	Crummy.G.A.	Sgmn.	India	*** March 1945
892	Dibble.A.H.	BSM	Sherborne	Left 21.2.45
893	Barley.J.	Gnr.	Swindon	Left 25.10.44 (K)
894	Foster.P.	Sgmn.	Leeds	Left 21.2.45
895	Goodwin.A.J.	Gnr.	Salford	*** March 1945
896	Harding.J.	Gnr	Rotherham	*** March 1945
897	Hewitson.J.H.	L/Cpl.	Durham	Left 21.2.45
898	Hill.P.S.W.	Gnr.	Walthamstow	Left 21.2.45
899	Hitchen.F.B.	L/Bdr.	Wakefield	Left 22.3.45 (S)
900	Humphries.A.	Gnr.	Burslem	Left 25.10.45 (K)

901	Jones.A.E.	L/Cpl.	Balsall Heath	Left 21.2.45
902	Leadbeatter.A.J.	L/Bdr.	Lewes	Died 18.11.44
903	Linton.L.A.	Sgmn.	Ewell	Left 25.10.44 (K)
904	McCoy.P.J.	Gnr.	Oldham	Left 21.2.45
905	McKay.J.L.	Gnr.	Swindon	Left 22.3.45 (S)
906	McKay.G.	Sgmn.	Glasgow	Left 25.10.44 (K)
907	Mathews.A.R.	Sgmn.	Birmingham	Left 25.10.44 (K)
908	Maynard.A.H.	L/Bdr.	Wokingham	Left 21.2.45
909	Neale.R.E.	L/Cpl.	Reading	Left 21.2.45
910	Pester.A.E.	Sgmn.	Plymouth	Left 21.2.43
911	Percy.E.T.T.	Gnr.	Cardiff	Left 6.12.44 (T)
912	Quilter.G.C.	Bdr.	Chelmsford	Left 21.2.45
913	Roberts.T.E.	Sgmn.	India	*** March 1945
914	Rogers.L.	L/Bdr.	Pontepore	Died 3.6.44
915	Rothery.H.	Sgmn.	Huddersfield	Died 7.5.44
916	Rowlands.F.W.	Sgmn.	Doncaster	*** March 1945
917	Rowe.F.O.	Gnr.	New Brighton	Left 25.10.44 (K)
918	Russell.L.	Gnr.	Sevenoaks	Left 21.2.45
919	Rylett.G.W.	Sgt.	Guernsey	Left 6.12.44 (T)
920	Scott.W.	L/Sgt.	India	Left 25.10.44 (K)
921	Stevenson.J.H.	Sgmn.	Staines.	*** March 1945
922	Waghorne	A.D.	Liverpool	Left 25.10.44 (K)
923	Walker.A.	Sgmn.	Plaistow	Left 21.2.45
924	White.J.H.	Gnr.	London	Left 21.2.45
925	Wood.H.	Sgmn.	Leeds	Left 6.12.44 (T)
926	Wood.S.	Sgmn.	Swinton	Left 23.3.45 (S)
927	Wright.F.	Gnr.	Newcastle /Tyne	Left 22.3.45 (S)
928	Young.R.	Sgmn.	Prescot	Left 21.2.45

A further seventy-five men came to Kinkaseki from No.2 Camp, Taichu, on 11 November 1943.

929	Chapman.G.W.	L/Sgt.	London	Left 22.3.45 (S)
930	Cull.H.J.	L/Sgt.	Downham	Left 30.3.45 (T)
931	Harris.L.J.	Sgt.	Llanelly	Left 22.3.45 (S)
932	Haskins.W.J.	L/Sgt.	Taunton	Left 25.10.44 (K)
933	Chatt.H.	Bdr.	Sunderland	*** March 1945
934	Cox.V.	Cpl.	Farnborough	Left 30.3.45 (T)
935	Davison.E.	Cpl.	Camden Town	Left 21.2.45
936	Hawtin.E.	Cpl.	London	Left 23.3.45 (S)
937	McDonald.W.	Bdr.	Leicester	Died 9.2.45
938	Wilson.B.J.	Cpl.	Norwich	Left 25.10.44 (K)
939	Daglish.J.G.	L/Bdr.	Sunderland	Left 22.3.45 (S)
940	Gibbins.E.	L/Bdr.	Sunderland	Left 22.3.45 (S)
941	Hall.A.E.T.	L/Bdr.	Bethnall Green	Left 25.10.44 (K)
942	Hunt.E.W.	L/Bdr.	Harpenden	Left 21.2.45
943	Knight.F.A.W.	L/Bdr.	London	Left 25.10.44 (K)
944	Amos.R.A.	Gnr.	Dunstable	Left 21.2.45
945	Atkinson.F.J.	Pte.	London	*** March 1945
946	Auty.H.	Tpr.	Bolton	Left 21.2.45
947	Baker.E.J.	Gnr.	Thornborough	Left 21.2.45
948	Barford.F.C.	Gnr.	Great Yarmouth	Left 21.2.45
949	Barton.E.	Tpr.	Wigan	Left 21.2.45
950	Bastin.R.G.	Gnr.	Clapton	Died 10.3.45
951	Biggin.T.A.	Gnr.	Workington	Died 24.8.45
952	Clarke.C.E.	Spr.	Kempston	Left 22.3.45 (S)
953	Cooper.E.	Pte.	Manchester	Left 30.3.45 (T)

954	Crouthers.A.	Gnr.	Sunderland	Left 21.2.45
955	Cullop.L.	Gnr.	Middlesborough	Died 10.1.45
956	Davies.D.B.	Pte.	Swansea	Left 21.2.45
957	Derbyshire.T.	Pte.	Wigan	Left 22,3,45 (S)
958	Dickinson/.S.	Spr.	Lincoln	Left 25.10.44 (K)
959	Dodds.S.	Gnr.	Benwell	Left 25.10.44 (K)
960	Edney.F.R.	Spr.	Penryn	*** March 1945
961	Ellis.W.	Pte.	Manchester	Left 30.3.45 (T)
962	Elwell.I.W.	Gnr.	Doncaster	*** March 1945
963	Evens.A.G.	Pte.	Luton	Left 30.3.45 (T)
964	Fern.G.	Pte.	Wolverhampton	*** March 1945
965	Findley.J.	Spr.	Montrose	*** March 1945
966	Garrett.G.	Pte.	Shoreditch	*** March 1945
967	Green.C.J.	Spr.	Liverpool	Left 21.2.45
968	Gregory.G.E.	Pte.	Hayes End	Left 21.2.45
969	Hannan.J.	Spr.	Bradford	*** March 1945
970	Harrington.S.J.A.	Gnr	Kidderminster	Left 25.10.44 (K)
971	Hennessy.J.J.	Tpr.	Dublin	Left 21.2.45
972	Higgins.J.	Tpr.	Bolton	*** March 1945
973	Holding.G.	Tpr.	Chorley	Left 21.2.45
974	Howard.R.D.	Spr.	Harrow	Left 21.2.45
975	King.B.G.	Spr.	Kentish Town	Left 22.3.45 (S)
976	Latham.G.	Pte.	Derry	*** March 1945
977	Lay.G.A.	Spr.	Birmingham	Left 21.2.45
978	Leslie.K.	Sgmn.	Guilford	*** March 1945
979	Long.G.E.	Pte.	Great Yarmouth	Left 21.2.45
980	Maltby.J.	Pte.	Nottingham	Left 21.2.45
981	Marrion.A.W.	Spr.	London.	Left 25.10.44 (K)

982	Marshall.J.R.	Gnr.	Sunderland	Left 22.3.45 (S)
983	Middleton.R.	Pte.	Aberdeenshire	*** March 1945
984	Milburn.J.	Gnr.	Leighton Bzzrd.	Left 25.10.44 (K)
985	Moffat.D.F.	Gnr.	Glasgow	*** March 1945
986	Morgan.C.	Spr.	Tredegar	Left 21.2.45
987	Mutch.J.	Pte.	Aberdeenshire	*** March 1945
988	Parsons.J.W.	Pte.	Deptford	Left 21.2.45
989	Price.F.R.	Sgmn.	Hayes	Left 30.3.45 (T)
990	Rush.M.	Pte.	Radcliffe	Left 21.2.45
991	Slade.E.	Gnr.	Luton	*** March 1945
992	Slater.N.	Spr.	Winlaton	Died 1.2.45
993	Spence.F.	Pte.	Durham	Left 25.10.4 (K)
994	Stevenson.F.G.	Pte.	Manchester	Left 21.2.45
995	Symonds.F.C.	Spr.	Sharnbrook	Left 25.10.44 (K)
996	Talbot.V.	Fus.	Strood	*** March 1945
997	Teasdale.J.	Gnr.	Hetton le Hole	Left 21.2.45
998	Tennant.W.	Gnr.	Glasgow.	*** March 1945
999	Walker.T.	Pte.	Glasgow	*** March 1945
1000	Washbrook.C.	Pte.	Bolton	Left 21.2.45
1001	Westacott.J.	Pte.	Streatham	*** March 1945
1002	Wheatley.W.S.	Gnr.	Durham	*** March 1945
1003	Wileman.G.W.	Spr.	Burton on Trent	Left 21.2.45
1004	White.W.	Sgt.	Bolton	Left 21.2.45

On 12 November 1943 a further seventy-five men came to Kinkaseki from No.3 Camp at Heito.

1005	Birch.D.E.	Cpl.	Amersham	***	March 1945
1006	Farbon.R.S.	Bdr.	Dunstable	Left 25.10.44 (K)	
1007	Gardner.A.J.	Bdr.	Porth	***	March 1945
1008	Greening.J.C.	Bdr.	Leighton Bzzrd.	Left 22.3.45 (S)	
1009	Harrison.D.W.	Cpl.	Newcastle/Tyne	***	March 1945
1010	Rawding.E.	Cpl.	Lincoln	Left 21.2.45	
1011	Stringer.S.G.	Bdr.	Esher	Left 25.10.44 (K)	
1012	Telfer.W.	Cpl.	Stenhousemuir	***	March 1945
1013	Young.W.L.	Cpl.	Sunderland	Left 22.3.45 (S)	
1014	Cadley.	L/Cpl.	Huddersfield	Left 30.3.45 (T)	
1015	Dixon.R.V.	L/Bdr.	Ramsgate	Left 21.2.45	
1016	Garrett.H.S.	L/Cpl.	Peckham	Left 21.2.45	
1017	Griffiths.W.	L/Bdr.	Bolton	Left 21.2.45	
1018	Hughes.C.	LAC	Glasgow	Left 21/2/45	
1019	Roberson.H.S.	L/Cpl.	Norwich	Left 21.2.45	
1020	Ross.W.	L/Cpl.	Glasgow	***	March 1945
1021	Tanner.C.R.	L/Bdr.	Shirley	***	March 1945
1022	Astill.H.	Pte.	London	Left 25.10.44 (K)	
1023	Bagwell.R.	Sgmn.	Preston	***	March 1945
1024	Baker,F.	Pte.	East Ham	***	March 1945
1025	Bentley.F.	Pte.	Bolton	Left 25.10.44 (K)	
1026	Bugg.H.	Pte.	Flackwell Heath	***	March 1945
1027	Butterworth.J.	Pte.	Rochdale	Left 22.3.45 (S)	
1028	Cooper.W.E.	Pte.	Manchester	Left 21.2.45	
1029	Cross.R.	Tpr.	Lancaster	***	March 1945
1030	Davies.J.	Pte.	Neyland	Left 21.2.45	
1031	Dick.W.G.	Pte.	Blackburn	***	March 1945
1032	Dobson.J.R.	Pte.	Twickenham	Left 25.10.44 (K)	

1033	Ellis.L.J.	Tpr.	Thundersley	Left 25.10.44 (K)
1034	Follon.A.J.	Pte.	Nottingham	Left 25.10.44 (K)
1035	Forham.L.	Pte.	Bexley Heath	Left 25.10.44 (K)
1036	Foster,G.J.	Sgmn.	Christchurch	*** March 1945
1037	Fox.A.R.	Pte.	Blackheath	Died 26.1.45
1038	Franklin.W.G.	Pte.	Hounslow	Left 25.10.44 (K)
1039	Gibbons.H.H.	Pte.	Darwen	Left 21.2.45
1040	Godwin.G.C.	Pte.	Manchester	Left 21.2.45
1041	Gough.J.	Pte.	Ashton U Lyne	*** March 1945
1042	Gregory.H.	Pte.	Bolton	Left 21.2.45
1043	Hammersley R.E.	Pte.	Lowestoft	Left 21.2.45
1044	Harris.B.	Tpr.	Bolton	Died 6.12.44
1045	Hills.H.S.	Pte.	Arlesay	*** March 1945
1046	Hindle.C.J.	Spr.	Clitheroe	Left 21.2.45
1047	Horsler.C.	Pte.	Luton	*** March 1945
1048	Kaye.R.	Spr.	Huddersfield	Died 9.12.43
1049	Keeley.J.H.	Pte.	London	*** March 1945
1050	Kilbride.A.E.	Pte.	London	*** March 1945
1051	Lemmer.L.R.	Pte.	Peckham	*** March 1945
1052	Lewis.S.J.	Spr.	Lymington	Left 22.3.45 (S)
1053	Mawdsley.F.I.	Gnr.	Dunstable	Left 21.2.45
1054	Mclaughlin.B.	Pte.	Glasgow	*** March 1945
1055	Morgan.A.D.	AC1	Llanelly	Left 21.2.45
1056	Owen.T.	Pte.	Manchester	Left 22.3.4 (S)
1057	Peatfield.J.	Pte.	Bolton	*** March 1945
1058	Poole.L.S.	Pte.	Chelmsford	*** March 1945
1059	Preston.E.	Gnr.	Altrincham	Left 21.2.45
1060	Quinn.J.E.	Gnr.	Newcastle/Tyne	Died 19.1.45

1061	Reed.R.J.	Pte.	Nottingham	*** March 1945
1062	Robinson.H.L.	Pte.	Ipswich	Left 25.10.44 (K)
1063	Ruscoe.A.	Pte.	Leigh	Died 29.11.44
1064	Scammell.J.	Pte.	Forrest Gate	Left 25.10.44 (K)
1065	Shaw.E.S.	Pte.	Watford	*** March 1945
1066	Smith.T.	Pte.	Rawtenstall	Left 25.10.44 (K)
1067	Soper F.J.	Spr.	Lympstone	*** March 1945
1068	Staniforth E.	Tpr.	Manchester	Left 25.10.44
1069	Stoves J.R.	Pte.	Newcastle	Left 22.3.45
1070	Tetley S.	Pte.	Morecombe	Left 25.10.44
1071	Thomson R.	Gnr.	Aberdeen	Died 11.12.44
1072	Tuttle.J.L.	Pte.	Hitchen	Left 21.2.45
1073	Wann.W.	Pte.	Mussleburgh	Left 21.2.45
1074	Webb.F.	Pte.	London	*** March 1945
1075	Williamson.B.	Spr.	Leicester	Left 30.3.45 (T)
1076	Weston.J.W.	LAC	Sheffield	Left 22.3.45 (S)
1077	Winchester.H.F.	Tpr.	Preston	Left 21.2.45
1078	Winter.W.	Pte.	Beccles	Left 25.10.44 (K)

Numbers 1079 to 1100 were not allotted.

On 26 October 1944 ten men from No.3 Camp, ten men from No.4 Camp and thirty men from No.6 Camp came to Kinkaseki.

1101	Johnson.E.A.	S/Sgt.	New Jersey USA	Left 21.2.45
1102	Raynis.A.J.	S/Sgt.	Brooklyn N.Y.	Left 21.2.45
1103	Smith.W.B.	Pfc.	California	Left 21.2.45
1104	Kondrasiewicz.J	Pfc.	Pennsylvania	*** March 1945

1105	Flynn.J.	Cpl.	Paisley	*** March 1945
1106	Murphy.J.	L/Cpl.	St Helens	*** March 1945
1107	Hodgson.G.E.	Pte.	Manchester	*** March 1945
1108	Hodson.F.	Tpr.	Ashton U Lyne	Left 30.3.45 (T)
1109	Timlin.T.	Pte.	Hamilton	*** March 1945
1110	Dean.B	Pfc.	Texas	Left 21.2.45
1111	Poole.C.A.E.	Pte.	Kentish Town	Left 21.2.45
1112	Whitmore.G.R.	Pte.	Leytonstone	Left 21.2.45
1113	Clack.E.A.	Sgmn.	Sheffield	Died 25.8.45
1114	Harrison.J.V.	Gnr.	Todmorden	*** March 1945
1115	Kerton.R.H.N.	Gnr.	Buxton	Left 22.3.45 (S)
1116	Lindsay.J.N.R.	Gnr.	Sheffield	*** March 1945
1117	Smith.H.W.C.	Sgmn.	New Barnett	Left 22.3.45 (S)
1118	Jauney.E.	AC2	London	*** March 1945
1119	Walters.R.A.	Gnr.	Chippenham	Left 21.2.45
1120	Howard.W.E.	Pte.	Alperton	Left 21.2.45
1121	Gandy.C.F.	QMS	Chelmsford	*** March 1945
1122	Farnell.C.H.	BSM	Hanley	*** March 1945
1123	Forrester.R.C.	Sgt.	Hednesford	*** March 1945
1124	Pring.C.J.	Sgt.	Exeter	*** March 1945
1125	Althem.J.	Bdr.	India	*** March 1945
1126	Beaney.W.E.	L.Bdr.	Ipswich	Left 22.3.45 (S)
1127	Bramley.E.V.	L/Cpl.	Manchester	*** March 1945
1128	Hirst.G.	L/Bdr.	Huddersfield	*** March 1945
1129	Rowe.H.G.	L/Cpl.	Arbroath	*** March 1945
1130	Schofield.R.	L/Cpl.	Oldham	*** March 1945
1131	Stevens.R.	L/Bdr.	Henley on Thames	*** March 1945
1132	Anderson.E.W.	Gnr.	Aberdeen	*** March 1945

1133	Angus.P.C.	Gnr.	Dundee	***	March 1945
1134	Blain.G.	Gnr.	Sandhurst	***	March 1945
1135	Bret.R.H.A.	Gnr.	Grimsby	***	March 1945
1136	Burmingham.J.A.L.	Sgmn.	Farnham	***	March 1945
1137	Furbank.H.	Gnr.	Norfolk	***	March 1945
1138	Heard.G.M.	Gnr.	Handsworth	***	March 1945
1139	Henson.J.	Gnr.	Ilkester	***	March 1945
1140	Hughes.F.K.	Gnr.	Swansea	***	March 1945
1141	Kay.F.W.	Gnr.	Hull	Left 22.3.45 (S)	
1142	Miller.J.	Sgmn.	Pontefract	***	March 1945
1143	Morris.W.J.	Gnr.	Maesycwmmer	Left 22.3.45 (S)	
1144	Robinson.A.	Sgmn.	Durham	***	March 1945
1145	Sporton.S.P.	Sgmn.	Chesterfield	***	March 1945
1146	Vickerstaff.N.S.	Sgmn.	Long Eaton	***	March 1945
1147	Warbrick.G.H.	Gnr.	Wexford	***	March 1945
1148	Gotobed.J.	Gnr.	Hollyoaks	***	March 1945
1149	Button.R.	Gnr.	East Kirby	***	March 1945
1150	Bird.H.	Pte.	Bradford	***	March 1945

Three doctors and three medical orderlies came to Kinkaseki from No. Camp (Kagi) and No.6 Camp (Taihoku) on 16 May 1945.

1151	Kern.C.V.	Capt.	Tulsa. USA
1152	Schneider.L	Capt.	Portland USA
1153	Lewis.C.V.	Capt.	Aberllefenni
1154	Brodsky.P.	Sgt.	Philadelphia USA
1155	Emsinas.A.Z.	Pfc.	Arizona USA
1156	Paradise.B.P.	Pfc.	Nebraska USA

297

No.	Name	Rank	Next of kin	Service No.		Address		Status
433	SMITH, D.D.	Lieut	HRS D.D.	4448/AAB 2350469	(W)	BERKELEY HOUSE CAWNPORE INDIA		LEFT 21-2-.. J E
434	SMITH, G.H.W.	Sgun	MRS	318093	(W)	DURBAN VILLA, 11 EAST BARNET ROAD NEW BARNET, HERTS	✓	LEFT 20.8.43
435	SMITH, H.	Gur	MRS H C	929386	(Gur)	27 MIDFIELD ROAD COALBURN LANARKSHIRE	S	DIED 24.9..
436	SMITH, J.	L/Bdr	MRS H.	1105142	(W)	43 KENDALL ST. SOUTH REDDISH STOCKPORT, CHESHIRE	✓ E	V E
437	SMITH, J.M.M	Gnr	MRS J	1510931	(W)	88 ASHLEY TERR ALLOA	✓ S	V R
438	SORRELL, P.	gur		1096284	(M)	48 FALKIRK ST HOXTON LONDON N.1.	E	LEFT 13.11.42
439	SOUTHERTON, H.H.	gur	HRS E	948483		448 BOLTON RD, SMALL HEATH BIRMINGHAM	✓ E	V E
440	SPEED, H.	Bdr		963019				LEFT 20.8.43
441	SPOONER, R.	Gur		961129				LEFT 13.11.43
442	SPURRIER, A.W.	gur		1089478				LEFT 8.11.43
443	STANHOPE, T.E.	Gur		1105143				LEFT 20.8.43
444	STEVENSON, J.D.McK.	Bdr	HRS J	859318	(W)	4, CARNEGIE PLACE PERTH	✓ S	V P
445	STEVENSON, W	gur		34214	(W)	10 EXETER DRIVE GLASGOW	S	LEFT 13.11.43
446	STEWART, G.H.	Major		125568			✓	LEFT 20.8.43
447	STEWART, J.H.F.	Capt	MRS J.H.F.	950239	(W)	STICKHILL RAVENSTRUTHER LANARK	S	LEFT 22.3.. R
448	STOCKFORD, R.	Gur		919276				LEFT 20.8.43
449	STONE, S.D.J.	Gur		114812				LEFT 8.11.43
450	STRONG, C.C.	L/Bdr	HRS C.C.	1089491	(W)	9 BYRON TERR SHOTTON COLLIERY DURHAM	✓ E	V E
451	SWAN, G.E	Gur	MRS G	309362		24 SCHOOLGATE LEICESTER LEICS	E S	LEFT 22.3.45 E
452	SWAN, W.	Gur		1105145				LEFT 13.11.43
453	SWEENEY, D.	Gur	MRS D	1451970		17 KEYDEN ST. GLASGOW N	S	DIED 18.9.43
454	SWEENEY, T.A.	gur	HRS T		(W)	53 MERKLAND ST PARTICK GLASGOW	✓ S	J R
455	TABEART, E.	Capt		2580992				LEFT 20.8.43
456	TA...	Sgt			(B)	127 RAMPART AVENUE KNIGHTSWOOD GLASGOW	S	LEFT 13.11.43

Copy of camp records.

	1457871			(W)	3 HARBOUR RD WIBSEY BRADFORD YORKS	✓	E	LEFT 20.8.4 X
457	TAYLOR, J	Gnr		(W)	40 ECCLESBOURNE GARDENS PALMERS GREEN LONDON N.13		E	LEFT 20.8 X
458	TAYLOR, L.V.	Gnr			3 STONEHILL PLACE JEDBURGH		S	LEFT 21.2.4 J R
459	TELFER, J.M.	Sqmn	MR J					LEFT 21.2.4
460	TERRY, E	Cnr	MRS W	(M)	7 WESTDALE LANE CARLTON, NOTTS		E	J F
461	THACKABERRY, G	Gnr	MRS J	(W)	21 KINNIG ST GLASGOW	✓	S	✓ P.
462	THOMAS, F	Sgt	MRS	(H)	16 HYNDLEE DR GLASGOW S.W.1	✓	S	LEFT 10.3.45 T P
463	THOMPSON, R.	L/Bdr						LEFT 20.8 X
464	THOMPSON, R.W.	Gnr		(W)	27 FLETCHER CRESC RASTRICK BRIGHOUSE YORKS	✓	E	LEFT 20.8 X
465	THORNTON, J.E.	Gnr	MRS J		1 CLAREMONT CEMETARY RD PUDSEY, nr LEEDS YORKS		E	LEFT 28.10.4 ∞
466	TITHERINGTON, T.A.	Sqmn	MR E.		46 FODEN ROAD GREAT BARR BIRMINGHAM 22	✓	E	✓ E
467	TOPPING, K.G.	Gnr		(F)	33 CHELERFORD AVE WHITLEY BAY, NUMBERLAND		E	LEFT 20.8.4 X
468	TOPPING, J	Gnr	MRS J.G.		46 PLANTHILL RD VICTORIA AVENUE MANCHESTER 9		E	LEFT 20.8.4 X
469	TOUGH, R.	L/Bdr						LEFT 20.8.4 X
470	TOWNLEY, W.	Gnr		(H)	27 TOTLAND RD COSHAM PORTSMOUTH HANTS		E	LEFT 2.3.4 S F
471	TRAVIS, N.S	L/Bdr	MRS L	(W)	BRIDGE YARD, 191 GUINNESS BLDGS BETYON OR VAUXHALL BURY ST EDMUNDS LONDON		E	LEFT 20.8 X
472	TRIM, J.J	Gnr		(W)	55 HOLT ST MIDDLESBOROUGH YORKS		E	LEFT 28.10.4 ∞
473	TUCK, S.H	Gnr	MRS I.M	(W)	29 CHATEL LANE SALTERHEBBLE HALIFAX YORKS		E	LEFT 8.11.4 O
474	TURNER, J	Gnr			41 NETHAN ST GLASGOW		S	LEFT 20.8.4 X
475	TURNER, M	Gnr			26 DORRIT ST LIVERPOOL 8 LANCS	✓	E	✓ E
476	TUTHILL, G.W.T.	Gnr	MRS D.	(H)	15 STANLEY RD TOTTENHAM LONDON N.15	✓	E	LEFT 10.3.45
477	VACHER, G.W.	Gnr	MRS G	(N)	68 MYDDLETON RD HORNSEY LONDON N.8	✓	S	✓ E
478	VACHER, W.M.	L/Bdr	MRS L					LEFT 8.11.4 O
479	VANSTONE, R.H.	Gnr			HOLMNEAD LANGHOLM DUMFRIESSHIRE		S	LEFT 28.10.4 ∞
480	VERE, A	Gnr	MRS J GRANT					

Copy of camp records.

Retrieving the buried camp records, 1946.

⊣⊦ APPENDIX TWO ⊦⊢

War Crime Trials

Full Name	Nickname	Status	Sentence
Col. Junichi Nakano	None	Commandant PoW Camps Taiwan	20 years
Col. Hideo Sazawa	None	Ditto	15 years
Major Taichi Uete	None	Ditto	Death
Capt.Yaychachi Immamura	None	Commandant Kinkaseki	15 years
Lieut. Koji Tamaki	None	2nd I.C. Kinkaseki	15 years
Lieut, Nobuo Suzuki	The Count	Camp officer	15 Years
Lieut. Iwao Tahara	None	Camp officer	7 years
Lieut. Yoshijiro Oita	None	Camp officer	7 years
Sgt.Maj. Tatsuo Furuo	None	Camp W.O.	10 years
Sgt. Mitoshi Nakajima	None	Guard	3 Years
Sgt. Toranosuke Tashiro	Sanitary Sid	Medical Staff	8 Years
Col. Mitsuo Ueno	Lancho	Medical Staff	2 years
Cpl.Shigeru Kuribayashi	So-so	Medical Staff	2 years
Mitsgi Toda	None	Mine Manager	1 year
Katsumi Nakamura	None	Chief of Mining Dept.	5 years
Cho Kon Toku	Frying Pan	*Hanchoe*	7 years
Takejoro Nagi	The Ghost	*Hanchoe*	10 years
Fumio Suenobu	Blackie	*Hanchoe*	3 years
Teruo Zushi	The Eagle	*Hanchoe*	10 years
Kozo Utsonomiya	Charley Chaplin	*Hanchoe*	4 years
Seichi Takeichi	Nelson	*Hanchoe*	2 years
Yonemura None	Mine liaison	Officer	Acquitted
Lieut. Tsumoru Ashida	None	Camp officer	Acquitted

ᛘ BIBLIOGRAPHY ᚱ

Benedict, Ruth, *The Chrysanthemum and the Sword*, Riverside Press, Cambridge, Massachusetts, 1946.

Caffrey, Kate, *Out in the Midday Sun*, Andre Deutsch Ltd., London 1974.

Chamberlain, William Henry, *Japan Over Asia*, Duckworth, London 1937.

Chamberlain, Basil Hall, *Japanese Things*, publ. 1905, Charles E.Tuttle Coy, Tokyo 1971.

Churchill, Winston S., *Triumph and Tragedy*, Cassell & Co. Ltd. London 1954.

Deacon, Richard, *A History of the Japanese Secret Service*, Taiwan, 1982.

Fisher, Charles A., *Three Times a Guest*, Cassell Ltd., London 1979.

Grew, Joseph C., *Ten Years in Japan*, Hammond, Hammond & Co.Ltd., London 1944.

Hachiya. Michihiko, *Hiroshima Diary – The Journal of a Japanese Physician – August 6 – September 30, 1945*, Victor Gollancz Ltd. 1955.

Hearn, Lafcardio, *Tohoro – Hints and Echoes of Japanese Inner Life*, Gay & Bird, London 1908.

Hsu, Shuhsi, *The War Conduct of the Japanese*, Kelly & Walsh, Shanghai, 1938.

Ishimaru, Lt. Commander Tota, *Japan Must Fight Britain*, Hurst & Blackett Ltd., London 1936.

Lord Russell of Liverpool, *The Nights of Bushido*, Cassell & Co.Ltd. London 1958.

Montgomery, Michael, *Imperialist Japan*, Christopher Helm, London 1987.

O'Conroy, Taid, *The Menace of Japan*, Paternoster Library, London 1933.

Percival, Lt.Gen.A.E., *War in Malaya*, Eyre & Spotiswoode, London 1946.

Pernikoff, Alexander, *Bushido, The Anatomy of Terror*, Hutchinson & Co.Ltd. London 1933.

Public Records Office – Kew

Rawlings, Leo, *The Dawn Came Up Like Thunder*, Rawlings Chapman Publications, London 1972.

Shigemitsu, Mamoru, *Japan and her Destiny*, Hutchinson, London 1958.

Shilony, Ben-Ami, *Politics and Culture in Wartime Japan*, Clarendon Press, Oxford 1981.

Simson, Brig. Ivan, *Singapore – Too Little Too Late*, Leo Cooper Ltd. London 1970.

Tsuji, Colonel Masanobu, *Singapore*, Constable & Coy, London 1962.

Tsurumi, Shunsuke, *An Intellectual History of Wartime Japan 1931-1945*, KPI Ltd., London 1982.

Utley, Freda, *Japan's Feet of Clay*, Faber & Faber Ltd., London 1936.

Van der Post, Laurens, *Night of the New Moon*, Hogarth Press, London 1970.

Westwood, J.N., *The Russo-Japanese War*, Sidwick & Johnson, London 1973.

Woodburn Kirby, Major General S., *The War Against Japan*, H.M.S.O. London 1957.

gelignite, use down the mine, 101, 102, 103, 151

General Hospital, 61

General Strike, 1926, 23

geta, 75, 155

Ghost, the, 95, 221, 222, 228

Giran, 225

gold mine, 243

Gore, L/Sgt. H., 21

Gourock, 28

Greater East Asia Co-prosperity Sphere, 54, 252

Griffiths, L/Cp J., 21, 117

Grundy, Bombardier George, 35

Gunn, Gnr.A., 21

Gurun, 36, 37, 38, 41, 42

H

H.M.S. Cythia, 28

H.M.S. Prince of Wales, 56

H.M.S. Repulse, 56

hammer men, 98

Hellyer, Lieutenant R.W., 79, 182

'High Nose Village', 242, 248

hiragana, 140, 141

Hirohito, Emperor, 134, 135, 189, 190, 191, 234, 251, 252, 253, 254

Hiroshima, 192, 201

Hiroshima, atomic bomb on, 192, 201

Hitoshi, Sgt, Nakajima,, 171

Hong Kong, 55, 56, 57, 211, 237

Howe, Gunner J., 186

Hsieh, Jie Chauag, 243

Hsintien, 245

Hudson, Lieut. H.A., 79

Hudson Reconnaissance planes, 56

I

ice-box, 107

Ichie, Lieutenant, 131

identification photographs, 105, 220

ideogram, 140

Immamura, Captain Yaychachi, 80, 135, 136, 137. 139, 147, 149, 150, 151, 153, 154, 171, 180, 181, 184, 186, 210, 212, 213, 214, 216, 224, 229

Imperial Rescript, 134, 137, 254

Inouye, Jukichi, 190

International Military Tribunal, 190, 209

International Red Cross, 119, 128, 167, 168, 181, 182, 202, 218, 220

J

Japanese Medical Officer, 115

Japanese Medical Sergeant, 81

Japanese Military Hospital, 213

jika tabi, 86

Jitra, 35

Johore Baru, 46